The Bite-size Bible

Edited by Andy Bianchi

Collins, a division of HarperCollins*Publishers*
77–85 Fulham Palace Road, London W6 8JB
www.collins.co.uk

First published in Great Britain in 2007 by HarperCollins*Publishers*

1

Compilation © HarperCollins Publishers 2007

Andrew Bianchi asserts the moral right to be identified as the editor of this work.

Scriptures are taken from the Contemporary English Version of the Bible, published by
HarperCollins Publishers, © American Bible Society.

A catalogue record for this book is available from the British Library.

ISBN-13 978 0 00 724851 3

Typeset by MATS, Southend-on-Sea, Essex
Printed and bound in Great Britain by
Clays Ltd, St Ives plc

CONDITIONS OF SALE

Contents

INTRODUCTION

WHAT IS THE BITE-SIZE BIBLE?

The Bible is a big book, so it can be hard to know where to start. In addition, many people may have only read it in the older translations, which are wonderfully poetic but can be hard to understand – and certainly make it more difficult to see how it can possibly apply today.

The *Bite-size Bible* tackles these problems head-on: it has been created to help anyone and everyone read the story of the Bible, so they can understand this important book and grapple with the issues it raises.

This is a shortened version of the whole Bible. The passages have been selected because, together, they give a clear view of what the Bible says as a whole. There are all the well-known stories that will help the reader feel instantly at home, as well as other passages that flesh out the main themes.

The text used is from the *Contemporary English Version*, which uses simple, modern English that makes for a clear understanding of what is going on. Using everyday words and phrases, it reflects the style of the original writers, who expressed themselves in ways that made sense to the audiences of their time.

HOW DOES IT WORK?

Just like a novel, the *Bite-size Bible* can easily be read from cover to cover, or you can dip in and out when you want. There are other ways to explore more systematically – you can rush through a few core passages, or follow a thread on a particular theme with the help of the lists you'll find on the pages at the back of the book.

You'll see the following logos appear alongside additional information throughout the book – here's what they all mean.

■ Core passages
To get a quick overview, the Core passages logo will guide you through the top 50 passages. At the end of each passage is a ■▶ which points you to the next passage to jump on to. Not exactly a full meal, but everything needed to get by.

Key verses

Each passage has a key verse picked out, which gives a flavour of the entire passage or makes a particular contribution towards a better understanding of the Bible overall.

The Arts

The Bible has inspired some of the greatest works of art, literature and music – from Michelangelo's Sistine Chapel to Andrew Lloyd Webber's *Joseph and the Amazing Technicolour Dreamcoat*. These are highlighted next to the relevant Bible passage, as well as some lesser known works, which demonstrate the wide-reaching influence of the Bible throughout the centuries. Along with the name of the artist, composer or writer, other details like the work's date and location give some background information to help anyone who wants to explore further.

Key themes

While the Bible was written many centuries ago, it still deals with the sort of situations and circumstances experienced today. Some of these themes, such as family life, food, animals and transport, are picked out where they occur, and act as a reminder of the centrality of these issues to human existence down the ages. These are listed at the back of the book, so you can follow a theme through the Bible.

See also

Often, reading one passage throws light upon another. Sometimes these complementary passages relate the same incident but from a different perspective, or they might simply deepen understanding of what each passage means in a wider context. References that appear in **bold** type may be found within the Bite-size Bible, others may need to be checked out within the full Bible.

KEY EVENTS IN THE BIBLE

Creation	Genesis 1.1–2.3
Noah's Ark	Genesis 6.5–7.23
Joseph and his brothers	Genesis 37.1–11
Plagues	Exodus 7.14–8.19
Exodus	Exodus 13.17–21
Ten Commandments	Exodus 19.1–20.21
The fall of Jericho	Joshua 6.1–20

David and Goliath	1 Samuel 17.40–51
Elijah brings down fire	1Kings 18.1–39
Daniel in the lions' den	Daniel 6.1–23
Jonah	Jonah 1.1–17
Birth of Jesus	Matthew 1.18–25
Baptism of Jesus	Matthew 3.13–17
Temptation of Jesus	Matthew 4.1–11
Last Supper	Matthew 26.26–29
Crucifixion of Jesus	Matthew 27.27–44
Resurrection of Jesus	Mark 16.1–8
Coming of the Holy Spirit	Acts 2.1–21
Conversion of Saul	Acts 9.1–9

KEY PEOPLE IN THE BIBLE

Abraham	Genesis 12.1–20
Adam	Genesis 2.4–25
David	1 Samuel 16.1–13
Elijah	1 Kings 17.1–7
Elisha	2 Kings 2.1–15
Eve	Genesis 2.4–25
Gideon	Judges 6.11–24
Isaac	Genesis 22.1–14
Jacob	Genesis 25.19–34
Jesus	Matthew 1.18–25
John the Baptist	Luke 1.57–80
Joshua	Joshua 1.1–9
Mary	Luke 1.26–38
Moses	Exodus 2.1–10
Noah	Genesis 6.5–7.23
Paul / Saul	Acts 9.1–9
Peter	Matthew 4.12–25
Samson	Judges 15.1–8
Samuel	1 Samuel 1.1–20
Solomon	1 Kings 1.11–39

THE LAW

The first five books of the Bible are traditionally called 'The Law'. They are also known as the books of Moses, and deal largely with the beginnings of the state of Israel. Central to this were the laws which the people were expected to observe when they got to the land God had chosen for them.

BEGINNINGS

GENESIS
1.1–2.3

God looked at what he had done. All of it was very good! Evening came and then morning – that was the sixth day.

FRANZ HAYDN
THE CREATION
1798

BIRDS AND ANIMALS

THE BEGINNING OF EVERYTHING

The word 'Genesis' means beginnings, and its content sets the tone for the rest of the Bible as it begins to answer the questions of why we are here and how we are meant to live.

In the beginning God created the heavens and the earth. The earth was barren, with no form of life; it was under a roaring ocean covered with darkness. But the Spirit of God was moving over the water.

God said, 'I command light to shine!' And light started shining. God looked at the light and saw that it was good. He separated light from darkness and named the light 'Day' and the darkness 'Night'. Evening came and then morning – that was the first day.

God said, 'I command a dome to separate the water above it from the water below it.'

And that's what happened. God made the dome and named it 'Sky'. Evening came and then morning – that was the second day.

God said, 'I command the water under the sky to come together in one place, so there will be dry ground.' And that's

See also JOB 38,
JOHN 1.1–5,
COLOSSIANS
1.15–20,
EXODUS 20.11

what happened. God named the dry ground 'Land', and he named the water 'Sea'. God looked at what he had done and saw that it was good.

God said, 'I command the earth to produce all kinds of plants, including fruit trees and grain.' And that's what happened. The earth produced all kinds of vegetation. God looked at what he had done, and it was good. Evening came and then morning – that was the third day.

God said, 'I command lights to appear in the sky and to separate day from night and to show the time for seasons, special days, and years. I command them to shine on the earth.' And that's what happened. God made two powerful lights, the brighter one to rule the day and the other to rule the night. He also made the stars. Then God put these lights in the sky to shine on the earth, to rule day and night, and to separate light from darkness. God looked at what he had done, and it was good. Evening came and then morning – that was the fourth day.

God said, 'I command the sea to be full of living creatures, and I command birds to fly above the earth.' So God made the giant sea monsters and all the living creatures that swim in the sea. He also made every kind of bird. God looked at what he had done, and it was good. Then he gave the living creatures his blessing – he told the sea creatures to live everywhere in the sea and the birds to live everywhere on earth.

Evening came and then morning – that was the fifth day.

God said, 'I command the earth to give life to all kinds of tame animals, wild animals, and reptiles.' And that's what happened. God made every one of them. Then he looked at what he had done, and it was good.

God said, 'Now we will make humans, and they will be like us. We will let them rule the fish, the birds, and all other living creatures.'

So God created humans to be like himself; he made men and women.

God gave them his blessing and said: Have a lot of children! Fill the earth with people and bring it under your control. Rule over the fish in the sea, the birds in the sky, and every animal on the earth.

I have provided all kinds of fruit and grain for you to eat. And I have given the green plants as food for everything else that breathes. These will be food for animals, both wild and tame, and for birds.

God looked at what he had done. All of it was very good! Evening came and then morning – that was the sixth day.

So the heavens and the earth and everything else were created. By the seventh day God had finished his work, and so he rested. God blessed the seventh day and made it special because on that day he rested from his work.

⟩ GENESIS 2.4–25

◻

GOD'S BEAUTIFUL GARDEN

**GENESIS
2.4–25**

But the Lord told him, 'You may eat fruit from any tree in the garden, except the one that has the power to let you know the difference between right and wrong. If you eat any fruit from that tree, you will die before the day is over!'

That's how God created the heavens and the earth.

When the Lord God made the heavens and the earth, no grass or plants were growing anywhere. God had not yet sent any rain, and there was no one to work the land.

But streams came up from the ground and watered the earth.

The Lord God took a handful of soil and made a man. God breathed life into the man, and the man started breathing. The Lord made a garden in a place called Eden, which was in the east, and he put the man there.

The Lord God placed all kinds of beautiful trees and fruit trees in the garden. Two other trees were in the middle of the garden. One of the trees gave life – the other gave the power to know the difference between right and wrong.

From Eden a river flowed out to water the garden, then it divided into four rivers.

The first one is the River Pishon that flows through the land of Havilah, where pure gold, rare perfumes, and precious

MICHELANGELO
THE CREATION OF
ADAM
SISTINE CHAPEL,
ROME 1511

FOOD AND DRINK

See also
ISAIAH 51.3,
EZEKIEL 31.9,
JOEL 2.3

stones are found. The second is the River Gihon that winds through Ethiopia. The River Tigris that flows east of Assyria is the third, and the fourth is the River Euphrates.

The Lord God put the man in the Garden of Eden to take care of it and to look after it. But the Lord told him, 'You may eat fruit from any tree in the garden, except the one that has the power to let you know the difference between right and wrong. If you eat any fruit from that tree, you will die before the day is over!'

The Lord God said, 'It isn't good for the man to live alone. I need to make a suitable partner for him.' So the Lord took some soil and made Birds and animals. He brought them to the man to see what names he would give each of them. Then the man named the tame animals and the birds and the wild animals. That's how they got their names.

None of these was the right kind of partner for the man. So the Lord God made him fall into a deep sleep, and he took out one of the man's ribs. Then after closing the man's side, the Lord made a woman out of the rib.

The Lord God brought her to the man, and the man exclaimed,

'Here is someone like me! She is part of my body, my own flesh and bones. She came from me, a man. So I will name her Woman!'

That's why a man will leave his own father and mother. He marries a woman, and the two of them become like one person.

Although the man and his wife were both naked, they were not ashamed.

▶ GENESIS 3.1–24

A FATEFUL DECISION

GENESIS
3.1–24

*The woman stared
at the fruit. It
looked beautiful and
tasty. She wanted
the wisdom that it
would give her, and
she ate some of the
fruit. Her husband
was there with her,
so she gave some to
him, and he ate it
too.*

JOHN MILTON
PARADISE LOST
1667

FOOD AND DRINK

See also **ROMANS
5.12–21,
1 CORINTHIANS
15. 21–23, 45–49,
2 CORINTHIANS
11.3**

The snake was more cunning than any of the other wild animals that the Lord God had made. One day it came to the woman and asked, 'Did God tell you not to eat fruit from any tree in the garden?'

The woman answered, 'God said we could eat fruit from any tree in the garden, except the one in the middle. He told us not to eat fruit from that tree or even to touch it. If we do, we will die.'

'No, you won't!' the snake replied. 'God understands what will happen on the day you eat fruit from that tree. You will see what you have done, and you will know the difference between right and wrong, just as God does.'

The woman stared at the fruit. It looked beautiful and tasty. She wanted the wisdom that it would give her, and she ate some of the fruit. Her husband was there with her, so she gave some to him, and he ate it too. Straight away they saw what they had done, and they realized they were naked. Then they sewed fig leaves together to make something to cover themselves.

Late in the afternoon a breeze began to blow, and the man and woman heard the Lord God walking in the garden. They were frightened and hid behind some trees.

The Lord called out to the man and asked, 'Where are you?'

The man answered, 'I was naked, and when I heard you walking through the garden, I was frightened and hid!'

'How did you know you were naked?' God asked. 'Did you eat any fruit from that tree in the middle of the garden?'

'It was the woman you put here with me,' the man said. 'She gave me some of the fruit, and I ate it.'

The Lord God then asked the woman, 'What have you done?'

'The snake tricked me,' she answered. 'And I ate some of that fruit.'

So the Lord God said to the snake:

'Because of what you have done, you will be the only animal to suffer this curse – for as long as you live, you will crawl on your stomach and eat dust.

You and this woman will hate each other; your descendants and hers will always be enemies. One of hers will strike you on the head, and you will strike him on the heel.'

Then the Lord said to the woman,

'You will suffer terribly when you give birth. But you will still desire your husband, and he will rule over you.'

The Lord said to the man,

'You listened to your wife and ate fruit from that tree. And so, the ground will be under a curse because of what you did. As long as you live, you will have to struggle to grow enough food.

Your food will be plants, but the ground will produce thorns and thistles. You will have to sweat to earn a living; you were made out of soil, and you will once again turn into soil.'

The man Adam named his wife Eve because she would become the mother of all who live.

Then the Lord God made clothes out of animal skins for the man and his wife.

The Lord said, 'These people now know the difference between right and wrong, just as we do. But they must not be allowed to eat fruit from the tree that lets them live for ever.' So the Lord God sent them out of the Garden of Eden, where they would have to work the ground from which the man had been made. Then God put winged creatures at the entrance to the garden and a flaming, flashing sword to guard the way to the life-giving tree.

GENESIS 6.5–7.23

GOD'S FLOOD AND NOAH'S ESCAPE

GENESIS 6.5–7.23

He was very sorry that he had made them, and he said, 'I'll destroy every living creature on earth! I'll wipe out people, animals, birds, and reptiles. I'm sorry I ever made them.'

RAPHAEL
NOAH AND HIS SONS BUILDING THE ARK
THE VATICAN
1517

BIRDS AND ANIMALS
TRAVEL AND TRANSPORT

See also
2 PETER 2.5,
2 PETER 3.5–6,
HEBREWS 11.7

Adam and Eve, now exiled from Eden, started a family. Later their firstborn son, Cain, killed his brother. This wicked act – and others like it – soon became commonplace. Many generations later God decided to intervene.

The Lord saw how bad the people on earth were and that everything they thought and planned was evil. He was very sorry that he had made them, and he said, 'I'll destroy every living creature on earth! I'll wipe out people, animals, birds, and reptiles. I'm sorry I ever made them.'

But the Lord was pleased with Noah, and this is the story about him. Noah was the only person who lived right and obeyed God. He had three sons: Shem, Ham, and Japheth.

God knew that everyone was terribly cruel and violent. So he told Noah:

Cruelty and violence have spread everywhere. Now I'm going to destroy the whole earth and all its people. Get some good timber and build a boat. Put rooms in it and cover it with tar inside and out. Make it one hundred and thirty-three metres long, twenty-two metres wide, and thirteen metres high. Build a roof on the boat and leave a space of about forty-four centimetres between the roof and the sides. Make the boat three storeys high and put a door on one side.

I'm going to send a flood that will destroy everything that breathes! Nothing will be left alive. But I solemnly promise that you, your wife, your sons, and your daughters-in-law will be kept safe in the boat.

Bring into the boat with you a male and a female of every kind of animal and bird, as well as a male and a female of every reptile. I don't want them to be destroyed. Store up enough food both for yourself and for them.

Noah did everything the Lord told him to do.
The Lord told Noah:

Take your whole family with you into the boat, because you are the only one on this earth who pleases me. Take seven pairs of every kind of animal that can be used for sacrifice and one pair of all others. Also take seven pairs of every kind of bird with you. Do this so there will always be Birds and animals on the earth. Seven days from now I will send rain that will last for forty days and nights, and I will destroy all other living creatures I have made.

Noah was six hundred years old when he went into the boat to escape the flood, and he did everything the Lord had told him to do. His wife, his sons, and his daughters-in-law all went inside with him. He obeyed God and took a male and a female of each kind of animal and bird into the boat with him. Seven days later a flood began to cover the earth.

Noah was six hundred years old when the water under the earth started gushing out everywhere. The sky opened like windows, and rain poured down for forty days and nights. All this began on the seventeenth day of the second month of the year. On that day Noah and his wife went into the boat with their three sons, Shem, Ham, and Japheth, and their wives. They took along every kind of animal, tame and wild, including the birds. Noah took a male and a female of every living creature with him, just as God had told him to do. And when they were all in the boat, God closed the door.

For forty days the rain poured down without stopping. And the water became deeper and deeper, until the boat started floating high above the ground. Finally, the mighty flood was so deep that even the highest mountain peaks were about seven metres below the surface of the water. Not a bird, animal, reptile, or human was left alive anywhere on earth. The Lord destroyed everything that breathed. Nothing was left alive except Noah and the others in the boat.

▮ GENESIS 8.3–19

NOAH LEAVES THE BOAT AT LAST

God said to Noah, 'You, your wife, your sons, and your daughters-in-law may now leave the boat. Let out the birds, animals, and reptiles, so they can mate and live all over the earth.'

BIRDS AND ANIMALS

For one hundred and fifty days the water slowly went down. Then on the seventeenth day of the seventh month of the year, the boat came to rest somewhere in the Ararat mountains. The water kept going down, and the mountain tops could be seen on the first day of the tenth month.

Forty days later Noah opened a window to send out a raven, but it kept flying around until the water had dried up. Noah wanted to find out if the water had gone down, and he sent out a dove. Deep water was still everywhere, and the dove could not find a place to land. So it flew back to the boat. Noah held out his hand and helped it back in.

Seven days later Noah sent the dove out again. It returned in the evening, holding in its beak a green leaf from an olive tree. Noah knew that the water was finally going down. He waited seven more days before sending the dove out again, and this time it did not return.

Noah was now six hundred and one years old. And by the first day of that year, almost all the water had gone away. Noah made an opening in the roof of the boat and saw that the ground was getting dry. By the twenty-seventh day of the second month, the earth was completely dry.

God said to Noah,

'You, your wife, your sons, and your daughters-in-law may now leave the boat. Let out the birds, animals, and reptiles, so they can mate and live all over the earth.' After Noah and his family had gone out of the boat, the living creatures left in groups of their own kind.

GENESIS 8.20–9.8–17

GENESIS 8.20–22, 9.8–17

Never again will I punish the earth for the sinful things its people do. All of them have evil thoughts from the time they are young, but I will never destroy everything that breathes, as I did this time.

AGREEMENTS AND PROMISES
BIRDS AND ANIMALS
FARMING AND PRODUCE

NEVER AGAIN

Noah built an altar where he could offer sacrifices to the Lord. Then he offered on the altar one of each kind of animal and bird that could be used for a sacrifice. The smell of the burning offering pleased God, and he said:

Never again will I punish the earth for the sinful things its people do. All of them have evil thoughts from the time they are young, but I will never destroy everything that breathes, as I did this time.

As long as the earth remains, there will be planting and harvest, cold and heat; winter and summer, day and night.

Again, God said to Noah and his sons:

I am going to make a solemn promise to you and to everyone who will live after you. This includes the birds and the animals that came out of the boat. I promise every living creature that the earth and those living on it will never again be destroyed by a flood.

The rainbow that I have put in the sky will be my sign to you and to every living creature on earth. It will remind you that I will keep this promise for ever.

When I send clouds over the earth, and a rainbow appears in the sky, I will remember my promise to you and to all other living creatures. Never again will I let flood waters destroy all life. When I see the rainbow in the sky, I will always remember the promise that I have made to every living creature. The rainbow will be the sign of that solemn promise.

▶ GENESIS 12.1–20

GOD FRUSTRATES THE PEOPLE'S PLANS

Noah's sons and their descendants began to spread all over the world as God had originally intended. Some, however, decided to make their home in one place rather than continue moving.

So the people had to stop building the city, because the Lord confused their language and scattered them all over the earth.

At first everyone spoke the same language, but after some of them moved from the east and settled in Babylonia, they said:

Let's build a city with a tower that reaches to the sky! We'll use hard bricks and tar instead of stone and mortar. We'll become famous, and we won't be scattered all over the world.

But when the Lord came down to look at the city and the tower, he said:

These people are working together because they all speak the same language. This is just the beginning. Soon they will be able to do anything they want. Come on! Let's go down and confuse them by making them speak different languages – then they won't be able to understand each other.

So the people had to stop building the city, because the Lord confused their language and scattered them all over the earth. That's how the city of Babel got its name.

ABRAHAM, ISAAC, JACOB AND JOSEPH

GOD PICKS OUT ABRAM

One of Noah's descendants, Abram, moved with his father from their homeland of Ur towards Canaan. When they reached a place called Haran, they settled there.

I will bless you and make your descendants into a great nation. You will become famous and be a blessing to others.

The Lord said to Abram:

Leave your country, your family, and your relatives and go to the land that I will show you. I will bless you and make your descendants into a great nation. You will become famous and be a blessing to others. I will bless anyone who blesses you, but I will put a curse on anyone who puts a curse on you. Everyone on earth will be blessed because of you.

Abram was seventy-five years old when the Lord told him to leave the city of Haran. He obeyed and left with his wife Sarai, his nephew Lot, and all the possessions and slaves they had got while in Haran.

When they came to the land of Canaan, Abram went as far as the sacred tree of Moreh in a place called Shechem. The Canaanites were still living in the land at that time, but the Lord appeared to Abram and promised, 'I will give this land to your family for ever.' Abram then built an altar there for the Lord.

The crops failed, and there was no food anywhere in the land. So Abram and his wife Sarai went to live in Egypt for a while. But just before they got there, he said, 'Sarai, you are really beautiful! When the Egyptians see how lovely you are, they will murder me because I am your husband. But they won't kill you. Please save my life by saying that you are my sister.'

As soon as Abram and Sarai arrived in Egypt, the Egyptians

AGREEMENTS AND PROMISES
BIRDS AND ANIMALS
FARMING AND PRODUCE
MARRIAGE AND FAMILY
TRAVEL AND TRANSPORT

See also
GENESIS 25.1,
GENESIS 46.1,
MATTHEW 1.1–17

noticed how beautiful she was. The king's officials told him about her, and she was taken to his house.

The king was good to Abram because of Sarai, and Abram was given sheep, cattle, donkeys, slaves, and camels.

Because of Sarai, the Lord struck the king and everyone in his palace with terrible diseases. Finally, the king sent for Abram and said to him, 'What have you done to me? Why didn't you tell me Sarai was your wife? Why did you make me believe she was your sister? Now I've married her. Take her and go! She's your wife.'

So the king told his men to let Abram and Sarai take their possessions and leave.

> GENESIS 22.1–14

ABRAHAM'S LOYALTY IS SEVERELY TESTED

God spoke to Abram again, confirming that he would keep all his promises. He also changed his name to Abraham, and that of his wife to Sarah. In due course – and despite her age – she gave birth to a son called Isaac.

'My son,' Abraham answered, 'God will provide the lamb.'

REMBRANDT
THE SACRIFICE OF
ABRAHAM
THE STATE
HERMITAGE
MUSEUM
ST PETERSBURG
1635

Some years later God decided to test Abraham, so he spoke to him.

Abraham answered, 'Here I am, Lord.'

The Lord said, 'Go and get Isaac, your only son, the one you dearly love! Take him to the land of Moriah, and I will show you a mountain where you must sacrifice him to me on the fires of an altar.' So Abraham got up early the next morning and chopped wood for the fire. He put a saddle on his donkey and left with Isaac and two servants for the place where God had told him to go.

Three days later Abraham looked into the distance and saw the place. He told his servants, 'Stay here with the donkey, while my son and I go over there to worship. We will come back.'

**BIRDS AND
ANIMALS
TRAVEL AND
TRANSPORT**

See also
EXODUS 12,
ISAIAH 53,
HEBREWS 10.1–18,
1 JOHN 2.1–2

Abraham put the wood on Isaac's shoulder, but he carried the hot coals and the knife. As the two of them walked along, Isaac said, 'Father, we have the coals and the wood, but where is the lamb for the sacrifice?'

'My son,' Abraham answered, 'God will provide the lamb.'

The two of them walked on, and when they reached the place that God had told him about, Abraham built an altar and placed the wood on it. Next, he tied up his son and put him on the wood. He then took the knife and got ready to kill his son.

But the Lord's angel shouted from heaven, 'Abraham! Abraham!'

'Here I am!' he answered.

'Don't hurt the boy or harm him in any way!' the angel said. 'Now I know that you truly obey God, because you were willing to offer him your only son.'

Abraham looked up and saw a ram caught by its horns in the bushes. So he took the ram and sacrificed it in place of his son.

Abraham named that place 'The Lord will Provide'. And even now people say, 'On the mountain of the Lord it will be provided.'

 EXODUS 1.1–22

GENESIS
24.1–27

THE SEARCH FOR ISAAC'S BRIDE

When Sarah died, Abraham decided it was time for Isaac to marry, but it was important that his son didn't marry just anyone...

'I thank you, Lord God of my master Abraham! You have led me to his relatives and kept your promise to him.'

Abraham was now a very old man. The Lord had made him rich, and he was successful in everything he did. One day, Abraham called in his most trusted servant and said to him, 'Solemnly promise me in the name of the Lord, who rules heaven and earth, that you won't choose a wife for my son Isaac from the people here in the land of Canaan. Instead, go back to the land where I was born and find a wife for him from among my relatives.'

BIRDS AND
ANIMALS
FOOD AND DRINK
MARRIAGE AND
FAMILY
TRAVEL AND
TRANSPORT

But the servant asked, 'What if the young woman I choose refuses to leave home and come here with me? Should I send Isaac there to look for a wife?'

'No!' Abraham answered. 'Don't ever do that, no matter what. The Lord who rules heaven brought me here from the land where I was born and promised that he would give this land to my descendants for ever. When you go back there, the Lord will send his angel ahead of you to help you find a wife for my son. If the woman refuses to come along, you don't have to keep this promise. But don't ever take my son back there.' So the servant gave Abraham his word that he would do everything he had been told to do.

Soon after that, the servant loaded ten of Abraham's camels with valuable gifts. Then he set out for the city in northern Syria, where Abraham's brother Nahor lived.

When he got there, he let the camels rest near the well outside the city. It was late afternoon, the time when the women came out for water. The servant prayed:

You, Lord, are the God my master Abraham worships. Please keep your promise to him and let me find a wife for Isaac today. The young women of the city will soon come to this well for water, and I'll ask one of them for a drink. If she gives me a drink and then offers to get some water for my camels, I'll know she is the one you have chosen and that you have kept your promise to my master.

While he was still praying, a beautiful unmarried young woman came by with a water jar on her shoulder. She was Rebekah, the daughter of Bethuel, the son of Abraham's brother Nahor and his wife Milcah. Rebekah walked past Abraham's servant, then went over to the well, and filled her water jar. When she started back, Abraham's servant ran to her and said, 'Please let me have a drink of water.'

'I'll be glad to,' she answered. Then she quickly took the jar from her shoulder and held it while he drank. After he had finished, she said, 'Now I'll give your camels all the water they want.' She quickly poured out water for them, and she kept going back for more, until his camels had drunk all they wanted. Abraham's servant did not say a word, but he watched everything Rebekah did, because he wanted to know for certain if this was the woman the Lord had chosen.

The servant had brought along an expensive gold ring and two large gold bracelets. When Rebekah had finished bringing the water, he gave her the ring for her nose and the bracelets for her arms. Then he said, 'Please tell me who your father is. Does he have room in his house for me and my men to spend the night?'

She answered, 'My father is Bethuel, the son of Nahor and Milcah. We have a place where you and your men can stay, and we also have enough straw and feed for your camels.'

Then the servant bowed his head and prayed, 'I thank you, Lord God of my master Abraham! You have led me to his relatives and kept your promise to him.'

**GENESIS
24.54–67**

REBEKAH AND ISAAC MEET AT LAST

Rebekah's father Laban invited Abraham's servant to his home to explain the reasons for his visit.

Isaac took Rebekah into the tent where his mother had lived before she died, and Rebekah became his wife. He loved her and was comforted over the loss of his mother.

BIRDS AND
ANIMALS
MARRIAGE AND
FAMILY
TRAVEL AND
TRANSPORT

Abraham's servant and the men with him ate and drank, then spent the night there. The next morning they got up, and the servant told Rebekah's mother and brother, 'I would like to go back to my master now.'

'Let Rebekah stay with us for a week or ten days,' they answered. 'Then she may go.'

But he said, 'Don't make me stay any longer. The Lord has already helped me find a wife for my master's son. Now let us return.'

They answered, 'Let's ask Rebekah what she wants to do.' They called her and asked, 'Are you willing to leave with this man at once?'

'Yes,' she answered.

So they agreed to let Rebekah and an old family servant woman leave immediately with Abraham's servant and his men. They gave Rebekah their blessing and said, 'We pray that

God will give you many children and grandchildren and that he will help them defeat their enemies.' Afterwards, Rebekah and the young women who were to travel with her prepared to leave. Then they got on camels and left with Abraham's servant and his men.

At that time Isaac was living in the southern part of Canaan near a place called 'The Well of the Living One who Sees Me'. One evening he was walking out in the fields, when suddenly he saw a group of people approaching on camels. So he started towards them. Rebekah saw him coming; she got down from her camel, and asked, 'Who is that man?'

'He is my master Isaac,' the servant answered. Then Rebekah covered her face with her veil.

The servant told Isaac everything that had happened.

Isaac took Rebekah into the tent where his mother had lived before she died, and Rebekah became his wife. He loved her and was comforted over the loss of his mother.

GENESIS
25.19–34

TENSIONS ARISE BETWEEN ESAU AND JACOB

On the death of his father Abraham, Isaac inherited all his wealth. God looked after Isaac in the same way that he had taken care of his father, giving him success in all that he did.

Esau would take the meat of wild animals to his father Isaac, and so Isaac loved him more, but Jacob was his mother's favourite son.

Isaac was the son of Abraham, and he was forty years old when he married Rebekah, the daughter of Bethuel. She was also the sister of Laban, the Aramean from northern Syria.

Almost twenty years later, Rebekah still had no children. So Isaac asked the Lord to let her have a child, and the Lord answered his prayer.

Before Rebekah gave birth, she knew she was going to have twins, because she could feel them inside her, fighting each other. She thought, 'Why is this happening to me?' Finally, she asked the Lord why her twins were fighting, and he told her:

'Your two sons will become two separate nations. The

Agreements and
Promises
Food and drink
Marriage and
family
Violence and
warfare

See also
ROMANS 9.10–13

younger of the two will be stronger, and the elder son will be his servant.'

When Rebekah gave birth, the first baby was covered with red hair, so he was named Esau. The second baby grabbed his brother's heel, so they named him Jacob. Isaac was sixty years old when they were born.

As Jacob and Esau grew older, Esau liked the outdoors and became a good hunter, while Jacob settled down and became a shepherd. Esau would take the meat of wild animals to his father Isaac, and so Isaac loved him more, but Jacob was his mother's favourite son.

One day, Jacob was cooking some stew, when Esau came home hungry and said, 'I'm starving to death! Give me some of that red stew at once!' That's how Esau got the name 'Edom'.

Jacob replied, 'Sell me your rights as the firstborn son.'

'I'm about to die,' Esau answered. 'What good will those rights do me?'

But Jacob said, 'Promise me your birthrights, here and now!' And that's what Esau did. Jacob then gave Esau some bread and some of the bean stew, and when Esau had finished eating and drinking, he just got up and left, showing how little he thought of his rights as the firstborn.

GENESIS
27.1–41

ISAAC'S PARTING WORDS TO HIS SONS

God told Isaac to live in the country of the Philistines. Here he prospered, becoming a powerful and wealthy man. Yet for all Isaac's success, the tension between his sons remained an issue.

Esau hated his
brother Jacob
because he had
stolen the blessing
that was supposed

After Isaac had become old and almost blind, he called in his firstborn son Esau, who asked him, 'Father, what can I do for you?'

Isaac replied, 'I am old and might die at any time. So take your bow and arrows, then go out in the fields, and kill a wild

*to be his. So he said
to himself, 'Just as
soon as my father
dies, I'll kill Jacob.'*

**AGREEMENTS AND
PROMISES
BIRDS AND
ANIMALS
FOOD AND DRINK**

See also
**GENESIS 49,
NUMBERS 11.8**

animal. Cook some of that tasty food that I love so much and bring it to me. I want to eat it once more and give you my blessing before I die.'

Rebekah had been listening, and as soon as Esau left to go hunting, she said to Jacob, 'I heard your father tell Esau to kill a wild animal and cook some tasty food for your father before he dies. Your father said this because he wants to bless your brother with the Lord as his witness. Now, my son, listen carefully to what I want you to do. Go and kill two of your best young goats and bring them to me. I'll cook the tasty food that your father loves so much. Then you can take it to him, so he can eat it and give you his blessing before he dies.'

'My brother Esau is a hairy man,' Jacob reminded her. 'And I am not. If my father touches me and realizes I am trying to trick him, he will put a curse on me instead of giving me a blessing.'

Rebekah insisted, 'Let his curse fall on me! Just do what I say and bring me the meat.' So Jacob brought the meat to his mother, and she cooked the tasty food that his father liked. Then she took Esau's best clothes and put them on Jacob. She also covered the smooth part of his hands and neck with goatskins and gave him some bread and the tasty food she had cooked.

Jacob went to his father and said, 'Father, here I am.'

'Which one of my sons are you?' his father asked.

Jacob replied, 'I am Esau, your firstborn, and I have done what you told me. Please sit up and eat the meat I have brought. Then you can give me your blessing.'

Isaac asked, 'My son, how did you find an animal so quickly?' 'The Lord your God was kind to me,' Jacob answered.

'My son,' Isaac said, 'come closer, where I can touch you and find out if you really are Esau.' Jacob went closer. His father touched him and said, 'You sound like Jacob, but your hands feel hairy like Esau's.' And so Isaac blessed Jacob, thinking he was Esau.

Isaac asked, 'Are you really my son Esau?'

'Yes, I am,' Jacob answered.

So Isaac told him, 'Serve me the wild meat, and I can give you my blessing.'

Jacob gave him some meat, and he ate it. He also gave him some wine, and he drank it. Then Isaac said, 'Son, come over here and kiss me.'

While Jacob was kissing him, Isaac caught the smell of his clothes and said:

'The smell of my son is like a field the Lord has blessed. God will bless you, my son, with dew from heaven and with fertile fields, rich with grain and grapes. Nations will be your servants and bow down to you. You will rule over your brothers, and they will kneel at your feet. Anyone who curses you will be cursed; anyone who blesses you will be blessed.'

Straight after Isaac had given Jacob his blessing and Jacob had gone, Esau came back from hunting. He cooked the tasty food, brought it to his father, and said, 'Father, please sit up and eat the meat I have brought you, so you can give me your blessing.'

'Who are you?' Isaac asked. 'I am Esau, your firstborn son.'

Isaac started trembling and said, 'Then who brought me some wild meat just before you came in? I ate it and gave him a blessing that cannot be taken back.'

Esau cried loudly and begged, 'Father, give me a blessing too!'

Isaac answered, 'Your brother tricked me and stole your blessing.'

Esau replied, 'My brother deserves the name Jacob, because he has already cheated me twice. The first time he cheated me out of my rights as the firstborn son, and now he has cheated me out of my blessing.' Then Esau asked his father, 'Don't you still have any blessing left for me?'

'My son,' Isaac answered, 'I have made Jacob the ruler over you and your brothers, and all of you will be his servants. I have also promised him all the grain and grapes that he needs. There's nothing left that I can do for you.'

'Father,' Esau asked, 'don't you have more than one

blessing? You can surely give me a blessing too!' Then Esau started crying again.

So his father said:

'Your home will be far from that fertile land, where dew comes down from the heavens. You will live by the power of your sword and be your brother's slave. But when you decide to be free, you will break loose.'

Esau hated his brother Jacob because he had stolen the blessing that was supposed to be his. So he said to himself, 'Just as soon as my father dies, I'll kill Jacob.'

JACOB'S AWESOME DREAM

GENESIS 28.10–17

Rebekah discovered that Esau was planning to kill Jacob, so she told him to run away and stay with her brother Laban until his brother's fury had died down.

Jacob woke up suddenly and thought, 'The Lord is in this place, and I didn't even know it.'

AGREEMENTS AND PROMISES
DREAMS AND VISIONS

Jacob left the town of Beersheba and started out for Haran. At sunset he stopped for the night and went to sleep, resting his head on a large rock. In a dream he saw a ladder that reached from earth to heaven, and God's angels were going up and down on it.

The Lord was standing beside the ladder and said:

I am the Lord God who was worshipped by Abraham and Isaac. I will give to you and your family the land on which you are now sleeping. Your descendants will spread over the earth in all directions and will become as numerous as the specks of dust. Your family will be a blessing to all people. Wherever you go, I will watch over you, then later I will bring you back to this land. I won't leave you – I will do all I have promised.

Jacob woke up suddenly and thought, 'The Lord is in this place, and I didn't even know it.' Then Jacob became frightened and said, 'This is a fearsome place! It must be the house of God and the ladder to heaven.'

JACOB MARRIES THE WRONG GIRL

After his strange dream, Jacob went on with his journey. As he did so he met a group of shepherds who knew his uncle. While they were talking, Laban's daughter Rachel arrived, and the two cousins met for the first time.

Jacob worked seven years for Laban, but the time seemed like only a few days, because he loved Rachel so much.

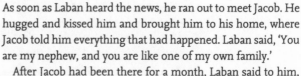

FOOD AND DRINK
MARRIAGE AND
FAMILY

As soon as Laban heard the news, he ran out to meet Jacob. He hugged and kissed him and brought him to his home, where Jacob told him everything that had happened. Laban said, 'You are my nephew, and you are like one of my own family.'

After Jacob had been there for a month, Laban said to him, 'You shouldn't have to work without pay, just because you are a relative of mine. What do you want me to give you?'

Laban had two daughters. Leah was older than Rachel, but her eyes didn't sparkle, while Rachel was beautiful and had a good figure. Since Jacob was in love with Rachel, he answered, 'If you will let me marry Rachel, I'll work seven years for you.'

Laban replied, 'It's better for me to let you marry Rachel than for someone else to have her. So stay and work for me.' Jacob worked seven years for Laban, but the time seemed like only a few days, because he loved Rachel so much.

Jacob said to Laban, 'The time is up, and I want to marry Rachel now!' So Laban gave a big feast and invited all their neighbours. But that evening he brought Leah to Jacob, who married her and spent the night with her. Laban also gave Zilpah to Leah as her servant woman.

The next morning Jacob found out that he had married Leah, and he asked Laban, 'Why did you do this to me? Didn't I work to get Rachel? Why did you trick me?'

Laban replied, 'In our country the elder daughter must get married first. After you spend this week with Leah, you may also marry Rachel. But you will have to work for me another seven years.'

At the end of the week of celebration, Laban let Jacob marry Rachel, and he gave her his servant woman Bilhah. Jacob loved Rachel more than he did Leah, but he had to work another seven years for Laban.

JACOB'S NIGHT TIME FIGHT

After working for his father-in-law many years, tensions arose between Jacob and Laban. Jacob, who with God's help had become very wealthy, decided to return home with his family and possessions.

Jacob said, 'I have seen God face to face, and I am still alive.' So he named the place Peniel.

TRAVEL AND TRANSPORT

Jacob got up in the middle of the night and took his wives, his eleven children, and everything he owned across to the other side of the River Jabbok for safety. Afterwards, Jacob went back and spent the rest of the night alone.

A man came and fought with Jacob until just before daybreak. When the man saw that he could not win, he struck Jacob on the hip and threw it out of joint. They kept on wrestling until the man said, 'Let go of me! It's almost daylight.'

You can't go until you bless me,' Jacob replied.

Then the man asked, 'What is your name?'

'Jacob,' he answered.

The man said, 'Your name will no longer be Jacob. You have wrestled with God and with men, and you have won. That's why your name will be Israel.'

Jacob said, 'Now tell me your name.' 'Don't you know who I am?' he asked. And he blessed Jacob.

Jacob said, 'I have seen God face to face, and I am still alive.' So he named the place Peniel.

JOSEPH'S DREAMS CAUSE RESENTMENT

When Jacob met his brother he was surprised to discover that Esau no longer harboured a grudge against him. Reconciled at last, the two brothers parted company.

Jacob had given Joseph a fine coat to show that he was his favourite son, and so Joseph's brothers hated him and would not be friendly to him.

Jacob lived in the land of Canaan, where his father Isaac had lived, and this is the story of his family.

When Jacob's son Joseph was seventeen years old, he took care of the sheep with his brothers, the sons of Bilhah and

ANDREW LLOYD
WEBBER AND TIM
RICE
JOSEPH AND THE
AMAZING
TECHNICOLOR
DREAMCOAT
1968

DREAMS AND
VISIONS
FARMING AND
PRODUCE
MARRIAGE AND
FAMILY

Zilpah. But he was always telling his father all sorts of bad things about his brothers.

Jacob loved Joseph more than he did any of his other sons, because Joseph was born after Jacob was very old. Jacob had given Joseph a fine coat to show that he was his favourite son, and so Joseph's brothers hated him and would not be friendly to him. One day, Joseph told his brothers what he had dreamed, and they hated him even more. Joseph said, 'Let me tell you about my dream. We were out in the field, tying up bundles of wheat. Suddenly my bundle stood up, and your bundles gathered around and bowed down to it.'

His brothers asked, 'Do you really think you are going to be king and rule over us?' Now they hated Joseph more than ever because of what he had said about his dream.

Joseph later had another dream, and he told his brothers, 'Listen to what else I dreamed. The sun, the moon, and eleven stars bowed down to me.'

When he told his father about this dream, his father became angry and said, 'What's that supposed to mean? Are your mother and I and your brothers all going to come and bow down in front of you?' Joseph's brothers were jealous of him, but his father kept wondering about the dream.

GENESIS
37.12–36

All Jacob's children
came to comfort
him, but he refused
to be comforted.
'No,' he said, 'I will
go to my grave,
mourning for my
son.' So Jacob kept
on grieving.

JOSEPH IS SOLD BY HIS BROTHERS

One day when Joseph's brothers had taken the sheep to a pasture near Shechem, his father Jacob said to him, 'I want you to go to your brothers. They are with the sheep near Shechem.'

'Yes, sir,' Joseph answered.

His father said, 'Go and find out how your brothers and the sheep are doing. Then come back and let me know.' So he sent him from Hebron Valley.

Joseph was near Shechem and wandering through the fields, when a man asked, 'What are you looking for?'

Joseph answered, 'I'm looking for my brothers who are watching the sheep. Can you tell me where they are?'

'They're not here any more,' the man replied. 'I overheard them say they were going to Dothan.'

Joseph left and found his brothers in Dothan. But before he got there, they saw him coming and made plans to kill him. They said to one another, 'Look, here comes the hero of those dreams! Let's kill him and throw him into a pit and say that some wild animal ate him. Then we'll see what happens to those dreams.'

Reuben heard this and tried to protect Joseph from them. 'Let's not kill him,' he said. 'Don't murder him or even harm him. Just throw him into a dry well out here in the desert.' Reuben planned to rescue Joseph later and take him back to his father.

When Joseph came to his brothers, they pulled off his fine coat and threw him into a dry well.

As Joseph's brothers sat down to eat, they looked up and saw a caravan of Ishmaelites coming from Gilead. Their camels were loaded with all kinds of spices that they were taking to Egypt. So Judah said, 'What will we gain if we kill our brother and hide his body? Let's sell him to the Ishmaelites and not harm him. After all, he is our brother.' And the others agreed.

When the Midianite merchants came by, Joseph's brothers took him out of the well, and for twenty pieces of silver they sold him to the Ishmaelites who took him to Egypt.

When Reuben returned to the well and did not find Joseph there, he tore his clothes in sorrow. Then he went back to his brothers and said, 'The boy is gone! What am I going to do?'

Joseph's brothers killed a goat and dipped Joseph's fine coat in its blood. After this, they took the coat to their father and said, 'We found this! Look at it carefully and see if it belongs to your son.'

Jacob knew it was Joseph's coat and said, 'It's my son's coat! Joseph has been torn to pieces and eaten by some wild animal.'

Jacob mourned for Joseph a long time, and to show his sorrow he tore his clothes and wore sackcloth. All Jacob's children came to comfort him, but he refused to be comforted.

'No,' he said, 'I will go to my grave, mourning for my son.' So Jacob kept on grieving.

Meanwhile, the Midianites had sold Joseph in Egypt to a man named Potiphar, who was the king's official in charge of the palace guard.

GENESIS
39.1–23

POTIPHAR'S WIFE TRIES TO SEDUCE JOSEPH

'No one in my master's house is more important than I am. The only thing he hasn't given me is you, and that's because you are his wife. I won't sin against God by doing such a terrible thing as this.'

REMBRANDT
JOSEPH ACCUSED BY
POTIPHAR'S WIFE
NATIONAL GALLERY
OF ART
WASHINGTON
1655

See also
1 CORINTHIANS
6.18,
HEBREWS 13.4

The Ishmaelites took Joseph to Egypt and sold him to Potiphar, the king's official in charge of the palace guard. So Joseph lived in the home of Potiphar, his Egyptian owner.

Soon Potiphar realized that the Lord was helping Joseph to be successful in whatever he did. Potiphar liked Joseph and made him his personal assistant, putting him in charge of his house and all his property. Because of Joseph, the Lord began to bless Potiphar's family and fields. Potiphar left everything up to Joseph, and with Joseph there, the only decision he had to make was what he wanted to eat.

Joseph was well-built and handsome, and Potiphar's wife soon noticed him. She asked him to make love to her, but he refused and said, 'My master isn't worried about anything in his house, because he has placed me in charge of everything he owns. No one in my master's house is more important than I am. The only thing he hasn't given me is you, and that's because you are his wife. I won't sin against God by doing such a terrible thing as this.' She kept begging Joseph day after day, but he refused to do what she wanted or even to go near her.

One day, Joseph went to Potiphar's house to do his work, and none of the other servants were there. Potiphar's wife grabbed hold of his coat and said, 'Make love to me!' Joseph ran out of the house, leaving her hanging on to his coat.

When this happened, she called in her servants and said, 'Look! This Hebrew has come just to make fools of us. He tried to rape me, but I screamed for help. And when he heard me scream, he ran out of the house, leaving his coat with me.'

Potiphar's wife kept Joseph's coat until her husband came home. Then she said, 'That Hebrew slave of yours tried to rape me! But when I screamed for help, he left his coat and ran out of the house.'

Potiphar became very angry and threw Joseph in the same prison where the king's prisoners were kept.

While Joseph was in prison, the Lord helped him and was good to him. He even made the jailer like Joseph so much that he put him in charge of the other prisoners and of everything that was done in the jail. The jailer did not worry about anything, because the Lord was with Joseph and made him successful in all that he did.

GENESIS
40.1–23

Everything happened just as Joseph had said it would, but the king's personal servant completely forgot about Joseph.

DREAMS AND VISIONS
FOOD AND DRINK

See also
NEHEMIAH 1

JOSEPH ADVISES HIS FELLOW INMATES

While Joseph was in prison, both the king's personal servant and his chief cook made the king angry. So he had them thrown into the same prison with Joseph. They spent a long time in prison, and Potiphar, the official in charge of the palace guard, made Joseph their servant.

One night each of the two men had a dream, but their dreams had different meanings. The next morning, when Joseph went to see the men, he could tell they were upset, and he asked, 'Why are you so worried today?'

'We each had a dream last night,' they answered, 'and there is no one to tell us what they mean.'

Joseph replied, 'Doesn't God know the meaning of dreams? Now tell me what you dreamed.'

The king's personal servant told Joseph, 'In my dream I saw a vine with three branches. As soon as it budded, it blossomed, and its grapes became ripe. I held the king's cup and squeezed the grapes into it, then I gave the cup to the king.'

Joseph said:

This is the meaning of your dream. The three branches

stand for three days, and in three days the king will pardon you. He will make you his personal servant again, and you will serve him his wine, just as you used to do. But when these good things happen, please don't forget to tell the king about me, so I can get out of this place. I was kidnapped from the land of the Hebrews, and here in Egypt I haven't done anything to deserve being thrown in jail.

When the chief cook saw that Joseph had given a good meaning to the dream, he told Joseph, 'I also had a dream. In it I was carrying three breadbaskets stacked on top of my head. The top basket was full of all kinds of baked things for the king, but birds were eating them.'
Joseph said:
This is the meaning of your dream. The three baskets are three days, and in three days the king will cut off your head. He will hang your body on a pole, and birds will come and peck at it.

Three days later, while the king was celebrating his birthday with a dinner for his officials, he sent for his personal servant and the chief cook. He put the personal servant back in his old job and had the cook put to death.
Everything happened just as Joseph had said it would, but the king's personal servant completely forgot about Joseph.

GENESIS 41.1–41

JOSEPH EXPLAINS THE KING'S DREAMS

'Your Majesty,' Joseph answered, 'I can't do it myself, but God can give a good meaning to your dreams.'

Two years later the king of Egypt dreamed he was standing beside the River Nile. Suddenly, seven fat, healthy cows came up from the river and started eating grass along the bank. Then seven ugly, skinny cows came up out of the river and ate the fat, healthy cows. When this happened, the king woke up.
The king went back to sleep and had another dream. This time seven full heads of grain were growing on a single stalk. Later, seven other heads of grain appeared, but they were thin

BIRDS AND
ANIMALS
DREAMS AND
VISIONS
FARMING AND
PRODUCE

See also EXODUS 7,
JEREMIAH 46.7–8,
RUTH 1.1, 2
SAMUEL 21.1,
1 KINGS 18.2

and scorched by the east wind. The thin heads of grain swallowed the seven full heads. Again the king woke up, and it had only been a dream. The next morning the king was upset. So he called in his magicians and wise men and told them what he had dreamed. None of them could tell him what the dreams meant.

The king's personal servant said:

Now I remember what I was supposed to do. When you were angry with me and your chief cook, you threw us both in jail in the house of the captain of the guard. One night we both had dreams, and each dream had a different meaning. A young Hebrew, who was a servant of the captain of the guard, was there with us at the time. When we told him our dreams, he explained what each of them meant, and everything happened just as he said it would. I got my job back, and the cook was put to death.

The king sent for Joseph, who was quickly brought out of jail. He shaved, changed his clothes, and went to the king.

The king said to him, 'I had a dream, yet no one can explain what it means. I am told that you can interpret dreams.'

'Your Majesty,' Joseph answered, 'I can't do it myself, but God can give a good meaning to your dreams.'

The king told Joseph:

I dreamed I was standing on the bank of the River Nile. I saw seven fat, healthy cows come up out of the river, and they began feeding on the grass. Next, seven skinny, bony cows came up out of the river. I have never seen such terrible looking cows anywhere in Egypt. The skinny cows ate the fat ones. But you couldn't tell it, because these skinny cows were just as skinny as they were before. Straight away, I woke up.

I also dreamed that I saw seven heads of grain growing on one stalk. The heads were full and ripe. Then seven other heads of grain came up. They were thin and scorched by a wind from the desert. These heads of grain swallowed the full ones. I told my dreams to the magicians, but none of them could tell me the meaning of the dreams.

Joseph replied:

Your Majesty, both of your dreams mean the same thing, and in them God has shown what he is going to do. The seven good cows stand for seven years, and so do the seven good heads of grain. The seven skinny, ugly cows that came up later also stand for seven years, as do the seven bad heads of grain that were scorched by the east wind. The dreams mean there will be seven years when there won't be enough grain.

It is just as I said – God has shown what he intends to do. For seven years Egypt will have more than enough grain, but that will be followed by seven years when there won't be enough. The good years of plenty will be forgotten, and everywhere in Egypt people will be starving. The famine will be so bad that no one will remember that once there had been plenty. God has given you two dreams to let you know that he has definitely decided to do this and that he will do it soon.

Your Majesty, you should find someone who is wise and will know what to do, so that you can put him in charge of all Egypt. Then appoint some other officials to collect one-fifth of every crop harvested in Egypt during the seven years when there is plenty. Give them the power to collect the grain during those good years and to store it in your cities. It can be stored until it is needed during the seven years when there won't be enough grain in Egypt. This will keep the country from being destroyed because of the lack of food.

The king and his officials liked this plan. So the king said to them, 'No one could possibly handle this better than Joseph, since the Spirit of God is with him.'

The king told Joseph, 'God is the one who has shown you these things. No one else is as wise as you are or knows as much as you do. I'm putting you in charge of my palace, and everybody will have to obey you. No one will be over you except me. You are now governor of all Egypt!'

JOSEPH'S BROTHERS GO TO EGYPT IN SEARCH OF FOOD

For seven years, while the harvests were very good, Joseph travelled the length and breadth of Egypt, storing as much food as possible in preparation for what was to come.

'We're being punished because of Joseph. We saw the trouble he was in, but we refused to help him when he begged us. That's why these terrible things are happening.'

FOOD AND DRINK
MARRIAGE AND FAMILY
TRAVEL AND TRANSPORT

See also
NUMBERS
13.1–31,
JOSHUA 2.1,
1 SAMUEL 24.9,
LUKE 20.20,21

Egypt's seven years of plenty came to an end, and the seven years of famine began, just as Joseph had said. There was not enough food in other countries, but all over Egypt there was plenty. When the famine finally struck Egypt, the people asked the king for food, but he said, 'Go to Joseph and do what he tells you to do.'

The famine became bad everywhere in Egypt, so Joseph opened the storehouses and sold the grain to the Egyptians. People from all over the world came to Egypt, because the famine was severe in their countries.

When Jacob found out there was grain in Egypt, he said to his sons, 'Why are you just sitting here, staring at one another? I have heard there is grain in Egypt. Now go down and buy some, so we won't starve to death.'

Ten of Joseph's brothers went to Egypt to buy grain. But Jacob did not send Joseph's younger brother Benjamin with them; he was afraid that something might happen to him. So Jacob's sons joined others from Canaan who were going to Egypt because of the terrible famine.

Since Joseph was governor of Egypt and in charge of selling grain, his brothers came to him and bowed with their faces to the ground. They did not recognize Joseph, but straight away he knew who they were, though he pretended not to know. Instead, he spoke harshly and asked, 'Where do you come from?'

'From the land of Canaan,' they answered. 'We've come here to buy grain.'

Joseph remembered what he had dreamed about them and said, 'You're spies! You've come here to find out where our country is weak.'

'No sir,' they replied. 'We're your servants, and we have only come to buy grain. We're honest men, and we come from the same family – we're not spies.'

'That isn't so!' Joseph insisted. 'You've come here to find out where our country is weak.'

But they explained, 'Sir, we come from a family of twelve brothers. The youngest is still with our father in Canaan, and one of our brothers is dead.'

Joseph replied:

It's just like I said. You're spies, and I'm going to find out who you really are. I swear by the life of the king that you won't leave this place until your youngest brother comes here. Choose one of you to go after your brother, while the rest of you stay here in jail. That will show whether you are telling the truth. But if you are lying, I swear by the life of the king that you are spies!

Joseph kept them all under guard for three days, before saying to them:

Since I respect God, I'll give you a chance to save your lives. If you are honest men, one of you must stay here in jail, and the rest of you can take the grain back to your starving families. But you must bring your youngest brother to me. Then I'll know that you are telling the truth, and you won't be put to death.

Joseph's brothers agreed and said to one another, 'We're being punished because of Joseph. We saw the trouble he was in, but we refused to help him when he begged us. That's why these terrible things are happening.'

Reuben spoke up, 'Didn't I tell you not to harm the boy? But you wouldn't listen, and now we have to pay the price for killing him.' They did not know that Joseph could understand them, since he was speaking through an interpreter. Joseph turned away from them and cried, but soon he turned back and spoke to them again. Then he had Simeon tied up and taken away while they watched.

*'I won't let my son
Benjamin go down
to Egypt with the
rest of you. His
brother is already
dead, and he is the
only son I have left.
I am an old man,
and if anything
happens to him on
the way, I'll die from
sorrow, and all of
you will be to
blame.'*

BIRDS AND
ANIMALS
FOOD AND DRINK

WORRYING NEWS FROM EGYPT

Joseph gave orders for his brothers' grain sacks to be filled with grain and for their money to be put in their sacks. He also gave orders for them to be given food for their journey home. After this was done, they each loaded the grain on their donkeys and left.

When they returned to the land of Canaan, they told their father Jacob everything that had happened to them:

The governor of Egypt was rude and treated us like spies. But we told him, 'We're honest men, not spies. We come from a family of twelve brothers. The youngest is still with our father in Canaan, and the other is dead.'

Then the governor of Egypt told us, 'I'll find out if you really are honest. Leave one of your brothers here with me, while you take the grain to your starving families. But bring your youngest brother to me, so I can be certain that you are honest men and not spies. After that, I'll let your other brother go free, and you can stay here and trade.'

When the brothers started emptying their sacks of grain, they found their money bags in them. They were frightened, and so was their father Jacob, who said, 'You have already taken my sons Joseph and Simeon from me. And now you want to take away Benjamin! Everything is against me.'

Reuben spoke up, 'Father, if I don't bring Benjamin back, you can kill both of my sons. Trust me with him, and I will bring him back.'

But Jacob said, 'I won't let my son Benjamin go down to Egypt with the rest of you. His brother is already dead, and he is the only son I have left. I am an old man, and if anything happens to him on the way, I'll die from sorrow, and all of you will be to blame.'

*When you go in to
see the governor, I
pray that God All-
Powerful will be
good to you and
that the governor
will let your other
brother and
Benjamin come
back home with
you. If I must lose
my children, I
suppose I must.*

FARMING AND
PRODUCE
FOOD AND DRINK
MARRIAGE AND
FAMILY

JACOB RELUCTANTLY ALLOWS BENJAMIN TO GO TO EGYPT

The famine in Canaan got worse, until finally, Jacob's family had eaten all the grain they had bought in Egypt. So Jacob said to his sons, 'Go back and buy some more grain.'

Judah replied, 'The governor strictly warned us that we would not be allowed to see him unless we brought our youngest brother with us. If you let us take Benjamin along, we will go and buy grain. But we won't go without him!'

Their father said:

If Benjamin must go with you, take the governor a gift of some of the best things from our own country, such as perfume, honey, spices, pistachio nuts, and almonds. Also take along twice the amount of money for the grain, because there must have been some mistake when the money was put back in your sacks. Take Benjamin with you and leave right away.

When you go in to see the governor, I pray that God All-Powerful will be good to you and that the governor will let your other brother and Benjamin come back home with you. If I must lose my children, I suppose I must.

The brothers took the gifts, twice the amount of money, and Benjamin. Then they hurried off to Egypt. When they stood in front of Joseph, he saw Benjamin and told the servant in charge of his house, 'Take these men to my house. Slaughter an animal and cook it, so they can eat with me at midday.'

When Joseph came home, they gave him the gifts they had brought, and they bowed down to him. After Joseph had asked how they were, he said, 'What about your elderly father? Is he still alive?'

They answered, 'Your servant our father is still alive and well.' And again they bowed down to Joseph.

When Joseph looked around and saw his brother Benjamin, he said, 'This must be your youngest brother, the one you told me about. God bless you, my son.'

Straight away he rushed off to his room and cried because of his love for Benjamin. After washing his face and returning, he was able to control himself and said, 'Serve the meal!'

Joseph was served at a table by himself, and his brothers were served at another. The Egyptians sat at yet another table, because Egyptians felt it was disgusting to eat with Hebrews. To the surprise of Joseph's brothers, they were seated in front of him according to their ages, from the eldest to the youngest. They were served food from Joseph's table, and Benjamin was given five times as much as each of the others. So Joseph's brothers drank with him and had a good time.

FROM
GENESIS
44.3–45.28

Since Joseph could no longer control his feelings in front of his servants, he sent them out of the room. When he was alone with his brothers, he told them, 'I am Joseph.'

BIRDS AND
ANIMALS
TRAVEL AND
TRANSPORT

JOSEPH TELLS HIS BROTHERS WHO HE REALLY IS

Early the next morning, the men were sent on their way with their donkeys. But they had not gone far from the city when Joseph told the servant, 'Go after those men! When you catch them, say, "My master has been good to you. So why have you stolen his silver cup?

When the servant caught up with them, he said exactly what Joseph had told him to say. But they replied, 'Sir, why do you say such things? We would never do anything like that! If you find that one of us has the cup, then kill him, and the rest of us will become your slaves.'

'Good!' the man replied, 'I'll do what you have said. But only the one who has the cup will become my slave. The rest of you can go free.'

Each of the brothers quickly put his sack on the ground and opened it. Joseph's servant started searching the sacks, beginning with the one that belonged to the eldest brother. When he came to Benjamin's sack, he found the cup. This upset the brothers so much that they began tearing their clothes in sorrow. Then they loaded their donkeys and returned to the city.

When Judah and his brothers got there, Joseph was still at home. So they bowed down to Joseph, who asked them, 'What have you done? Didn't you know I could find out?'

'Sir, what can we say?' Judah replied. 'How can we prove we are innocent? God has shown that we are guilty. And now all of us are your slaves, especially the one who had the cup.'

Joseph told them, 'I would never punish all of you. Only the one who was caught with the cup will become my slave. The rest of you are free to go home to your father.'

Judah went over to Joseph and said:

Sir, you have as much power as the king himself, and I am only your slave. Please don't get angry if I speak. You asked us if our father was still alive and if we had any more brothers. So we told you, 'Our father is a very old man. In fact, he was already old when Benjamin was born. Benjamin's brother is dead. Now Benjamin is the only one of the two brothers who is still alive, and our father loves him very much.'

You ordered us to bring him here, so you could see him for yourself. We told you that our father would die if Benjamin left him. But you warned us that we could never see you again, unless our youngest brother came with us. So we returned to our father and reported what you had said.

Later our father told us to come back here and buy more grain. But we answered, 'We can't go back to Egypt without our youngest brother. We will never be let in to see the governor, unless he is with us.'

Sir, our father then reminded us that his favourite wife had given birth to two sons. One of them was already missing and had not been seen for a long time. My father thinks the boy was torn to pieces by some wild animal, and he said, 'I am an old man. If you take Benjamin from me, and something happens to him, I will die of a broken heart.'

That's why Benjamin must be with us when I go back to my father. He loves him so much that he will die if Benjamin doesn't come back with me. I promised my father that I would bring him safely home. If I don't, I told my father he could blame me the rest of my life.

Sir, I am your slave. Please let me stay here in place of Benjamin and let him return home with his brothers. How can I face my father if Benjamin isn't with me? I couldn't bear to see my father in such sorrow.

Since Joseph could no longer control his feelings in front of his servants, he sent them out of the room. When he was alone with his brothers, he told them, 'I am Joseph.'

Don't worry or blame yourselves for what you did. God is the one who sent me ahead of you to save lives.

There has already been a famine for two years, and for five more years no one will plough fields or harvest grain. But God sent me on ahead of you to keep your families alive and to save you in this wonderful way. After all, you weren't really the ones who sent me here – it was God. He made me the highest official in the king's court and placed me over all Egypt.

Now hurry back and tell my father that his son Joseph says, 'God has made me ruler of Egypt. Come here as quickly as you can.

Joseph's brothers left Egypt, and when they arrived in Canaan, they told their father that Joseph was still alive and was the ruler of Egypt. But their father was so surprised that he could not believe them. Then they told him everything Joseph had said. When he saw the wagons Joseph had sent, he felt much better and said, 'Now I can believe you! My son Joseph must really be alive, and I will get to see him before I die.'

Escape from Egypt

EXODUS
1.1–22

THE ISRAELITES ARE VICTIMISED

Once he had discovered that his son Joseph was still alive and living in Egypt, Jacob moved his family to settle there. After all Joseph had done for Egypt, Jacob and his family were welcomed with open arms; but as time passed, Joseph's actions were forgotten, and things changed.

The Egyptians were cruel to the people of Israel and forced them to make bricks and to mix mortar and to work in the fields.

DIR. BRENDA CHAPMAN AND STEVE HICKNER
THE PRINCE OF EGYPT
1998

MARRIAGE AND FAMILY

See also
GENESIS 4.17,
GENESIS 11.1–9

When Jacob went to Egypt, his son Joseph was already there. So Jacob took his eleven other sons and their families. They were: Reuben, Simeon, Levi, Judah, Issachar, Zebulun, Benjamin, Dan, Naphtali, Gad, and Asher. Altogether, Jacob had seventy children, grandchildren, and great-grandchildren who went with him.

After Joseph, his brothers, and everyone else in that generation had died, the people of Israel became so numerous that the whole region of Goshen was full of them.

Many years later a new king came to power. He did not know what Joseph had done for Egypt, and he told the Egyptians:

There are too many of those Israelites in our country, and they are becoming more powerful than we are. If we don't outsmart them, their families will keep growing larger. And if our country goes to war, they could easily fight on the side of our enemies and escape from Egypt.

The Egyptians put slave bosses in charge of the people of Israel and tried to wear them down with hard work. Those bosses forced them to build the cities of Pithom and Rameses, where the king could store his supplies. But even though the Israelites were ill-treated, their families grew larger, and they took over more land. Because of this, the Egyptians hated them more than before and made them work so hard that their lives were miserable. The Egyptians were cruel to the people of Israel and forced them to make bricks and to mix mortar and to work in the fields.

Finally, the king called in Shiphrah and Puah, the two women who helped the Hebrew mothers when they gave birth. He told them, 'If a Hebrew woman gives birth to a girl, let the child live. If the baby is a boy, kill him!'

But the two women were faithful to God and did not kill the boys, even though the king had told them to. The king called them in again and asked, 'Why are you letting those baby boys live?'

They answered, 'Hebrew women have their babies much quicker than Egyptian women. By the time we arrive, their babies are already born.' God was good to the two women because they truly respected him, and he blessed them with children of their own.

The Hebrews kept increasing until finally, the king gave a command to everyone in the nation, 'As soon as a Hebrew boy is born, throw him into the River Nile! But you can let the girls live.'

> EXODUS 2.1–10

A BABY SET ADRIFT ON THE RIVER NILE

EXODUS
2.1–10

And when he was old enough, she took him to the king's daughter, who adopted him. She named him Moses because she said, 'I pulled him out of the water.'

A man from the Levi tribe married a woman from the same tribe, and she later had a baby boy. He was a beautiful child, and she kept him inside for three months. But when she could no longer keep him hidden, she made a basket out of reeds and covered it with tar. She put him in the basket and placed it in the tall grass along the edge of the River Nile. The baby's elder sister stood at a distance to see what would happen to him.

About that time one of the king's daughters came down to take a bath in the river, while her servant women walked along

HOGARTH
MOSES BROUGHT
TO PHARAOH'S
DAUGHTER
THOMAS CORAN
FOUNDATION FOR
CHILDREN
LONDON 1746

MARRIAGE AND
FAMILY

See also
HEBREWS 11.23

the river bank. She saw the basket in the tall grass and sent one of the young women to pull it out of the water. When the king's daughter opened the basket, she saw the baby and felt sorry for him because he was crying. She said, 'This must be one of the Hebrew babies.'

At once the baby's elder sister came up and asked, 'Do you want me to get a Hebrew woman to take care of the baby for you?'

'Yes,' the king's daughter answered. So the girl brought the baby's mother, and the king's daughter told her, 'Take care of this child, and I will pay you.'

The baby's mother carried him home and took care of him. And when he was old enough, she took him to the king's daughter, who adopted him. She named him Moses because she said, 'I pulled him out of the water.'

> EXODUS 3.1–4.16

EXODUS
2.11–22

When the king heard what Moses had done, the king wanted to kill him. But Moses escaped and went to the land of Midian.

BIRDS AND
ANIMALS

MOSES ESCAPES EGYPTIAN JUSTICE

After Moses had grown up, he went out to where his own people were hard at work, and he saw an Egyptian beating one of them. Moses looked around to see if anyone was watching, then he killed the Egyptian and hid his body in the sand.

When Moses went out the next day, he saw two Hebrews fighting. So he went to the man who had started the fight and asked, 'Why are you beating up one of your own people?'

The man answered, 'Who put you in charge of us and made you our judge? Are you planning to kill me, just as you killed that Egyptian?'

This frightened Moses because he was sure that people must have found out what had happened. When the king heard what Moses had done, the king wanted to kill him. But Moses escaped and went to the land of Midian.

One day, Moses was sitting there by a well, when the seven daughters of Jethro, the priest of Midian, came up to water their father's sheep and goats. Some shepherds tried to chase them away, but Moses came to their rescue and watered their animals. When Jethro's daughters returned home, their father asked, 'Why have you come back so early today?'

They answered, 'An Egyptian rescued us from the shepherds, and he even watered our sheep and goats.'

'Where is he?' Jethro asked. 'Why did you leave him out there? Invite him to eat with us.'

Moses agreed to stay on with Jethro, who later let his daughter Zipporah marry Moses.

GOD GIVES MOSES A JOB TO DO

FROM EXODUS 3.1–4.16

Although that king of Egypt died, the Israelites remained in terrible slavery. They cried out to God, who took pity on them. He revealed his rescue plan to Moses, who was not keen on carrying it out.

But the Lord answered, 'Who makes people able to speak or makes them deaf or unable to speak? Who gives them sight or makes them blind? Don't you know that I am the one who does these things?

One day, Moses was taking care of the sheep and goats of his father-in-law Jethro, the priest of Midian, and Moses decided to lead them across the desert to Sinai, the holy mountain. There an angel of the Lord appeared to him from a burning bush. Moses saw that the bush was on fire, but it was not burning up. 'This is strange!' he said to himself. 'I'll go over and see why the bush isn't burning up.'

When the Lord saw Moses coming near the bush, he called him by name, and Moses answered, 'Here I am.'

God replied, 'Don't come any closer. Take off your sandals – the ground where you are standing is holy. I am the God who was worshipped by your ancestors Abraham, Isaac, and Jacob.'

Moses was afraid to look at God, and so he hid his face.

The Lord said:

I have seen how my people are suffering as slaves in Egypt, and I have heard them beg for my help because of the way they are being ill-treated. I feel sorry for them, and I have come down to rescue them from the Egyptians. I will bring

M CHAGALL
MOSES BEFORE THE BURNING BUSH
MUSÉE NATIONAL
MESSAGE BIBLIQUE
NICE C.1960

THE LAW   EXODUS   **47**

See also
1 KINGS 18.38,
DANIEL 3.27,
NUMBERS 12.10,
2 KINGS 5.1,
MATTHEW 8.2–3

my people out of Egypt into a country where there is good land, rich with milk and honey. Now go to the king! I am sending you to lead my people out of his country.

But Moses said, 'Who am I to go to the king and lead your people out of Egypt?'

God replied, 'I will be with you. And you will know that I am the one who sent you, when you worship me on this mountain after you have led my people out of Egypt.'

Moses asked the Lord, 'Suppose everyone refuses to listen to my message, and no one believes that you really appeared to me?'

The Lord answered, 'What's that in your hand?'

'A walking stick,' Moses replied.

'Throw it down!' the Lord commanded. So Moses threw the stick on the ground. It immediately turned into a snake, and Moses jumped back.

'Pick it up by the tail!' the Lord told him. And when Moses did this, the snake turned back into a walking stick.

'Do this,' the Lord said, 'and the Israelites will believe that you have seen me, the God who was worshipped by their ancestors Abraham, Isaac, and Jacob.'

Next, the Lord commanded Moses, 'Put your hand inside your shirt.' Moses obeyed, and when he took it out, his hand had turned white as snow – like someone with leprosy.

'Put your hand back inside your shirt,' the Lord told him. Moses did so, and when he took it out again, it was as healthy as the rest of his body.

Moses replied, 'I have never been a good speaker. I wasn't one before you spoke to me, and I'm not one now. I am slow at speaking, and I can never think of what to say.'

But the Lord answered, 'Who makes people able to speak or makes them deaf or unable to speak? Who gives them sight or makes them blind? Don't you know that I am the one who does these things?

Now go! When you speak, I will be with you and give you the words to say.'

Moses begged, 'Lord, please send someone else to do it.'

The Lord became irritated with Moses and said:

What about your brother Aaron, the Levite? I know he is a good speaker. He is already on his way here to visit you, and he will be happy to see you again. Aaron will speak to the people for you, and you will be like me, telling Aaron what to say. I will be with both of you as you speak, and I will tell each of you what to do.

➤ EXODUS 12.21–34

FROM EXODUS
5.1–6.13

MOSES DEMANDS FREEDOM FOR HIS COUNTRYMEN

Moses duly met up with Aaron and together they returned to Egypt. They told the Israelite leaders everything God had said and done. The Israelites were very excited at the prospect of leaving their life of slavery behind.

'Who is this Lord and why should I obey him?' the king replied. 'I refuse to let you and your people go!'

Moses and Aaron went to the king of Egypt and told him, 'The Lord God says, "Let my people go into the desert, so they can honour me with a celebration there."'

'Who is this Lord and why should I obey him?' the king replied. 'I refuse to let you and your people go!'

They answered, 'The Lord God of the Hebrews, has appeared to us. Please let us walk three days into the desert where we can offer sacrifices to him. If you don't, he may strike us down with terrible troubles or with war.'

The king said, 'Moses and Aaron, why are you keeping these people from working? Look how many you are keeping from doing their work. Now everyone get back to work!'

That same day the king gave orders to his slave bosses and to the men directly in charge of the Israelite slaves. He told them:

Don't give the slaves any more straw to put in their bricks. Force them to find their own straw wherever they can, but they must make the same number of bricks as before. They are lazy, or else they would not beg me to let them go and sacrifice to their God. Make them work so hard that they won't have time to listen to these lies.

The slave bosses and the men in charge of the slaves went out and told them, 'The king says he will not give you any more straw. Go and find your own straw wherever you can, but you must still make as many bricks as before.'

The men knew they were in deep trouble when they were ordered to make the same number of bricks each day. After they left the king, they went to see Moses and Aaron, who had been waiting for them. Then the men said, 'We hope the Lord will punish both of you for making the king and his officials hate us. Now they even have an excuse to kill us.'

Then the Lord told Moses to demand that the king of Egypt let the Israelites leave. But Moses replied, 'I'm not a powerful speaker. If the Israelites won't listen to me, why should the king of Egypt?' But the Lord sent Aaron and Moses with a message for the Israelites and for the king; he also ordered Aaron and Moses to free the people from Egypt.

Exodus
7.14–8.19

DISASTERS BEGIN TO STRIKE EGYPT

Moses and his brother went back to meet the king, and to show him God's power Aaron threw his staff on the ground. It immediately turned into a snake. Despite this miracle, the king refused to pay attention to what they said.

The magicians told the king, 'God has done this.' But, as the Lord had said, the king was too stubborn to listen.

The Lord said to Moses:

The Egyptian king stubbornly refuses to change his mind and let the people go. Tomorrow morning take the stick that turned into a snake, then wait beside the River Nile for the king. Tell him, 'The Lord God of the Hebrews sent me to order you to release his people, so they can worship him in the desert. But until now, you have paid no attention.

'The Lord is going to do something to show you that he really is the Lord. I will strike the Nile with this stick, and the water will turn into blood. The fish will die, the river will stink, and none of you Egyptians will be able to drink the water.'

Moses, then command Aaron to hold his stick over the water. And when he does, every drop of water in Egypt will turn into blood, including rivers, canals, ponds, and even the water in buckets and jars.

Moses and Aaron obeyed the Lord. Aaron held out his stick, then struck the Nile, as the king and his officials watched. The river turned into blood, the fish died, and the water smelt so bad that none of the Egyptians could drink it. Blood was everywhere in Egypt.

But the Egyptian magicians used their secret powers to do the same thing. The king did just as the Lord had said – he stubbornly refused to listen. Then he went back to his palace and never gave it a second thought. The Egyptians had to dig holes along the banks of the Nile for drinking water, because water from the river was unfit to drink.

Seven days after the Lord had struck the Nile, he said to Moses:

Go to the palace and tell the king of Egypt that I order him to let my people go, so they can worship me. If he refuses, I will cover his entire country with frogs. Warn the king that the Nile will be full of frogs, and from there they will spread into the royal palace, including the king's bedroom and even his bed. Frogs will enter the homes of his officials and will find their way into ovens and into the bowls of bread dough. Frogs will be crawling on everyone – the king, his officials, and every citizen of Egypt.

Moses, now command Aaron to hold his stick over the water. Then frogs will come from all rivers, canals, and ponds in Egypt, and they will cover the land.

Aaron obeyed, and suddenly frogs were everywhere in Egypt. But the magicians used their secret powers to do the same thing.

The king sent for Moses and Aaron and told them, 'If you

ask the Lord to take these frogs away from me and my people, I will let your people go and offer sacrifices to him.'

'All right,' Moses answered. 'You choose the time when I am to pray for the frogs to stop bothering you, your officials, and your people, and for them to leave your houses and be found only in the river.'

'Do it tomorrow!' the king replied. 'As you wish,' Moses agreed. 'Then everyone will discover that there is no god like the Lord, and frogs will no longer be found anywhere, except in the Nile.'

After Moses and Aaron left the palace, Moses begged the Lord to do something about the frogs he had sent as punishment for the king. The Lord listened to Moses, and frogs died everywhere – in houses, yards, and fields. The dead frogs were placed in piles, and the whole country began to stink. But when the king saw that things were now better, he again did just as the Lord had said and stubbornly refused to listen to Moses and Aaron.

The Lord said to Moses, 'Command Aaron to strike the ground with his walking stick, and everywhere in Egypt the dust will turn into gnats.' They obeyed, and when Aaron struck the ground with the stick, gnats started swarming on people and animals. In fact, every speck of dust in Egypt turned into a gnat. When the magicians tried to use their secret powers to do this, they failed, and gnats stayed on people and animals.

The magicians told the king, 'God has done this.'

But, as the Lord had said, the king was too stubborn to listen.

FROM EXODUS
8.20–9.12

THINGS GET WORSE FOR THE EGYPTIANS

But the king turned stubborn again and would not let the people go.

The Lord said to Moses:

Early tomorrow morning, while the king is on his way to the river, go and say to him, 'The Lord commands you to let his people go, so they can worship him. If you don't, he will send swarms of flies to attack you, your officials, and every citizen of your country. Houses will be full of flies, and the ground will crawl with them.

'The Lord's people in Goshen won't be bothered by flies, but your people in the rest of the country will be tormented by them. That's how you will know that the Lord is here in Egypt. This miracle will happen tomorrow.'

The Lord kept his promise – the palace and the homes of the royal officials swarmed with flies, and the rest of the country was infested with them as well. Then the king sent for Moses and Aaron and told them, 'Go and sacrifice to your God, but stay here in Egypt.'

'That's impossible!' Moses replied. 'Any sacrifices we offer to the Lord our God would disgust the Egyptians, and they would stone us to death. No indeed! The Lord has ordered us to walk three days into the desert before offering sacrifices to him, and that's what we have to do.'

Then the king told him, 'I'll let you go into the desert to offer sacrifices, if you don't go very far. But in the meantime, pray for me.'

'Your Majesty,' Moses replied, 'I'll pray for you as soon as I leave, and by tomorrow the flies will stop bothering you, your officials, and the citizens of your country. Only make sure that you're telling the truth this time and that you really intend to let our people offer sacrifices to the Lord.'

After leaving the palace, Moses prayed, and the Lord answered his prayer. Not a fly was left to pester the king, his officials, or anyone else in Egypt. But the king turned stubborn again and would not let the people go. The Lord sent Moses with this message for the king of Egypt:

The Lord God of the Hebrews commands you to let his people go, so they can worship him. If you keep refusing, he will bring a terrible disease on your horses and donkeys, your camels and cattle, and your sheep and goats. But the Lord will protect the animals that belong to the people of Israel, and none of theirs will die. Tomorrow is the day the Lord has set to do this.

It happened the next day – all the animals belonging to the Egyptians died, but the Israelites did not lose even one. When the king found out, he was still too stubborn to let the people go.

The Lord said to Moses and Aaron:

Take a few handfuls of ashes from a stove and let Moses throw them into the air. Be sure the king is watching. The ashes will blow across the land of Egypt, causing sores to break out on people and animals.

So they took a few handfuls of ashes and went to the king. Moses threw them into the air, and sores immediately broke out on the Egyptians and their animals. The magicians were suffering so much from the sores, that they could not even come to Moses. Everything happened just as the Lord had told Moses – he made the king too stubborn to listen to Moses and Aaron.

Exodus
9.13–10.29

I did this because I want you to tell your children and your grandchildren about my miracles and about my harsh treatment of the Egyptians. Then all of you will know that I am the Lord.

BIRDS AND
ANIMALS
FARMING AND
PRODUCE
MIRACLES AND
WONDERS

EGYPT IS BROUGHT TO ITS KNEES

The Lord told Moses to get up early the next morning and say to the king:

The Lord God of the Hebrews commands you to let his people go, so they can worship him! If you don't, he will send his worst plagues to strike you, your officials, and everyone else in your country. Then you will find out that no one can oppose the Lord. In fact, he could already have sent a terrible disease and wiped you from the face of the earth. But he has kept you alive, just to show you his power and to bring honour to himself everywhere in the world.

You are still determined not to let the Lord's people go. All right. At this time tomorrow, he will bring on Egypt the worst hailstorm in its history. You had better give orders for every person and every animal in Egypt to take shelter. If they don't, they will die.

Some of the king's officials were frightened by what the Lord had said, and they hurried off to make sure their slaves and animals were safe. But others paid no attention to his threats

See also
JOSHUA 10.11,
REVELATION 16.21

and left their slaves and animals out in the open.

Then the Lord told Moses, 'Stretch your arm towards the sky, so that hailstones will fall on people, animals, and crops in the land of Egypt.' Moses pointed his walking stick towards the sky, and hailstones started falling everywhere. Thunder roared, and lightning flashed back and forth, striking the ground. This was the worst storm in the history of Egypt. People, animals, and crops were pounded by the hailstones, and bark was stripped from trees. Only Goshen, where the Israelites lived, was safe from the storm.

The king sent for Moses and Aaron and told them, 'Now I have really sinned! My people and I are guilty, and the Lord is right. We can't stand any more of this thunder and hail. Please ask the Lord to make it stop. Your people can go – you don't have to stay in Egypt any longer.'

Moses answered, 'As soon as I leave the city, I will lift my arms in prayer. When the thunder and hail stop, you will know that the earth belongs to the Lord. But I am certain that neither you nor your officials really fear the Lord God.'

Meanwhile, the flax and barley crops had been destroyed by the storm because they were ready to ripen. But the wheat crops ripen later, and they were not damaged.

After Moses left the royal palace and the city, he lifted his arms in prayer to the Lord, and the thunder, hail, and drenching rain stopped. When the king realized that the storm was over, he disobeyed once more. He and his officials were so stubborn that he refused to let the Israelites go. This was exactly what the Lord had said would happen.

The Lord said to Moses:

Go back to the king. I have made him and his officials stubborn, so that I could work these miracles. I did this because I want you to tell your children and your grand-children about my miracles and about my harsh treatment of the Egyptians. Then all of you will know that I am the Lord.

Moses and Aaron went to the king and told him that the Lord God of the Hebrews had said:

How long will you stubbornly refuse to obey? Release my people so they can worship me. Do this by tomorrow, or I will cover your country with so many locusts that you won't be able to see the ground. Most of your crops were ruined by the hailstones, but these locusts will destroy what little is left, including the trees. Your palace, the homes of your officials, and all other houses in Egypt will overflow with more locusts than have ever been seen in this country.

After Moses left the palace, the king's officials asked, 'Your Majesty, how much longer is this man going to be a troublemaker? Why don't you let the people leave, so they can worship the Lord their God? Don't you know that Egypt is a disaster?'

The king had Moses and Aaron brought back, and he said, 'All right, you may go and worship the Lord your God. But first tell me who will be going.'

'Everyone, young and old,' Moses answered. 'We will even take our sheep, goats, and cattle, because we want to hold a celebration in honour of the Lord.' The king replied, 'The Lord had better watch over you on the day I let you leave with your families! You're up to no good. Do you want to worship the Lord? All right, take only the men and go.' Then Moses and Aaron were chased out of the palace.

The Lord told Moses, 'Stretch your arm towards Egypt. Swarms of locusts will come and eat everything left by the hail.'

Moses held out his walking stick, and the Lord sent an east wind that blew across Egypt the rest of the day and all that night. By morning, locusts were swarming everywhere. Never before had there been so many locusts in Egypt, and never again will there be so many. The ground was black with locusts, and they ate everything left on the trees and in the fields. Nothing green remained in Egypt – not a tree or a plant.

At once the king sent for Moses and Aaron. He told them, 'I have sinned against the Lord your God and against you. Forgive me one more time and ask the Lord to stop these insects from killing every living plant.'

Moses left the palace and prayed. Then the Lord sent a

strong west wind that swept the locusts into the Red Sea. Not one locust was left anywhere in Egypt, but the Lord made the king so stubborn that he still refused to let the Israelites go.

The Lord said to Moses, 'Stretch your arm towards the sky, and everything will be covered with darkness thick enough to touch.' Moses stretched his arm towards the sky, and Egypt was covered with darkness for three days. During that time, the Egyptians could not see each other or leave their homes, but there was light where the Israelites lived.

The king sent for Moses and told him, 'Go and worship the Lord! And take your families with you. Just leave your sheep, goats, and cattle.'

'No!' Moses replied. 'You must let us offer sacrifices to the Lord our God, and we won't know which animals we will need until we get there. That's why we can't leave even one of them here.'

This time the Lord made the king so stubborn that he said to Moses, 'Get out and stay out! If you ever come back, you're dead!'

'Have it your way,' Moses answered. 'You won't see me again.'

FROM EXODUS
12.21–34

DEATH STALKS THROUGH EGYPT

God told Moses that one final, terrifying disaster would strike Egypt, after which the king would finally let them go.

During that night the Lord will go through the country of Egypt and kill the firstborn son in every Egyptian family. He will see where you have put the blood, and he

Moses called the leaders of Israel together and said:

Each family is to pick out a sheep and kill it for Passover. Make a brush from a few small branches of a hyssop plant and dip the brush in the bowl that has the blood of the animal in it. Then brush some of the blood above the door and on the posts at each side of the door of your house. After this, everyone is to stay inside.

During that night the Lord will go through the country of Egypt and kill the firstborn son in every Egyptian family. He

will not come into
your house.

J.M.W. TURNER
THE TENTH PLAGUE
OF EGYPT
1802

BIRDS AND
ANIMALS
FOOD AND DRINK
MARRIAGE AND
FAMILY
MIRACLES AND
WONDERS

See also
NUMBERS 9,
MATTHEW
26.26–29,
1 CORINTHIANS
5.7

will see where you have put the blood, and he will not come into your house. His angel that brings death will pass over and not kill your firstborn sons.

After you have entered the country promised to you by the Lord, you and your children must continue to celebrate Passover each year.

Then they left and did what Moses and Aaron had told them to do.

At midnight the Lord killed the firstborn son of every Egyptian family, from the son of the king to the son of every prisoner in jail. He also killed the firstborn male of every animal that belonged to the Egyptians.

That night the king, his officials, and everyone else in Egypt got up and started crying bitterly. In every Egyptian home, someone was dead.

During the night the king sent for Moses and Aaron and told them, 'Get your people out of my country and leave us alone! Go and worship the Lord, as you have asked. Take your sheep, goats, and cattle, and get out. But ask your God to be kind to me.'

The Egyptians did everything they could to get the Israelites to leave their country fast. They said, 'Please hurry and leave. If you don't, we will all be dead.' So the Israelites quickly made some bread dough and put it in pans. But they did not mix any yeast in the dough to make it rise. They wrapped cloth around the pans and carried them on their shoulders.

EXODUS 14.5–29

THE ISRAELITES BEGIN THEIR JOURNEY HOME

As the Israelites left they asked the Egyptians for gold, silver and clothes. Their former captives were so happy to see them go that they gave them everything they needed for the journey.

During the day the Lord went ahead of his people in a thick cloud, and during the night he went ahead of them in a flaming fire. That way the Lord could lead them at all times, whether day or night.

After the king had finally let the people go, the Lord did not lead them through Philistine territory, though that was the shortest way. God had said, 'If they are attacked, they may decide to return to Egypt.' So he led them around through the desert and towards the Red Sea.

The Israelites left Egypt, prepared for battle.

Moses made them take along the bones of Joseph, whose dying words had been, 'God will come to your rescue, and when he does, be sure to take along my bones.'

The people of Israel left Succoth and camped at Etham at the border of Egypt near the desert. During the day the Lord went ahead of his people in a thick cloud, and during the night he went ahead of them in a flaming fire. That way the Lord could lead them at all times, whether day or night.

GOD DESTROYS THE EGYPTIAN ARMY

When the people were gone, the king changed his mind once more and chased after the Israelites. But God laid a trap for him and his army.

But Moses answered, 'Don't be afraid! Be brave, and you will see the Lord save you today. These Egyptians will never bother you again.'

When the king of Egypt heard that the Israelites had finally left, he and his officials changed their minds and said, 'Look what we have done! We let them get away, and they will no longer be our slaves.'

The king got his war chariot and army ready. He commanded his officers in charge of his six hundred best chariots and all his other chariots to start after the Israelites. The Lord

BIRDS AND
ANIMALS
MIRACLES AND
WONDERS
VIOLENCE AND
WARFARE

See also JOSHUA
3.1–17

made the king so stubborn that he went after them, even though the Israelites proudly went on their way. But the king's horses and chariots and soldiers caught up with them while they were camping by the Red Sea near Pi-Hahiroth and Baal-Zephon.

When the Israelites saw the king coming with his army, they were frightened and begged the Lord for help. They also complained to Moses, 'Wasn't there enough room in Egypt to bury us? Is that why you brought us out here to die in the desert? Why did you bring us out of Egypt anyway? While we were there, didn't we tell you to leave us alone? We would rather be slaves in Egypt than die in this desert!'

But Moses answered, 'Don't be afraid! Be brave, and you will see the Lord save you today. These Egyptians will never bother you again. The Lord will fight for you, and you won't have to do a thing.'

The Lord said to Moses, 'Why do you keep calling out to me for help? Tell the Israelites to move forward. Then hold your walking stick over the sea. The water will open up and make a road where they can walk through on dry ground. I will make the Egyptians so stubborn that they will go after you. Then I will be praised because of what happens to the king and his chariots and cavalry. The Egyptians will know for sure that I am the Lord.'

All this time God's angel had gone ahead of Israel's army, but now he moved behind them. A large cloud had also gone ahead of them, but now it moved between the Egyptians and the Israelites. The cloud gave light to the Israelites, but made it dark for the Egyptians, and during the night they could not come any closer.

Moses stretched his arm over the sea, and the Lord sent a strong east wind that blew all night until there was dry land where the water had been. The sea opened up, and the Israelites walked through on dry land with a wall of water on each side.

The Egyptian chariots and cavalry went after them. But before daylight the Lord looked down at the Egyptian army from the fiery cloud and made them panic. Their chariot wheels got stuck, and it was hard for them to move. So the Egyptians said to one another, 'Let's leave these people alone! The Lord is on their side and is fighting against us.'

The Lord told Moses, 'Stretch your arm towards the sea – the water will cover the Egyptians and their cavalry and chariots.' Moses stretched out his arm, and at daybreak the water rushed towards the Egyptians. They tried to run away, but the Lord drowned them in the sea. The water came and covered the chariots, the cavalry, and the whole Egyptian army that had followed the Israelites into the sea. Not one of them was left alive. But the sea had made a wall of water on each side of the Israelites; so they walked through on dry land.

▶ EXODUS 19.1–20.21

GOD'S PEOPLE IN THE DESERT

Exodus
16.1–31

FOOD FOR EVERYONE

Moses led the people from the Red Sea into the desert. When they were unable to find anything to drink, God miraculously provided water for them but they were soon worrying again.

'I have heard my people complain. Now tell them that each evening they will have meat and each morning they will have more than enough bread. Then they will know that I am the Lord their God.'

MIRACLES AND WONDERS

See also
JOHN 6.1–51

On the fifteenth day of the second month after the Israelites had escaped from Egypt, they left Elim and started through the western edge of the Sinai Desert in the direction of Mount Sinai. There in the desert they started complaining to Moses and Aaron, 'We wish the Lord had killed us in Egypt. When we lived there, we could at least sit down and eat all the bread and meat we wanted. But you have brought us out here into this desert, where we are going to starve.'

The Lord said to Moses, 'I will send bread down from heaven like rain. Each day the people can go out and gather only enough for that day. That's how I will see if they obey me. But on the sixth day of each week they must gather and cook twice as much.'

Moses and Aaron told the people, 'This evening you will know that the Lord was the one who rescued you from Egypt. And in the morning you will see his glorious power, because he has heard your complaints against him. Why should you grumble to us? Who are we?'

Then Moses continued, 'You will know it is the Lord when he gives you meat each evening and more than enough bread each morning. He is really the one you are complaining about, not us – we are nobodies – but the Lord has heard your complaints.'

Moses turned to Aaron and said, 'Bring the people together, because the Lord has heard their complaints.'

Aaron was speaking to them, when everyone looked out towards the desert and saw the bright glory of the Lord in a cloud. The Lord said to Moses, 'I have heard my people complain. Now tell them that each evening they will have meat and each morning they will have more than enough bread. Then they will know that I am the Lord their God.'

That evening a lot of quails came and landed everywhere in the camp, and the next morning dew covered the ground. After the dew had gone, the desert was covered with thin flakes that looked like frost. The people had never seen anything like this, and they started asking each other, 'What is it?'

Moses answered, 'This is the bread that the Lord has given you to eat. And he orders you to gather about two litres for each person in your family – that should be more than enough.'

They did as they were told. Some gathered more and some gathered less, according to their needs, and none was left over.

Moses told them not to keep any overnight. Some of them disobeyed, but the next morning what they kept was stinking and full of worms, and Moses was angry.

Each morning everyone gathered as much as they needed, and in the heat of the day the rest melted. However, on the sixth day of the week, everyone gathered enough to have four litres, instead of two. When the leaders reported this to Moses, he told them that the Lord had said, 'Tomorrow is the Sabbath, a sacred day of rest in honour of me. So gather all you want to bake or boil, and make sure you save enough for tomorrow.'

The people obeyed, and the next morning the food smelt fine and had no worms. 'You may eat the food,' Moses said. 'Today is the Sabbath in honour of the Lord, and there won't be any of this food on the ground today. You will find it there for the first six days of the week, but not on the Sabbath.'

A few of the Israelites did go out to look for some, but there was none. Then the Lord said, 'Moses, how long will you people keep disobeying my laws and teachings? Remember that I was the one who gave you the Sabbath. That's why on the sixth day I provide enough bread for two days. Everyone is to stay at home and rest on the Sabbath.' And so they rested on the Sabbath.

The Israelites called the bread manna. It was white like coriander seed and delicious as wafers made with honey.

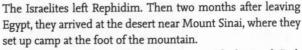

FROM EXODUS
19.1–20.21

TEN COMMANDMENTS

Now that the food issue was resolved, the people continued their journey into the wilderness, towards an historic encounter with God.

I am the Lord your
God, the one who
brought you out of
Egypt where you
were slaves.

DIR. CECIL B
DEMILLE
THE TEN
COMMANDMENTS
1956

See also
1 KINGS 19.1–16,
MATTHEW 5.1–7.29

The Israelites left Rephidim. Then two months after leaving Egypt, they arrived at the desert near Mount Sinai, where they set up camp at the foot of the mountain.

Moses went up the mountain to meet with the Lord God, who told him to say to the people:

You saw what I did in Egypt, and you know how I brought you here to me, just as a mighty eagle carries its young. Now if you will faithfully obey me, you will be my very own people. The whole world is mine, but you will be my holy nation and serve me as priests. Moses, that is what you must tell the Israelites.

After Moses had gone back down, he told the people what the Lord had said.

God said to the people of Israel:

I am the Lord your God, the one who brought you out of Egypt where you were slaves.

Do not worship any god except me.

Do not make idols that look like anything in the sky or on earth or in the sea under the earth. Don't bow down and worship idols. I am the Lord your God, and I demand all your love. If you reject me, I will punish your families for three or four generations. But if you love me and obey my laws, I will be kind to your families for thousands of generations.

Do not misuse my name. I am the Lord your God, and I will punish anyone who misuses my name.

Remember that the Sabbath Day belongs to me. You have six days when you can do your work, but the seventh day of each week belongs to me, your God. No one is to work on that day – not you, your children, your slaves, your animals, or the foreigners who live in your towns. In six days I made the sky, the earth, the seas, and everything in them, but on the seventh day I rested. That's why I made the Sabbath a special day that belongs to me.

Respect your father and your mother, and you will live a long time in the land I am giving you.

Do not murder.

Be faithful in marriage.

Do not steal.

Do not tell lies about others.

Do not want to take anything that belongs to someone else. Don't want to take anyone's house, wife or husband, slaves, oxen, donkeys or anything else.

The people trembled with fear when they heard the thunder and the trumpet and saw the lightning and the smoke coming from the mountain. They stood a long way off and said to Moses, 'If you speak to us, we will listen. But don't let God speak to us, or we will die!'

'Don't be afraid!' Moses replied. 'God has come only to test you, so that by obeying him you won't sin.' But when Moses went near the thick cloud where God was, the people stayed a long way off.

➤ JOSHUA 3.1–17

EXODUS
32.1–20

THE ISRAELITES WASTE NO TIME IN DISOBEYING GOD

While Moses was on the mountain, God gave him many other laws to guide the people when they settled in the land they had been promised. But while their leader was talking to God, the people down below became impatient and took matters into their own hands.

After the people saw that Moses had been on the mountain for

Remember the solemn promise you made to Abraham, Isaac, and Jacob. You promised that some day they would have as many descendants as there are stars in the sky and that you would give them land.

TINTORETTO
WORSHIP OF THE
GOLDEN CALF
WASHINGTON
1560

See also
ISAIAH 44.9–20

a long time, they went to Aaron and said, 'Make us an image of a god who will lead and protect us. Moses brought us out of Egypt, but nobody knows what has happened to him.'

Aaron told them, 'Bring me the gold earrings that your wives and sons and daughters are wearing.' Everybody took off their earrings and brought them to Aaron, then he melted them and made an idol in the shape of a young bull. All the people said to one another, 'This is the god who brought us out of Egypt!'

When Aaron saw what was happening, he built an altar in front of the idol and said, 'Tomorrow we will celebrate in honour of the Lord.' The people got up early the next morning and killed some animals to be used for sacrifices and others to be eaten. Then everyone ate and drank so much that they began to carry on like wild people.

The Lord said to Moses:

Hurry back down! Those people you led out of Egypt are acting like fools. They have already stopped obeying me and have made themselves an idol in the shape of a young bull. They have bowed down to it, offered sacrifices, and said that it is the god who brought them out of Egypt. Moses, I have seen how stubborn these people are, and I'm angry enough to destroy them, so don't try to stop me. But I will make your descendants into a great nation.

Moses tried to get the Lord God to change his mind:

Our Lord, you used your mighty power to bring these people out of Egypt. Now don't become angry and destroy them. If you do, the Egyptians will say that you brought your people out here into the mountains just to get rid of them. Please don't be angry with your people. Don't destroy them!

Remember the solemn promise you made to Abraham, Isaac, and Jacob. You promised that some day they would have as many descendants as there are stars in the sky and that you would give them land.

So even though the Lord had threatened to destroy the people, he changed his mind and let them live.

Moses went back down the mountain with the two flat

stones on which God had written all his laws with his own hand, and he had used both sides of the stones.

When Joshua heard the noisy shouts of the people, he said to Moses, 'A battle must be going on down in the camp.'

But Moses replied, 'It doesn't sound like they are shouting because they have won or lost a battle. They are singing wildly!'

As Moses got closer to the camp, he saw the idol, and he also saw the people dancing around. This made him so angry that he threw down the stones and broke them to pieces at the foot of the mountain. He melted the idol the people had made, and he ground it into powder. He scattered it in their water and made them drink it.

SCOUTING ENEMY TERRITORY

FROM
NUMBERS
13.1–33

When God had finished giving Moses the laws and commandments his people were to follow, the Israelites continued their journey through the desert. Moses led them until they reached the borders of the land they had been promised. Here they set up camp, in preparation for the final push into their new home.

The land we explored is rich with milk and honey.

FOOD AND DRINK

See also
JOSHUA 2.1–24,
LUKE 20.20–21,
DEUTERONOMY
1.19–46

The Lord said to Moses, 'Choose a leader from each tribe and send them into Canaan to explore the land I am giving you.'

So Moses sent twelve tribal leaders from Israel's camp in the Paran Desert with orders to explore the land of Canaan. And here are their names:

Shammua son of Zaccur from Reuben, Shaphat son of Hori from Simeon, Caleb son of Jephunneh from Judah, Igal son of Joseph from Issachar, Joshua son of Nun from Ephraim, Palti son of Raphu from Benjamin, Gaddiel son of Sodi from Zebulun, Gaddi son of Susi from Manasseh, Ammiel son of Gemalli from Dan, Sethur son of Michael from Asher, Nahbi son of Vophsi from Naphtali, and Geuel son of Machi from Gad.

The twelve men left to explore Canaan from the Zin Desert in the south all the way to the town of Rehob near Lebo-Hamath in the north. As they went through the Southern Desert, they came to the town of Hebron, which was seven years older than the Egyptian town of Zoan. In Hebron, they saw the three Anakim clans of Ahiman, Sheshai, and Talmai. When they got to Bunch Valley, they cut off a branch with such a huge bunch of grapes, that it took two men to carry it on a pole. That's why the place was called Bunch Valley. Along with the grapes, they also took back pomegranates and figs.

After exploring the land of Canaan for forty days, the twelve men returned to Kadesh in the Paran Desert and told Moses, Aaron, and the people what they had seen. They showed them the fruit and said:

Look at this fruit! The land we explored is rich with milk and honey. But the people who live there are strong, and their cities are large and walled. We even saw the three Anakim clans. Besides that, the Amalekites live in the Southern Desert; the Hittites, Jebusites, and Amorites are in the hill country; and the Canaanites live along the Mediterranean Sea and the River Jordan.

Caleb calmed down the crowd and said, 'Let's go and take the land. I know we can do it!'

But the other men replied, 'Those people are much too strong for us.' Then they started spreading rumours and saying, 'We won't be able to grow anything in that soil. And the people are like giants. In fact, we saw the Nephilim who are the ancestors of the Anakim. They were so big that we felt as small as grasshoppers.'

NUMBERS
20.2–12

DYING OF THIRST IN THE DESERT

The people were afraid and refused to move into Canaan. God was angry and promised that of all the Israelite adults, only Joshua and Caleb would ever live there. So the people began a nomadic life in the desert.

But the Lord said to Moses and Aaron, 'Because you refused to believe in my power, these people did not respect me. And so, you will not be the ones to lead them into the land I have promised.'

FOOD AND DRINK

See also JOHN 7.37–44

The Israelites had no water, so they went to Moses and Aaron and complained, 'Moses, we'd be better off if we had died along with the others in front of the Lord's sacred tent. You brought us into this desert, and now we and our livestock are going to die! Egypt was better than this horrible place. At least there we had grain and figs and grapevines and pomegranates. But now we don't even have any water.'

Moses and Aaron went to the entrance to the sacred tent, where they bowed down. The Lord appeared to them in all his glory and said, 'Moses, get your walking stick. Then you and Aaron call the people together and command that rock to give you water. That's how you will provide water for the people of Israel and their livestock.'

Moses obeyed and took his stick from the sacred tent. After he and Aaron had gathered the people around the rock, he said, 'Look, you rebellious people, and you will see water flow from this rock!' He raised his stick in the air and struck the rock two times. At once, water gushed from the rock, and the people and their livestock had water to drink.

But the Lord said to Moses and Aaron, 'Because you refused to believe in my power, these people did not respect me. And so, you will not be the ones to lead them into the land I have promised.'

NUMBERS
21.4–9

SNAKE BITES

During their exile in the desert Aaron died, and everyone mourned his death for a month. As they continued to wander, the people's impatience was a recurrent theme.

'Make a snake out of bronze and place it on top of a pole. Anyone who gets bitten can look at the snake and won't die.'

The Israelites had to go around the territory of Edom, so when they left Mount Hor, they headed south towards the Red Sea. But along the way, the people became so impatient that they complained against God and said to Moses, 'Did you bring us out of Egypt, just to let us die in the desert? There's no water out here, and we can't stand this awful food!'

Then the Lord sent poisonous snakes that bit and killed

many of them.

Some of the people went to Moses and admitted, 'It was wrong of us to insult you and the Lord. Now please ask him to make these snakes go away.'

Moses prayed, and the Lord answered, 'Make a snake out of bronze and place it on top of a pole. Anyone who gets bitten can look at the snake and won't die.'

Moses obeyed the Lord. And all of those who looked at the bronze snake lived, even though they had been bitten by the poisonous snakes.

**DEUTERONOMY
6.1–9**

THE MOST IMPORTANT LAW OF ALL

After wandering in the desert for forty years, the Israelites returned again to the borders of Canaan. Moses spoke to the people, reminding them of all God had said and all that had happened since their departure from Egypt.

And if you and your descendants want to live a long time, you must always worship the Lord and obey his laws.

AGREEMENTS AND PROMISES

See also MARK
12.28–34

Moses said to Israel:

The Lord told me to give you these laws and teachings, so you can obey them in the land he is giving you. Soon you will cross the River Jordan and take that land. And if you and your descendants want to live a long time, you must always worship the Lord and obey his laws. Pay attention, Israel! Our ancestors worshipped the Lord, and he promised to give us this land that is rich with milk and honey. Be careful to obey him, and you will become a successful and powerful nation.

Listen, Israel! The Lord our God is the only true God! So love the Lord your God with all your heart, soul, and strength. Memorize his laws and tell them to your children over and over again. Talk about them all the time, whether you're at home or walking along the road or going to bed at night, or getting up in the morning. Write down copies and tie them to your wrists and foreheads to help you obey them. Write these laws on the door frames of your homes and on your town gates.

HISTORY

This section tells how the Israelites conquered, and settled in, the land God had promised them. It explains how the monarchy came into being and then tells of the successes and failures of a long line of kings. At the end, after the people are carried into exile by foreign powers, some return and begin the process of re-establishing their lives.

THE PROMISED LAND

JOSHUA 1.1–9

GOD PREPARES JOSHUA FOR THE INVASION

On the brink of the land God had promised his people, Moses spoke to the Israelites one last time, encouraging them to trust and follow the Lord. Before he died, God took Moses to the top of a mountain and showed him the promised land. As his final act, Moses appointed Joshua his successor, to lead the people in their conquest of the land.

I've commanded you to be strong and brave. Don't ever be afraid or discouraged! I am the Lord your God, and I will be there to help you wherever you go.

Moses, the Lord's servant, was dead. So the Lord spoke to Joshua son of Nun, who had been the assistant of Moses. The Lord said:

My servant Moses is dead. Now you must lead Israel across the River Jordan into the land I'm giving to all of you. Wherever you go, I'll give you that land, as I promised Moses. It will reach from the Southern Desert to the Lebanon Mountains in the north, and to the north-east as far as the great River Euphrates. It will include the land of the Hittites, and the land from here at the River Jordan to the Mediterranean Sea on the west. Joshua, I will always be with you and help you as I helped Moses, and no one will ever be able to defeat you.

**AGREEMENTS AND
PROMISES**

See also
JOSHUA 3.1–17,
2 KINGS 2. 7–13,
2 KINGS 5.10,
MATTHEW 3.6

Long ago I promised the ancestors of Israel that I would give this land to their descendants. So be strong and brave! Be careful to do everything my servant Moses taught you. Never stop reading The Book of the Law he gave you. Day and night you must think about what it says. If you obey it completely, you and Israel will be able to take this land.

I've commanded you to be strong and brave. Don't ever be afraid or discouraged! I am the Lord your God, and I will be there to help you wherever you go.

JOSHUA 2.1–24

JOSHUA SPENDS SPIES INTO JERICHO

I know that the Lord has given Israel this land. Everyone shakes with fear because of you.

See also
NUMBERS
13.1–31,
LUKE 20.20–21,
JOSHUA 6.22–25,
MATTHEW 1.5,
HEBREWS 11.31,
JAMES 2.25

Joshua chose two men as spies and sent them from their camp at Acacia with these instructions: 'Go across the river and find out as much as you can about the whole region, especially about the town of Jericho.'

The two spies left the Israelite camp at Acacia and went to Jericho, where they decided to spend the night at the house of a prostitute named Rahab.

But someone found out about them and told the king of Jericho, 'Some Israelite men came here tonight, and they are spies.' So the king sent soldiers to Rahab's house to arrest the spies.

Meanwhile, Rahab had taken the men up to the flat roof of her house and had hidden them under some piles of flax plants that she had put there to dry.

The soldiers came to her door and demanded, 'Let us have the men who are staying at your house. They are spies.'

She answered, 'Some men did come to my house, but I didn't know where they had come from. They left about sunset, just before it was time to close the town gate. I don't know where they were going, but if you hurry, perhaps you can catch them.'

The guards at the town gate let the soldiers leave Jericho, but they closed the gate again as soon as the soldiers went through. Then the soldiers headed towards the River Jordan to look for the spies at the place where people cross the river.

Rahab went back up to her roof. The spies were still awake, so she told them:

I know that the Lord has given Israel this land. Everyone shakes with fear because of you. We heard how the Lord dried up the Red Sea so you could leave Egypt. And we heard how you destroyed Sihon and Og, those two Amorite kings east of the River Jordan. We know that the Lord your God rules heaven and earth, and we've lost our courage and our will to fight.

Please promise me in the Lord's name that you will be as kind to my family as I have been to you. Do something to show that you won't let your people kill my father and mother and my brothers and sisters and their families.

'Rahab,' the spies answered, 'if you keep quiet about what we're doing, we promise to be kind to you when the Lord gives us this land. We pray that the Lord will kill us if we don't keep our promise!'

Rahab's house was built into the town wall, and one of the windows in her house faced outside the wall. She gave the spies a rope, showed them the window, and said, 'Use this rope to let yourselves down to the ground outside the wall. Then hide in the hills. The men who are looking for you won't be able to find you there. They'll give up and come back after a few days, and you can be on your way.'

The spies said:

You made us promise to let you and your family live. We will keep our promise, but you can't tell anyone why we were here. You must tie this red rope on your window when we attack, and your father and mother, your brothers, and everyone else in your family must be here with you. We'll take the blame if anyone who stays in this house gets hurt. But anyone who leaves your house will be killed, and it won't be our fault.

'I'll do exactly what you said,' Rahab promised. Then she sent them on their way and tied the red rope to the window.

The spies hid in the hills for three days while the king's soldiers looked for them along the roads. As soon as the soldiers gave up and returned to Jericho, the two spies went down into the Jordan valley and crossed the river. They reported to Joshua and told him everything that had happened. 'We're sure the Lord has given us the whole country,' they said. 'The people there shake with fear every time they think of us.'

CROSSING THE RIVER

FROM JOSHUA
3.1–17

But the living God will be with you and will force them out of the land when you attack

See also EXODUS
14.5–29

Early the next morning, Joshua and the Israelites packed up and left Acacia. They went to the River Jordan and camped there that night.

Joshua spoke to the people:

Come here and listen to what the Lord our God said he will do! The Canaanites, the Hittites, the Hivites, the Perizzites, the Girgashites, the Amorites, and the Jebusites control the land on the other side of the river. But the living God will be with you and will force them out of the land when you attack. And now, God is going to prove that he's powerful enough to force them out. Just watch the sacred chest that belongs to the Lord, the ruler of the whole earth. As soon as the priests carrying the chest step into the Jordan, the water will stop flowing and pile up as if someone had built a dam across the river.

The Lord has also said that each of the twelve tribes should choose one man to represent it.

The Israelites packed up and left camp. The priests carrying the chest walked in front, until they came to the River Jordan. The water in the river had risen over its banks, as it often does in springtime. But as soon as the feet of the priests touched the water, the river stopped flowing, and the water started piling up at the town of Adam near Zarethan. No water flowed towards the Dead Sea, and the priests stood in the middle of the dry river bed near Jericho while everyone else crossed over.

 JOSHUA 21.43–45

JOSHUA 6.1–20

THE ANNIHILATION OF JERICHO

The priests blew their trumpets again, and the soldiers shouted as loud as they could. The walls of Jericho fell flat. Then the soldiers rushed up the hill, went straight into the town, and captured it.

When all the Israelites had crossed the Jordan, they took twelve stones from the river bed, and set them up as a memorial to what had taken place.

Meanwhile, the people of Jericho had been locking the gates in their town wall because they were afraid of the Israelites. No one could go out or come in.

The Lord said to Joshua:

With my help, you and your army will defeat the king of Jericho and his army, and you will capture the town. Here is how to do it: march slowly around Jericho once a day for six days. Take along the sacred chest and make seven priests walk in front of it, carrying trumpets.

But on the seventh day, march slowly around the town seven times while the priests blow their trumpets. Then the priests will blast on their trumpets, and everyone else will shout. The wall will fall down, and your soldiers can go straight in from every side.

MIRACLES AND
WONDERS
VIOLENCE AND
WARFARE

See also
EXODUS 25.21,
DEUTERONOMY
10.5,
1 SAMUEL 4

Joshua called the priests together and said, 'Take the chest and make seven priests carry trumpets and march ahead of it.'

Next, he gave the army their orders: 'March slowly around Jericho. A few of you will go ahead of the chest to guard it, but most of you will follow it. Don't shout the battle cry or yell or even talk until the day I tell you to. Then let out a shout!'

As soon as Joshua finished giving the orders, the army started marching. One group of soldiers led the way, with seven priests marching behind them and blowing trumpets.

Then came the priests carrying the chest, followed by the rest of the soldiers.

They obeyed Joshua's orders and carried the chest once around the town before returning to camp for the night.

Early the next morning, Joshua and everyone else started marching around Jericho in the same order as the day before. One group of soldiers was in front, followed by the seven priests with trumpets and the priests who carried the chest. The rest of the army came next. The seven priests blew their trumpets while everyone marched slowly around Jericho and back to camp. They did this once a day for six days.

On the seventh day, the army got up at daybreak. They marched slowly around Jericho as they had done for the past six days, except on this day they went around seven times. Then the priests blew the trumpets, and Joshua yelled:

Get ready to shout! The Lord will let you capture this town. But you must destroy it and everything in it, to show that it now belongs to the Lord. The woman Rahab helped the spies we sent, so protect her and the others who are inside her house. But kill everyone else in the town. The silver and gold and everything made of bronze and iron belong to the Lord and must be put in his treasury. Be careful to follow these instructions, because if you see something you want and take it, the Lord will destroy Israel. And it will be all your fault.

The priests blew their trumpets again, and the soldiers shouted as loud as they could. The walls of Jericho fell flat. Then the soldiers rushed up the hill, went straight into the town, and captured it.

JOSHUA
21.43–45

The Lord gave the Israelites the land he had promised their ancestors, and they captured it and settled in it.

VIOLENCE AND
WARFARE

THE PEOPLE OF ISRAEL OCCUPY THE LAND

After their victory at Jericho, the Israelites continued their conquest of the land.

The Lord gave the Israelites the land he had promised their ancestors, and they captured it and settled in it. There still were enemies around Israel, but the Lord kept his promise to let his people live in peace. And whenever the Israelites did have to go to war, no enemy could defeat them. The Lord always helped Israel win. The Lord promised to do many good things for Israel, and he kept his promise every time.

> 1 SAMUEL 7.15–8.22

JOSHUA
24.14–25

But if you don't want to worship the Lord, then choose now! Will you worship the same idols your ancestors did? Or since you're living on land that once belonged to the Amorites, perhaps you'll worship their gods. I won't. My family

JOSHUA WARNS THE PEOPLE TO FOLLOW GOD

The people enjoyed a period of peace under Joshua's leadership. He called them together at Shechem, where they renewed the agreement between themselves and God.

Then Joshua told the people:
Worship the Lord, obey him, and always be faithful. Get rid of the idols your ancestors worshipped when they lived on the other side of the River Euphrates and in Egypt. But if you don't want to worship the Lord, then choose now! Will you worship the same idols your ancestors did? Or since you're living on land that once belonged to the Amorites, perhaps you'll worship their gods. I won't. My family and I are going to worship and obey the Lord!

The people answered:
We could never worship other gods or stop worshipping the Lord. The Lord is our God. We were slaves in Egypt as our

*and I are going to
worship and obey
the Lord!*

ancestors had been, but we saw the Lord work miracles to set our people free and to bring us out of Egypt. Even though other nations were all around us, the Lord protected us wherever we went. And when we fought the Amorites and the other nations that lived in this land, the Lord made them run away. Yes, we will worship and obey the Lord, because the Lord is our God.

Joshua said:

The Lord is fearsome; he is the one true God, and I don't think you are able to worship and obey him in the ways he demands. You would have to be completely faithful, and if you sin or rebel, he won't let you get away with it. If you turn your backs on the Lord and worship the gods of other nations, the Lord will turn against you. He will make terrible things happen to you and wipe you out, even though he had been good to you before.

But the people shouted, 'We won't worship any other gods. We will worship and obey only the Lord!'

Joshua said, 'You have heard yourselves say that you will worship and obey the Lord. Isn't that true?'

'Yes, it's true,' they answered.

Joshua said, 'But you still have some idols, like those the other nations worship. Get rid of your idols! You must decide once and for all that you really want to obey the Lord God of Israel.'

The people said, 'The Lord is our God, and we will worship and obey only him.'

Joshua helped Israel make an agreement with the Lord that day at Shechem.

STORIES OF GOD'S PEOPLE

FROM JUDGES
6.11–24

GOD SINGLES OUT GIDEON FOR MILITARY SERVICE

After Joshua's death, many of the Israelites forgot the Lord, and the surrounding nations began to cause them trouble. During this unsettling period God picked special men and women to lead his people against their enemies. These leaders became known as judges.

'Gideon,' the Lord answered, 'you can rescue Israel because I am going to help you! Defeating the Midianites will be as easy as beating up one man.'

*BIRDS AND
ANIMALS
FARMING AND
PRODUCE
MIRACLES AND
WONDERS*

GENESIS 16.7,
EXODUS 23.20,
1 KINGS 19.1–16,
2 KINGS 19.35,
MATTHEW 1.20,
LUKE 1.11,
LUKE 1.26,
ACTS 12.7

One day an angel from the Lord went to the town of Ophrah and sat down under the big tree that belonged to Joash, a member of the Abiezer clan. Joash's son Gideon was nearby, threshing grain in a shallow pit, where he could not be seen by the Midianites.

The angel appeared and spoke to Gideon, 'The Lord is helping you, and you are a strong warrior.'

Gideon answered, 'Please don't take this wrong, but if the Lord is helping us, then why have all these awful things happened? We've heard how the Lord performed miracles and rescued our ancestors from Egypt. But those things happened long ago. Now the Lord has abandoned us to the Midianites.'

'Gideon,' the Lord answered, 'you can rescue Israel because I am going to help you! Defeating the Midianites will be as easy as beating up one man.'

Gideon said, 'It's hard to believe that I'm actually talking to the Lord. Please do something so I'll know that you really are the Lord. And wait here until I bring you an offering.'

'All right, I'll wait,' the Lord answered.

Gideon went home and killed a young goat, then started boiling the meat. Next, he opened a big sack of flour and made it into thin bread. When the meat was done, he put it in a basket and poured the broth into a clay cooking pot. He took the meat, the broth, and the bread and placed them under the big tree.

God's angel said, 'Gideon, put the meat and the bread on this rock, and pour the broth over them.' Gideon did as he was told. The angel was holding a walking stick, and he touched the meat and the bread with the end of the stick. Flames jumped from the rock and burnt up the meat and the bread. When Gideon looked, the angel was gone.

Gideon realized that he had seen one of the Lord's angels. 'Oh!' he moaned. 'Now I'm going to die.'

'Calm down!' the Lord told Gideon. 'There's nothing to be afraid of. You're not going to die.'

Gideon built an altar for worshipping the Lord and called it 'The Lord Calms our Fears'. It still stands there in Ophrah, a town in the territory of the Abiezer clan.

**JUDGES
6.33–40**

All the Midianites, Amalekites, and other eastern nations got together and crossed the River Jordan. Then they invaded the land of Israel and set up camp in Jezreel Valley.

MIRACLES AND WONDERS

GIDEON IS NOT SO SURE

All the Midianites, Amalekites, and other eastern nations got together and crossed the River Jordan. Then they invaded the land of Israel and set up camp in Jezreel Valley.

The Lord's Spirit took control of Gideon, and Gideon blew a signal on a trumpet to tell the men in the Abiezer clan to follow him. He also sent messengers to the tribes of Manasseh, Asher, Zebulun, and Naphtali, telling the men of these tribes to come and join his army. Then they set out towards the enemy camp.

Gideon prayed to God, 'I know that you promised to help me rescue Israel, but I need proof. Tonight I'll put some wool on the stone floor of that threshing-place over there. If you really will help me rescue Israel, then tomorrow morning let there be dew on the wool, but let the stone floor be dry.'

And that's just what happened. Early the next morning, Gideon got up and checked the wool. He squeezed out enough water to fill a bowl. But Gideon prayed to God again. 'Don't be angry with me,' Gideon said. 'Let me try this just one more time, so I'll really be sure you'll help me. Only this time, let the wool be dry and the stone floor be wet with dew.'

That night, God made the stone floor wet with dew, but he kept the wool dry.

JUDGES 7.2–8

GIDEON REDUCES THE SIZE OF HIS ARMY

The Lord said, 'Gideon, your army is too big. I can't let you win with this many soldiers. The Israelites would think that they had won the battle all by themselves and that I didn't have anything to do with it.'

The Lord said, 'Gideon, your army is too big. I can't let you win with this many soldiers. The Israelites would think that they had won the battle all by themselves and that I didn't have anything to do with it. So call your troops together and tell them that anyone who is really afraid can leave Mount Gilead and go home.'

Twenty-two thousand men returned home, leaving Gideon with only ten thousand soldiers.

'Gideon,' the Lord said, 'you still have too many soldiers. Take them down to the spring and I'll test them. I'll tell you which ones can go along with you and which ones must go back home.'

When Gideon led his army down to the spring, the Lord told him, 'Watch how each man gets a drink of water. Then divide them into two groups – those who lap the water like a dog and those who kneel down to drink.'

Three hundred men scooped up water in their hands and lapped it, and the rest knelt to get a drink. The Lord said, 'Gideon, your army will be made up of everyone who lapped the water from their hands. Send the others home. I'm going to rescue Israel by helping you and your army of three hundred defeat the Midianites.'

Then Gideon gave these orders, 'You three hundred men stay here. The rest of you may go home, but leave your food and trumpets with us.'

Gideon's army camp was on top of a hill overlooking the Midianite camp in the valley.

GIDEON'S TINY BAND DESTROYS THE MIDIANITES

Gideon said, 'When we get to the enemy camp, spread out and surround it. Then wait for me to blow a signal on my trumpet. As soon as you hear it, blow your trumpets and shout, "Fight for the Lord! Fight for Gideon!"'

DREAMS AND VISIONS
MIRACLES AND WONDERS
VIOLENCE AND WARFARE

That night, the Lord said to Gideon. 'Get up! Attack the Midianite camp. I am going to let you defeat them, but if you're still afraid, you and your servant Purah should sneak down to their camp. When you hear what the Midianites are saying, you'll be brave enough to attack.'

Gideon and Purah worked their way to the edge of the enemy camp, where soldiers were on guard duty. The camp was huge. The Midianites, Amalekites, and other eastern nations covered the valley like a swarm of locusts. And it would be easier to count the grains of sand on a beach than to count their camels. Gideon overheard one enemy guard telling another, 'I had a dream about a flat loaf of barley bread that came tumbling into our camp. It hit the headquarters tent, and the tent tipped over and fell down.'

The other soldier answered, 'Your dream must have been about Gideon, the Israelite commander. It means God will let him and his army defeat the Midianite army and everyone else in our camp.'

As soon as Gideon heard about the dream and what it meant, he bowed down to praise God. Then he went back to the Israelite camp and shouted, 'Let's go! The Lord is going to let us defeat the Midianite army.'

Gideon divided his little army into three groups of one hundred men, and he gave each soldier a trumpet and a large clay jar with a burning torch inside. Gideon said, 'When we get to the enemy camp, spread out and surround it. Then wait for me to blow a signal on my trumpet. As soon as you hear it, blow your trumpets and shout, "Fight for the Lord! Fight for Gideon!"

Gideon and his group reached the edge of the enemy camp a few hours after dark, just after the new guards had come on duty. Gideon and his soldiers blew their trumpets and smashed the clay jars that were hiding the torches. The rest of Gideon's soldiers blew the trumpets they were holding in their right hands. Then they smashed the jars and held the burning torches in their left hands. Everyone shouted, 'Fight with your swords for the Lord and for Gideon!'

The enemy soldiers started yelling and tried to run away.

JUDGES 15.1–8   SAMSON AND HIS TEMPER TANTRUMS

The Israelites rebelled against God and he allowed the Philistines to conquer them. During this time a man called Samson, who had long hair and huge strength as a result of a vow made to God, fell in love with a Philistine woman, but after an argument with her family, he left her on their wedding day.

'This time,' Samson answered, 'I have a good reason for really hurting some Philistines.'

BIRDS AND
ANIMALS
VIOLENCE AND
WARFARE

Later, during the wheat harvest, Samson went to visit the young woman he thought was still his wife. He brought along a young goat as a gift and said to her father, 'I want to go into my wife's bedroom.'

'You can't do that,' he replied. 'When you left the way you did, I thought you were divorcing her. So I arranged for her to marry one of the young men who were at your party. But my younger daughter is even prettier, and you can have her as your wife.'

'This time,' Samson answered, 'I have a good reason for really hurting some Philistines.'

Samson went out and caught three hundred foxes and tied them together in pairs with oil-soaked rags around their tails. Then Samson took the foxes into the Philistine wheat fields that were ready to be harvested. He set the rags on fire and let the foxes go. The wheat fields went up in flames, and so did the stacks of wheat that had already been cut. Even the Philistine vineyards and olive orchards burnt.

Some of the Philistines started asking around, 'Who could have done such a thing?'

'It was Samson,' someone told them. 'He married the daughter of that man in Timnah, but then the man gave

Samson's wife to one of the men at the wedding.'

The Philistine leaders went to Timnah and burnt to death Samson's wife and her father.

When Samson found out what they had done, he went to them and said, 'You killed them! And I won't rest until I get even with you.' Then Samson started hacking them to pieces with his sword.

Samson left Philistia and went to live in the cave at Etam Rock.

JUDGES
16.4–22

THE SECRET OF SAMSON'S STRENGTH

The Philistines tried to capture Samson, but because of his incredible strength he was able to kill many of his would-be captors, and escape.

Finally, Samson told her the truth. 'I have belonged to God ever since I was born, so my hair has never been cut. If it were ever cut off, my strength would leave me, and I would be as weak as anyone else.'

P RUBENS
SAMSON AND
DELILAH
THE NATIONAL
GALLERY
LONDON
1609

Some time later, Samson fell in love with a woman named Delilah, who lived in Sorek Valley. The Philistine rulers went to Delilah and said, 'Trick Samson into telling you what makes him so strong and what can make him weak. Then we can tie him up so he can't get away. If you find out his secret, we will each give you eleven hundred pieces of silver.'

The next time Samson was at Delilah's house, she asked, 'Samson, what makes you so strong? How can I tie you up so you can't get away? Come on, you can tell me.'

Samson answered, 'If someone ties me up with seven new bowstrings that have never been dried, it will make me just as weak as anyone else.'

The Philistine rulers gave seven new bowstrings to Delilah. They also told some of their soldiers to go to Delilah's house and hide in the room where Samson and Delilah were. If the bowstrings made Samson weak, they would be able to capture him.

Delilah tied up Samson with the bowstrings and shouted, 'Samson, the Philistines are attacking!'

Samson snapped the bowstrings, as though they were pieces

of scorched string. The Philistines had not found out why Samson was so strong.

'You lied and made me look like a fool,' Delilah said. 'Now tell me. How can I really tie you up?'

Samson answered, 'Use some new ropes. If I'm tied up with ropes that have never been used, I'll be just as weak as anyone else.'

Delilah got new ropes and again some Philistines hid in the room. Then she tied up Samson's arms and shouted, 'Samson, the Philistines are attacking!'

Samson snapped the ropes as if they were threads.

'You're still lying and making a fool of me,' Delilah said. 'Tell me how I can tie you up!'

'My hair is in seven braids,' Samson replied. 'If you weave my braids into the threads on a loom and nail the loom to a wall, then I will be as weak as anyone else.'

While Samson was asleep, Delilah wove his braids into the threads on a loom and nailed the loom to a wall. Then she shouted, 'Samson, the Philistines are attacking!'

Samson woke up and pulled the loom free from its posts in the ground and from the nails in the wall. Then he pulled his hair free from the woven cloth.

'Samson,' Delilah said, 'you claim to love me, but you don't mean it! You've made me look like a fool three times now, and you still haven't told me why you are so strong.' Delilah started nagging and pestering him day after day, until he couldn't stand it any longer.

Finally, Samson told her the truth. 'I have belonged to God ever since I was born, so my hair has never been cut. If it were ever cut off, my strength would leave me, and I would be as weak as anyone else.'

Delilah realized that he was telling the truth. So she sent someone to tell the Philistine rulers, 'Come to my house one more time. Samson has finally told me the truth.'

The Philistine rulers went to Delilah's house, and they brought along the silver they had promised her. Delilah had lulled Samson to sleep with his head resting in her lap. She signalled to one of the Philistine men as she began cutting off Samson's seven braids. And by the time she had finished, Samson's strength was gone. Delilah tied him up and shouted, 'Samson, the Philistines are attacking!'

Samson woke up and thought, 'I'll break loose and escape, just as I always do.' He did not realize that the Lord had stopped helping him.

The Philistines grabbed Samson and put out his eyes. They took him to the prison in Gaza and chained him up. Then they put him to work, turning a millstone to grind grain. But they didn't cut his hair any more, so it started growing back.

SAMSON'S SUICIDE MISSION

JUDGES
16.23–30

Samson killed more Philistines when he died than he had killed during his entire life.

VIOLENCE AND
WARFARE

The Philistine rulers threw a big party and sacrificed a lot of animals to their god Dagon. The rulers said:

Samson was our enemy, but our god Dagon helped us capture him!

Everyone there was having a good time, and they shouted, 'Bring out Samson – he's still good for a few more laughs!'

The rulers had Samson brought from the prison, and when the people saw him, this is how they praised their god:

Samson ruined our crops and killed our people. He was our enemy, but our god captured him.

They made fun of Samson for a while, then they told him to stand near the columns that supported the roof. A young man was leading Samson by the hand, and Samson said to him, 'I need to lean against something. Take me over to the columns that hold up the roof.'

The Philistine rulers were celebrating in a temple packed with people and with three thousand more on the flat roof. They had all been watching Samson and making fun of him.

Samson prayed, 'Please remember me, Lord God. The Philistines put out my eyes, but make me strong one last time, so I can take revenge for at least one of my eyes!'

Samson was standing between the two middle columns that held up the roof. He felt around and found one column with his right hand, and the other with his left hand. Then he shouted, 'Let me die with the Philistines!' He pushed against the columns as hard as he could, and the temple collapsed with the Philistine rulers and everyone else still inside. Samson killed more Philistines when he died than he had killed during his entire life.

RUTH 1.6–18

TRAGEDY STRIKES IN A FOREIGN LAND

During this period of the judges there was famine in Judah. An Israelite called Elimelech settled in Moab, where his two sons married local women. Later Elimelech and both his children died, leaving his wife Naomi and her daughters-in-law to fend for themselves.

'Please don't tell me to leave you and return home! I will go where you go, I will live where you live; I will die where you die and be buried beside you.'

W BLAKE
NAOMI ENTREATING RUTH AND ORPAH TO RETURN TO THE LAND OF MOAB VICTORIA AND ALBERT MUSEUM LONDON
1795

When Naomi heard that the Lord had given his people a good harvest, she and her two daughters-in-law got ready to leave Moab and go to Judah. As they were on their way there, Naomi said to them, 'Don't you want to go back home to your own mothers? You were kind to my husband and sons, and you have always been kind to me. I pray that the Lord will be just as kind to you. May he give each of you another husband and a home of your own.'

Naomi kissed them. They cried and said, 'We want to go with you and live among your people.'

But she replied, 'My daughters, why don't you return home? What good will it do you to go with me? Do you think I could have more sons for you to marry? You must go back home, because I am too old to marry again. Even if I got married tonight and later had more sons, would you wait for them to become old enough to marry? No, my daughters! Life is harder for me than it is for you, because the Lord has turned against me.'

They cried again. Orpah kissed her mother-in-law goodbye,

AGREEMENTS AND
PROMISES
MARRIAGE AND
FAMILY

See also
MATTHEW 1.5

but Ruth held on to her. Naomi then said to Ruth, 'Look, your sister-in-law is going back to her people and to her gods! Why don't you go with her?' Ruth answered,

'Please don't tell me to leave you and return home! I will go where you go, I will live where you live; I will die where you die and be buried beside you. May the Lord punish me if we are ever separated, even by death!'

When Naomi saw that Ruth had made up her mind to go with her, she stopped urging her to go back.

RUTH 2.1–13

HARVEST TIME HELP

Naomi took Ruth with her and went back to her home town of Bethlehem.

'I pray that the Lord God of Israel will reward you for what you have done. And now that you have come to him for protection, I pray that he will bless you.'

FARMING AND
PRODUCE

One day, Ruth said to Naomi, 'Let me see if I can find someone who will let me pick up the grain left in the fields by the harvest workers.'

Naomi answered, 'Go ahead, my daughter.' So straight away, Ruth went out to pick up grain in a field owned by Boaz. He was a relative of Naomi's husband Elimelech, as well as a rich and important man.

When Boaz left Bethlehem and went out to his field, he said to the harvest workers, 'The Lord bless you!'

They replied, 'And may the Lord bless you!'

Then Boaz asked the man in charge of the harvest workers, 'Who is that young woman?'

The man answered, 'She is the one who came back from Moab with Naomi. She asked if she could pick up grain left by the harvest workers, and she has been working all morning without a moment's rest.'

Boaz went over to Ruth and said, 'I think it would be best for you not to pick up grain in anyone else's field. Stay here with the women and follow along behind them, as they gather up what the men have cut. I have warned the men not to bother you, and whenever you are thirsty, you can drink from the water jars they have filled.'

Ruth bowed down to the ground and said, 'You know I come from another country. Why are you so good to me?'

Boaz answered, 'I've heard how you've helped your mother-in-law ever since your husband died. You even left your own father and mother to come and live in a foreign land among people you don't know. I pray that the Lord God of Israel will reward you for what you have done. And now that you have come to him for protection, I pray that he will bless you.'

Ruth replied, 'Sir, it's good of you to speak kindly to me and make me feel so welcome. I'm not even one of your servants.'

RUTH 3.1–14

FINDING A HUSBAND FOR RUTH

Boaz told his workers to allow Ruth to gather all the grain she wanted without being harassed in any way.

One day, Naomi said to Ruth: It's time I found you a husband, who will give you a home and take care of you.

One day, Naomi said to Ruth:

It's time I found you a husband, who will give you a home and take care of you.

You have been picking up grain beside the women who work for Boaz, and you know he is a relative of ours. Tonight he will be threshing the grain. Now take a bath and put on some perfume, then dress in your best clothes. Go where he is working, but don't let him see you until he has finished eating and drinking. Watch where he goes to spend the night, then when he is asleep, lift the cover and lie down at his feet. He will tell you what to do.

Ruth answered, 'I'll do whatever you say.' She went out to the place where Boaz was working and did what Naomi had told her.

After Boaz finished eating and drinking and was feeling happy, he went over and fell asleep near the pile of grain. Ruth slipped over quietly. She lifted the cover and lay down near his feet.

In the middle of the night, Boaz suddenly woke up and was

shocked to see a woman lying at his feet. 'Who are you?' he asked.

'Sir, I am Ruth,' she answered, 'and you are the relative who is supposed to take care of me. So spread the edge of your cover over me.'

Boaz replied:

The Lord bless you! This shows how truly loyal you are to your family. You could have looked for a younger man, either rich or poor, but you didn't. Don't worry, I'll do what you have asked. You are respected by everyone in town.

It's true that I am one of the relatives who is supposed to take care of you, but there is someone who is an even closer relative. Stay here until morning, then I will find out if he is willing to look after you. If he isn't, I promise by the living God to do it myself. Now go back to sleep until morning.

Ruth lay down again, but she got up before daylight, because Boaz did not want anyone to know she had been there.

RUTH 4.1–13

BOAZ AND RUTH MARRY

Boaz married Ruth, and the Lord blessed her with a son.

SALVADOR DALI
FAMILIA RUTH
MOABITIDIS
BIBLIA SACRA PUB.
1969

Meanwhile, Boaz had gone to the meeting place at the town gate and was sitting there when the other close relative came by. So Boaz invited him to come over and sit down, and he did. Then Boaz got ten of the town leaders and also asked them to sit down. After they had sat down, he said to the man:

Naomi has come back from Moab and is selling the land that belonged to her husband Elimelech. I am telling you about this, since you are his closest relative and have the right to buy the property. If you want it, you can buy it now. These ten men and the others standing here can be witnesses. But if you don't want the property, let me know, because I am next in line.

The man replied, 'I will buy it!'

'If you do buy it from Naomi,' Boaz told him, 'you must also marry Ruth. Then if you have a son by her, the property will stay in the family of Ruth's first husband.'

The man answered, 'If that's the case, I don't want to buy it! That would make problems with the property I already own. You may buy it yourself, because I cannot.'

To make a sale legal in those days, one person would take off a sandal and give it to the other. So after the man had agreed to let Boaz buy the property, he took off one of his sandals and handed it to Boaz.

Boaz told the town leaders and everyone else:

All of you are witnesses that today I have bought from Naomi the property that belonged to Elimelech and his two sons, Chilion and Mahlon. You are also witnesses that I have agreed to marry Mahlon's widow Ruth, the Moabite woman. This will keep the property in his family's name, and he will be remembered in this town.

The town leaders and the others standing there said:

We are witnesses to this. And we pray that the Lord will give your wife many children, just as he did Leah and Rachel, the wives of Jacob. May you be a rich man in the tribe of Ephrath and an important man in Bethlehem. May the children you have by this young woman make your family as famous as the family of Perez, the son of Tamar and Judah.

Boaz married Ruth, and the Lord blessed her with a son.

A king for Israel

A MOTHER'S CRY FOR HELP

The period of the judges was in many ways an unsettling one for the Israelites. They increasingly cast envious eyes on their stronger, more stable neighbours, whose success they attributed to the existence of powerful kings. It was to be the role of Samuel, the last great judge, to bring the monarchy to God's people.

'Lord All-Powerful, I am your servant, but I am so miserable! Please let me have a son. I will give him to you for as long as he lives, and his hair will never be cut.'

AGREEMENTS AND PROMISES
FOOD AND DRINK
MARRIAGE AND FAMILY

Elkanah lived in Ramah, a town in the hill country of Ephraim. His great-great-grandfather was Zuph, so Elkanah was a member of the Zuph clan of the Ephraim tribe. Elkanah's father was Jeroham, his grandfather was Elihu, and his great-grandfather was Tohu.

Elkanah had two wives, Hannah and Peninnah. Although Peninnah had children, Hannah did not have any.

Once a year Elkanah travelled from his home town to Shiloh, where he worshipped the Lord All-Powerful and offered sacrifices. Eli was the Lord's priest there, and his two sons Hophni and Phinehas served with him as priests.

Whenever Elkanah offered a sacrifice, he gave some of the meat to Peninnah and some to each of her sons and daughters. But he gave Hannah even more, because he loved Hannah very much, even though the Lord had kept her from having children of her own.

Peninnah liked to make Hannah feel miserable about not having any children, especially when the family went to the house of the Lord each year.

One day, Elkanah was there offering a sacrifice, when Hannah began crying and refused to eat. So Elkanah asked, 'Hannah, why are you crying? Why won't you eat? Why do you feel so bad? Don't I mean more to you than ten sons?'

When the sacrifice had been offered, and they had eaten the meal, Hannah got up and went to pray. Eli was sitting in his chair near the door to the place of worship. Hannah was broken hearted and was crying as she prayed, 'Lord All-Powerful, I am your servant, but I am so miserable! Please let me have a son. I will give him to you for as long as he lives, and his hair will never be cut.'

Hannah prayed silently to the Lord for a long time. But her lips were moving, and Eli thought she was drunk. 'How long are you going to stay drunk?' he asked. 'Sober up!'

'Sir, please don't think I'm no good!' Hannah answered. 'I'm not drunk, and I haven't been drinking. But I do feel miserable and terribly upset. I've been praying all this time, telling the Lord about my problems.'

Eli replied, 'You may go home now and stop worrying. I'm sure the God of Israel will answer your prayer.'

'Sir, thank you for being so kind to me,' Hannah said. Then she left, and after eating something, she felt much better.

Elkanah and his family got up early the next morning and worshipped the Lord. Then they went back home to Ramah. Later the Lord blessed Elkanah and Hannah with a son. She named him Samuel because she had asked the Lord for him.

1 SAMUEL
3.1–10

A VOICE IN THE NIGHT

As soon as Samuel was old enough, Hannah took him, just as she had promised, to the house of the Lord, where God's sacred chest was kept. He lived there under the care and guidance of Eli the priest.

The Lord then stood beside Samuel and called out as he had done before, 'Samuel! Samuel!' 'I'm listening,' Samuel answered. 'What do you want me to do?'

Samuel served the Lord by helping Eli the priest, who was by that time almost blind. In those days, the Lord hardly ever spoke directly to people, and he did not appear to them in dreams very often. But one night, Eli was asleep in his room, and Samuel was sleeping on a mat near the sacred chest in the Lord's house. They had not been asleep very long when the Lord called out Samuel's name.

'Here I am!' Samuel answered. Then he ran to Eli and said, 'Here I am. What do you want?'

'I didn't call you,' Eli answered. 'Go back to bed.'

Samuel went back.

Again the Lord called out Samuel's name. Samuel got up and went to Eli. 'Here I am,' he said. 'What do you want?'

Eli told him, 'Son, I didn't call you. Go back to sleep.'

The Lord had not spoken to Samuel before, and Samuel did not recognize the voice. When the Lord called out his name for the third time, Samuel went to Eli again and said, 'Here I am. What do you want?'

Eli finally realized that it was the Lord who was speaking to Samuel. So he said, 'Go back and lie down! If someone speaks to you again, answer, "I'm listening, Lord. What do you want me to do?"'

Once again Samuel went back and lay down. The Lord then stood beside Samuel and called out as he had done before, 'Samuel! Samuel!'

'I'm listening,' Samuel answered. 'What do you want me to do?'

1 SAMUEL
7.15–8.22

WE WANT A KING!

God looked after Samuel as he grew up, using him to speak to all the people. His wisdom was respected and he travelled throughout the country giving advice, and telling everyone how to live in a way that pleased God.

'Do what they want,' the Lord answered. 'Give them a king.' Samuel told the people to go back to their homes.

Samuel was a leader in Israel all his life. Every year he would go around to the towns of Bethel, Gilgal, and Mizpah where he served as judge for the people. Then he would go back to his home in Ramah and do the same thing there. He also had an altar built for the Lord at Ramah.

Samuel had two sons. The elder one was Joel, and the younger one was Abijah. When Samuel was getting old, he let them be leaders at Beersheba. But they were not like their father. They were dishonest and accepted bribes to give unfair decisions.

See also
DEUTERONOMY
17.14–20

One day the nation's leaders came to Samuel at Ramah and said, 'You are an old man. You set a good example for your sons, but they haven't followed it. Now we want a king to be our leader, just like all the other nations. Choose one for us!'

Samuel was upset to hear the leaders say they wanted a king, so he prayed about it. The Lord answered:

Samuel, do everything they want you to do. I am really the one they have rejected as their king. Ever since the day I rescued my people from Egypt, they have turned from me to worship idols. Now they are turning away from you. Do everything they ask, but warn them and tell them how a king will treat them.

Samuel told the people who were asking for a king what the Lord had said:

If you have a king, this is how he will treat you. He will force your sons to join his army. Some of them will ride in his chariots, some will serve in the cavalry, and others will run ahead of his own chariot. Some of them will be officers in charge of a thousand soldiers, and others will be in charge of fifty. Still others will have to farm the king's land and harvest his crops, or make weapons and parts for his chariots. Your daughters will have to make perfume or do his cooking and baking.

The king will take your best fields, as well as your vineyards, and olive orchards and give them to his own officials. He will also take a tenth of your grain and grapes and give it to his officers and officials.

The king will take your slaves and your best young men and your donkeys and make them do his work. He will also take a tenth of your sheep and goats. You will become the king's slaves, and you will finally cry out for the Lord to save you from the king you wanted. But the Lord won't answer your prayers.

The people would not listen to Samuel. 'No!' they said. 'We want to be like other nations. We want a king to rule us and lead us in battle.'

Samuel listened to them and then told the Lord exactly what they had said. 'Do what they want,' the Lord answered. 'Give them a king.'

Samuel told the people to go back to their homes.

 1 SAMUEL 10.17–27

1 SAMUEL
9.1–10.1

Samuel looked at Saul, and the Lord told Samuel, 'This is the man I told you about. He's the one who will rule Israel.'

BIRDS AND
ANIMALS
FOOD AND DRINK

See also
1 SAMUEL 11,
1 SAMUEL 13.1–15,
1 SAMUEL
16.14–23,
1 SAMUEL 18.1–11,
1 SAMUEL 31,
GENESIS 27.1–41

ISRAEL'S FIRST KING

Kish was a wealthy man who belonged to the tribe of Benjamin. His father was Abiel, his grandfather was Zeror, his great-grandfather was Becorath, and his great-great-grand-father was Aphiah. Kish had a son named Saul, who was better looking and more than a head taller than anyone else in all Israel.

Kish owned some donkeys, but they had run off. So he told Saul, 'Take one of the servants and go and look for the donkeys.'

Saul and the servant went through the hill country of Ephraim and the territory of Shalishah, but they could not find the donkeys. Then they went through the territories of Shaalim and Benjamin, but still there was no sign of the donkeys. Finally they came to the territory where the clan of Zuph lived. 'Let's go back home,' Saul told his servant. 'If we don't go back soon, my father will stop worrying about the donkeys and start worrying about us!'

'Wait!' the servant answered. 'There's a man of God who lives in a town near here. He's amazing! Everything he says comes true. Let's talk to him. Perhaps he can tell us where to look.'

Saul said, 'How can we talk to the prophet when I don't have anything to give him? We don't even have any bread left in our sacks. What can we give him?'

'I have a small piece of silver,' the servant answered. 'We can give him that, and then he will tell us where to look for the donkeys.'

'Great!' Saul replied. 'Let's go to the man who can see

visions!' He said this because in those days God would answer questions by giving visions to prophets.

Saul and his servant went to the town where the prophet lived. As they were going up the hill to the town, they met some young women coming out to get water, and the two men said to them, 'We're looking for the man who can see visions. Is he in town?'

'Yes, he is,' they replied. 'He's in town today because there's going to be a sacrifice and a sacred meal at the place of worship. In fact, he's just ahead of you. Hurry and you should find him just inside the town gate. He's on his way out to the place of worship to eat with the invited guests. They can't start eating until he blesses the sacrifice. If you go now, you should find him.'

They went to the town, and just as they were going through the gate, Samuel was coming out on his way to the place of worship.

The day before Saul came, the Lord had told Samuel, 'I've seen how my people are suffering, and I've heard their call for help. About this time tomorrow I'll send you a man from the tribe of Benjamin, who will rescue my people from the Philistines. I want you to pour olive oil on his head to show that he will be their leader.'

Samuel looked at Saul, and the Lord told Samuel, 'This is the man I told you about. He's the one who will rule Israel.'

Saul went over to Samuel in the gateway and said, 'A man who can see visions lives here in town. Could you tell me the way to his house?'

'I am the one who sees visions!' Samuel answered. 'Go on up to the place of worship. You will eat with me today, and in the morning I'll answer your questions. Don't worry about your donkeys that ran off three days ago. They've already been found. Everything of value in Israel now belongs to you and your family.'

'Why are you telling me this?' Saul asked. 'I'm from Benjamin, the smallest tribe in Israel, and my clan is the least important in the tribe.'

Samuel took Saul and his servant into the dining room at the place of worship. About thirty people were there for the dinner, but Samuel gave Saul and his servant the places of honour. Then Samuel told the cook, 'I gave you the best piece of meat and told you to set it aside. Bring it here now.'

The cook brought the meat over and set it down in front of Saul. 'This is for you,' Samuel told him. 'Go ahead and eat it. I had this piece saved especially for you, and I invited these guests to eat with you.'

After Saul and Samuel had finished eating, they went down from the place of worship and back into town. A bed was set up for Saul on the flat roof of Samuel's house, and Saul slept there.

About sunrise the next morning, Samuel called up to Saul on the roof, 'Time to get up! I'll help you get started on your way.'

Saul got up. He and Samuel left together and had almost reached the edge of town when Samuel stopped and said, 'Tell your servant to go on. Stay here with me for a few minutes, and I'll tell you what God has told me.'

After the servant had gone, Samuel took a small jar of olive oil and poured it on Saul's head. Then he kissed Saul and told him:

The Lord has chosen you to be the leader and ruler of his people.

1 SAMUEL
10.17–27

SAUL ACCLAIMED AS KING

Saul left Samuel and returned to his father, but soon he was called to a meeting, together with all the people.

'Look closely at the man the Lord has chosen!' Samuel told the crowd. 'There is no one like him!' The crowd shouted, 'Long live the king!'

Samuel sent messengers to tell the Israelites to come to Mizpah and meet with the Lord. When everyone had arrived, Samuel said:

The Lord God of Israel told me to remind you that he had rescued you from the Egyptians and from the other nations that abused you.

God has rescued you from your troubles and hard times.

But you have rejected your God and have asked for a king. Now each tribe and clan must come near the place of worship so the Lord can choose a king.

Samuel brought each tribe, one after the other, to the altar, and the Lord chose the Benjamin tribe. Next, Samuel brought each clan of Benjamin there, and the Lord chose the Matri clan. Finally, Saul the son of Kish was chosen. But when they looked for him, he was nowhere to be found.

The people prayed, 'Our Lord, is Saul here?'

'Yes,' the Lord answered, 'he is hiding behind the baggage.'

The people ran and got Saul and brought him into the middle of the crowd. He was more than a head taller than anyone else. 'Look closely at the man the Lord has chosen!' Samuel told the crowd. 'There is no one like him!'

The crowd shouted, 'Long live the king!'

Samuel explained the rights and duties of a king and wrote them all in a book. He put the book in a temple building at one of the places where the Lord was worshipped. Then Samuel sent everyone home.

God had encouraged some young men to become followers of Saul, and when he returned to his home town of Gibeah, they went with him. But some worthless fools said, 'How can someone like Saul rescue us from our enemies?' They did not want Saul to be their king, and so they didn't bring him any gifts. But Saul kept calm.

▶ 1 SAMUEL 16.1–13

FINDING A BETTER KING FOR ISRAEL

Saul ruled Israel for forty-two years, but he did not always obey God as he should. So God spoke to Samuel, telling him of his decision to choose a new king.

People judge others by what they look like, but I judge people by what is in their hearts.'

RAPHAEL
SAMUEL ANOINTS DAVID KING
THE VATICAN
ROME
c. 1519

See also
RUTH 1.19,
MICAH 5.2,
MATTHEW 2.1,
LUKE 2.4,
2 SAMUEL 5.1–10

One day he said, 'Samuel, I've rejected Saul, and I refuse to let him be king any longer. Stop feeling sad about him. Put some olive oil in a small container and go and visit a man named Jesse, who lives in Bethlehem. I've chosen one of his sons to be my king.'

Samuel answered, 'If I do that, Saul will find out and have me killed.'

'Take a calf with you,' the Lord replied. 'Tell everyone that you've come to offer it as a sacrifice to me, then invite Jesse to the sacrifice. When I show you which one of his sons I have chosen, pour the olive oil on his head.'

Samuel did what the Lord told him and went to Bethlehem. The town leaders went to meet him, but they were terribly afraid and asked, 'Is this a friendly visit?'

'Yes, it is!' Samuel answered. 'I've come to offer a sacrifice to the Lord. Get yourselves ready to take part in the sacrifice and come with me.' Samuel also invited Jesse and his sons to come to the sacrifice, and he got them ready to take part.

When Jesse and his sons arrived, Samuel noticed Jesse's eldest son, Eliab. 'He must be the one the Lord has chosen,' Samuel said to himself.

But the Lord told him, 'Samuel, don't think Eliab is the one just because he's tall and handsome. He isn't the one I've chosen. People judge others by what they look like, but I judge people by what is in their hearts.'

Jesse told his son Abinadab to go over to Samuel, but Samuel said, 'No, the Lord hasn't chosen him.'

Next, Jesse sent his son Shammah to him, and Samuel said, 'The Lord hasn't chosen him either.'

Jesse sent all seven of his sons over to Samuel. Finally, Samuel said, 'Jesse, the Lord hasn't chosen any of these young men.

Do you have any more sons?'

'Yes,' Jesse answered. 'My youngest son David is out taking care of the sheep.'

'Send for him!' Samuel said. 'We won't start the ceremony until he gets here.'

Jesse sent for David. He was a healthy, good-looking boy with a sparkle in his eyes. As soon as David came, the Lord told Samuel, 'He's the one! Get up and pour the olive oil on his head.'

Samuel poured the oil on David's head while his brothers watched. At that moment, the Spirit of the Lord took control of David and stayed with him from then on.

Samuel returned home to Ramah.

▶ 2 SAMUEL 5.1–10

David's rise

From
1 Samuel
17.4–39

GOLIATH LAYS DOWN THE GAUNTLET

While Saul was still king, the Philistines gathered an army to go and fight against the Israelites. The two armies pitched their tents on opposing hillsides, waiting to see which would be the first to make a move.

Sir, I have killed lions and bears that way, and I can kill this worthless Philistine. He shouldn't have made fun of the army of the living God!

The Philistine army had a hero named Goliath who was from the town of Gath and was about three metres tall.

Goliath went out and shouted to the army of Israel:

Why are you lining up for battle? I'm the best soldier in our army, and all of you are in Saul's army. Choose your best soldier to come out and fight me! If he can kill me, our people will be your slaves. But if I kill him, your people will be our slaves. Here and now I challenge Israel's whole army! Choose someone to fight me!

Saul and his men heard what Goliath said, but they were so frightened of Goliath that they couldn't do a thing.

BIRDS AND ANIMALS
FOOD AND DRINK
VIOLENCE AND WARFARE

One day, Jesse told David, 'Hurry and take this sack of roasted grain and these ten loaves of bread to your brothers at the army camp. And here are ten large chunks of cheese to take to their commanding officer. Find out how your brothers are doing and bring back something that shows that they're all right. They're with Saul's army, fighting the Philistines in Elah Valley.'

David obeyed his father. He got up early the next morning and left someone else in charge of the sheep; then he loaded the supplies and started off. He reached the army camp just as the soldiers were taking their places and shouting the battle cry.

While David was talking with them, Goliath came out from the line of Philistines and started boasting as usual. David heard him.

David asked some soldiers standing nearby, 'What will a man get for killing this Philistine and stopping him from insulting our people? Who does that worthless Philistine think he is? He's making fun of the army of the living God!'

The soldiers told David what the king would give the man who killed Goliath.

Some soldiers overheard David talking, so they told Saul what David had said. Saul sent for David, and David came. 'Your Majesty,' he said, 'this Philistine shouldn't turn us into cowards. I'll go out and fight him myself!'

'You don't have a chance against him,' Saul replied. 'You're only a boy, and he's been a soldier all his life.'

But David told him:

Your Majesty, I take care of my father's sheep. And when one of them is dragged off by a lion or a bear, I go after it and beat the wild animal until it lets the sheep go. If the wild animal turns and attacks me, I grab it by the throat and kill it.

Sir, I have killed lions and bears that way, and I can kill this worthless Philistine. He shouldn't have made fun of the army of the living God! The Lord has rescued me from the claws of lions and bears, and he will keep me safe from the hands of this Philistine.

'All right,' Saul answered, 'go ahead and fight him. And I hope the Lord will help you.'

Saul had his own military clothes and armour put on David, and he gave David a bronze helmet to wear. David strapped on a sword and tried to walk around, but he was not used to wearing those things.

'I can't move with all this stuff on,' David said. 'I'm just not used to it.'

DAVID'S SURPRISE VICTORY

CARAVAGGIO

*DAVID WITH THE
HEAD OF GOLIATH*
KUNST-
HISTORISCHES
MUSEUM
VIENNA
1606–07

**VIOLENCE AND
WARFARE**

David took off the armour and picked up his shepherd's stick. He went out to a stream and picked up five smooth stones and put them in his leather bag. Then with his sling in his hand, he went straight towards Goliath.

Goliath came towards David, walking behind the soldier who was carrying his shield. When Goliath saw that David was just a healthy, good-looking boy, he made fun of him. 'Do you think I'm a dog?' Goliath asked. 'Is that why you've come after me with a stick?' He cursed David in the name of the Philistine gods and shouted, 'Come on! When I'm finished with you, I'll feed you to the birds and wild animals!'

David answered:

You've come out to fight me with a sword and a spear and a dagger. But I've come out to fight you in the name of the Lord All-Powerful. He is the God of Israel's army, and you have insulted him too!

Today the Lord will help me defeat you. I'll knock you down and cut off your head, and I'll feed the bodies of the other Philistine soldiers to the birds and wild animals. Then the whole world will know that Israel has a real God. Everybody here will see that the Lord doesn't need swords or spears to save his people. The Lord always wins his battles, and he will help us defeat you.

When Goliath started forward, David ran towards him. He put a stone in his sling and swung the sling around by its straps. When he let go of one strap, the stone flew out and hit Goliath on the forehead. It cracked his skull, and he fell face down on the ground. David defeated Goliath with a sling and a stone. He killed him without even using a sword.

David ran over and pulled out Goliath's sword. Then he used it to cut off Goliath's head.

When the Philistines saw what had happened to their hero, they started running away.

SAUL BECOMES JEALOUS OF DAVID

When the Israelites saw the Philistines retreat they gave chase, killing many of them. David was a hero, but his newfound popularity grated with Saul.

David had killed Goliath, the battle was over, and the Israelite army set out for home. As the army went along, women came out of each Israelite town to welcome King Saul. They were singing happy songs and dancing to the music of tambourines and harps. They sang:

Saul has killed a thousand enemies; David has killed ten thousand enemies!

This song made Saul very angry, and he thought, 'They are saying that David has killed ten times more enemies than I ever did. Next they will want to make him king.' Saul never again trusted David.

The next day the Lord let an evil spirit take control of Saul, and he began acting like a mad man inside his house. David came to play the harp for Saul as usual, but this time Saul had a spear in his hand. Saul thought, 'I'll pin David to the wall.' He threw the spear at David twice, but David dodged and got away both times.

SAUL ATTACKS DAVID

David's fame as an army general grew and grew – as did Saul's envy.

One day, Saul told his son Jonathan and his officers to kill David. But Jonathan liked David a lot, and he warned David, 'My father is trying to have you killed, so be very careful. Hide in a field tomorrow morning, and I'll bring him there. Then I'll talk to him about you, and if I find out anything, I'll let you know.'

The next morning, Jonathan reminded Saul about the many good things David had done for him. Then he said, 'Why do you want to kill David? He hasn't done anything to you. He has

AGREEMENTS AND
PROMISES
VIOLENCE AND
WARFARE

See also
JUDGES 5.3,
2 SAMUEL 6.1–23,
PSALMS,
AMOS 5.23,
EPHESIANS 5.19,
REVELATION 18.22

served in your army and has always done what's best for you. He even risked his life to kill Goliath. The Lord helped Israel win a great victory that day, and it made you happy.'

Saul agreed and promised, 'I swear by the living Lord that I won't have David killed!'

Jonathan called to David and told him what Saul had said. Then he brought David to Saul, and David served in Saul's army just as he had done before.

The next time there was a war with the Philistines, David fought hard and forced them to retreat.

One night, David was in Saul's home, playing the harp for him. Saul was sitting there, holding a spear, when an evil spirit from the Lord took control of him. Saul tried to pin David to the wall with the spear, but David dodged, and it stuck in the wall. David ran out of the house and escaped.

Saul sent guards to watch David's house all night and then to kill him in the morning.

Michal, David's wife, told him, 'If you don't escape tonight, they'll kill you tomorrow!' She helped David go through a window and climb down to the ground. As David ran off, Michal put a statue in his bed. She put goat hair on its head and dressed it in some of David's clothes.

The next morning, Saul sent guards to arrest David. But Michal told them, 'David is sick.'

Saul sent the guards back and told them, 'Get David out of his bed and bring him to me, so I can have him killed.'

When the guards went in, all they found in the bed was the statue with the goat hair on its head.

'Why have you tricked me this way?' Saul asked Michal. 'You helped my enemy get away!'

She answered, 'He said he would kill me if I didn't help him escape!'

Meanwhile, David went to Samuel at Ramah and told him what Saul had done. Then Samuel and David went to Prophets Village and stayed there.

A MESSAGE IN THE ARROWS

Jonathan said, 'Take
care of yourself. And
remember, we have
each asked the Lord
to watch and make
sure that we and
our descendants
keep our promise for
ever.' David left and
Jonathan went back
to town.

REMBRANDT
DAVID'S FAREWELL
FROM JONATHAN
THE STATE
HERMITAGE
MUSEUM
ST PETERSBURG
1642

David escaped from Prophets Village. Then he ran to see Jonathan and asked, 'Why does your father Saul want to kill me? What have I done wrong?'

'My father can't be trying to kill you! He never does anything without telling me about it. Why would he hide this from me? It can't be true!'

'Jonathan, I swear it's true! But your father knows how much you like me, and he didn't want to break your heart. That's why he didn't tell you. I swear by the living Lord and by your own life that I'm only one step ahead of death.'

David answered:

Tomorrow is the New Moon Festival, and I'm supposed to have dinner with your father. But instead, I'll hide in a field until the evening of the next day. If Saul wonders where I am, tell him, 'David asked me to let him go to his home town of Bethlehem, so he could take part in a sacrifice his family makes there every year.'

If your father says it's all right, then I'm safe. But if he gets angry, you'll know he wants to harm me.

After this Jonathan said:

Tomorrow is the New Moon Festival, and people will wonder where you are, because your place will be empty. By the day after tomorrow, everyone will think you've been gone a long time. Then go to the place where you hid before and stay beside Going-Away Rock. I'll shoot three arrows at a target off to the side of the rock.

So David hid there in the field.

During the New Moon Festival, Saul sat down to eat by the wall, just as he always did. Jonathan sat across from him, and Abner sat next to him. But David's place was empty. Saul didn't say anything that day, because he was thinking, 'Something must have happened to make David unfit to be at the Festival. Yes, something must have happened.'

The day after the New Moon Festival, when David's place

was still empty, Saul asked Jonathan, 'Why hasn't that son of Jesse come to eat with us? He wasn't here yesterday, and he still isn't here today!' Jonathan answered,

'The reason David hasn't come to eat with you is that he begged me to let him go to Bethlehem. He said, "Please let me go. My family is offering a sacrifice, and my brother told me I have to be there. Do me this favour and let me slip away to see my brothers."'

Saul was furious with Jonathan and yelled, 'You're no son of mine, you traitor! I know you've chosen to be loyal to that son of Jesse. You should be ashamed of yourself! And your own mother should be ashamed that you were ever born. You'll never be safe, and your kingdom will be in danger as long as that son of Jesse is alive. Turn him over to me now! He deserves to die!'

'Why do you want to kill David?' Jonathan asked. 'What has he done?'

Saul threw his spear at Jonathan and tried to kill him. Then Jonathan was sure that his father really did want to kill David.

In the morning, Jonathan went out to the field to meet David. He took a servant boy along and told him, 'When I shoot the arrows, you run and find them for me.'

The boy started running, and Jonathan shot an arrow so that it would go beyond him.

Jonathan gave his weapons to the boy and told him, 'Take these back into town.'

After the boy had gone, David got up from beside the mound and bowed very low three times. Then he and Jonathan kissed each other and cried, but David cried louder. Jonathan said, 'Take care of yourself. And remember, we have each asked the Lord to watch and make sure that we and our descendants keep our promise for ever.'

David left and Jonathan went back to town.

DAVID'S LOYALTY TO SAUL

David was forced to live as a fugitive, moving from place to place in order not to be found by Saul and his men, who remained intent on catching him.

You can see for yourself that the Lord gave me the chance to catch you in the cave today. Some of my men wanted to kill you, but I wouldn't let them do it. I told them, 'I will not harm the Lord's chosen king!'

See also 1 SAMUEL 26.1–25

When Saul got back from fighting off the Philistines, he heard that David was in the desert around En-Gedi. Saul led three thousand of Israel's best soldiers out to look for David and his men near Wild Goat Rocks at En-Gedi. There were some sheep pens along the side of the road, and one of them was built around the entrance to a cave. Saul went into the cave to relieve himself.

David and his men were hiding at the back of the cave. They whispered to David, 'The Lord told you he was going to let you defeat your enemies and do whatever you want with them. This must be the day the Lord was talking about.'

David sneaked over and cut off a small piece of Saul's robe, but Saul didn't notice a thing. Afterwards, David was sorry that he had even done that, and he told his men, 'Stop talking foolishly. We're not going to attack Saul. He's my king, and I pray that the Lord will keep me from doing anything to harm his chosen king.'

Saul left the cave and started down the road. Soon, David also got up and left the cave. 'Your Majesty!' he shouted from a distance.

Saul turned around to look. David bowed down very low and said:

Your Majesty, why do you listen to people who say that I'm trying to harm you? You can see for yourself that the Lord gave me the chance to catch you in the cave today. Some of my men wanted to kill you, but I wouldn't let them do it. I told them, 'I will not harm the Lord's chosen king!' Your Majesty, look at what I'm holding. You can see that it's a piece of your robe. If I could cut off a piece of your robe, I could have killed you. But I let you live, and that should prove I'm not trying to harm you or to rebel. I haven't done anything to you, and yet you keep trying to ambush and kill me.

'David, my son – is that you?' Saul asked. Then he started crying and said:

David, you're a better person than I am. You treated me with kindness, even though I've been cruel to you.

FROM
1 SAMUEL
26.1–25

DAVID SPARES SAUL'S LIFE AGAIN

Saul and David parted and although they had been reconciled, the king was soon hunting after David again.

'David, you had the chance to kill me today. But you didn't. I was very wrong about you. It was a terrible mistake for me to try to kill you. I've acted like a fool, but I'll never try to harm you again. You're like a son to me, so please come back.'

See also
NUMBERS
13.1–31,
JOSHUA 2.1–24,
LUKE 20.20–21,
1 SAMUEL 24.1–17

Once again, some people from Ziph went to Gibeah to talk with Saul. 'David has a hide-out on Mount Hachilah near Jeshimon out in the desert,' they told him.

Saul took three thousand of Israel's best soldiers and went to look for David there in Ziph Desert. Saul set up camp on Mount Hachilah, which is across the road from Jeshimon. But David was hiding out in the desert.

When David heard that Saul was following him, he sent some spies to find out if it was true.

That same night, David and Abishai crept into the camp. Saul was sleeping, and his spear was stuck in the ground not far from his head. Abner and the soldiers were sound asleep all around him.

Abishai whispered, 'This time God has let you get your hands on your enemy! I'll pin him to the ground with one thrust of his own spear.'

'Don't kill him!' David whispered back. 'The Lord will punish anyone who kills his chosen king. But I pray that the Lord will keep me from harming his chosen king. Let's grab his spear and his water jar and get out of here!'

David took the spear and the water jar, then left the camp. None of Saul's soldiers knew what had happened or even woke up – the Lord had made all of them fall sound asleep. David and Abishai crossed the valley and went to the top of the next hill, where they were at a safe distance. 'Abner!' David shouted towards Saul's army. 'Can you hear me?'

Abner shouted back. 'Who dares disturb the king?'

'Abner, what kind of a man are you?' David replied. 'Aren't you supposed to be the best soldier in Israel? Then why didn't you protect your king? Anyone who went into your camp could have killed him tonight. You're a complete failure! I swear by the living Lord that you and your men deserve to die for not protecting the Lord's chosen king. Look and see if you can find the king's spear and the water jar that were near his head.'

Saul could tell it was David's voice, and he called out, 'David, my son! Is that you?'

'Yes it is, Your Majesty. Why are you after me? Have I done something wrong, or have I committed a crime? 'David, you had the chance to kill me today. But you didn't. I was very wrong about you. It was a terrible mistake for me to try to kill you. I've acted like a fool, but I'll never try to harm you again. You're like a son to me, so please come back.' 'David, my son, I pray that the Lord will bless you and make you successful!' Saul went back home. David also left.

2 SAMUEL
1.1–16

DAVID MOURNS SAUL'S DEATH

The Philistines gathered an army to fight the Israelites. Saul and his sons met them in battle, but the king was killed. His death sparked off a civil war within the country.

David said to him, 'Why weren't you afraid to kill the Lord's chosen king? And you even told what you did. It's your own fault that you're going to die!' Then David told one of his soldiers, 'Come here and kill this man!'

Saul was dead.

Meanwhile, David had defeated the Amalekites and returned to Ziklag. Three days later, a soldier came from Saul's army. His clothes were torn, and earth was on his head. He went to David and knelt down in front of him.

David asked, 'Where did you come from?'

The man answered, 'From Israel's army. I barely escaped with my life.'

'Who won the battle?' David asked.

The man said, 'Our army turned and ran, but many were wounded and died. Even King Saul and his son Jonathan are dead.'

David asked, 'How do you know Saul and Jonathan are dead?'

The young man replied:

I was on Mount Gilboa and saw King Saul leaning on his spear. The enemy's war chariots and cavalry were closing in on him. When he turned round and saw me, he called me over. I went and asked what he wanted.

Saul asked me, 'Who are you?'

'An Amalekite,' I answered.

Then he said, 'Kill me! I'm dying, and I'm in terrible pain.'

So I killed him. I knew he was too badly wounded to live much longer. Then I took his crown and his arm-band, and I brought them to you, Your Majesty. Here they are.

Straight away, David and his soldiers tore their clothes in sorrow. They cried all day long and would not eat anything. Everyone was sad because Saul, his son Jonathan, and many of the Lord's people had been killed in the battle.

David asked the young man, 'Where is your home?'

The man replied, 'My father is an Amalekite, but we live in Israel.'

David said to him, 'Why weren't you afraid to kill the Lord's chosen king? And you even told what you did. It's your own fault that you're going to die!'

Then David told one of his soldiers, 'Come here and kill this man!'

DAVID IS CROWNED KING

2 SAMUEL
5.1–10

For several years there was a bitter war between Saul's family and David, who grew stronger as time went by.

Then the leaders poured olive oil on David's head to show that he was

Israel's leaders met with David at Hebron and said, 'We are your relatives. Even when Saul was king, you led our nation in battle. And the Lord promised that some day you would rule Israel and take care of us like a shepherd.'

now the king of Israel.

VIOLENCE AND WARFARE

See also 1 SAMUEL 16.1–13

During the meeting, David made an agreement with the leaders and asked the Lord to be their witness. Then the leaders poured olive oil on David's head to show that he was now the king of Israel.

David was thirty years old when he became king, and he ruled for forty years. He lived in Hebron for the first seven and a half years and ruled only Judah. Then he moved to Jerusalem, where he ruled both Israel and Judah for thirty-three years.

The Jebusites lived in Jerusalem, and David led his army there to attack them. The Jebusites did not think he could get in, so they told him, 'You can't get in here! We could drive you away, even if we couldn't see or walk!'

David told his troops, 'You will have to go up through the water tunnel to get those Jebusites. I hate people like them who can't walk or see.'

That's why there is still a rule that says, 'Only people who can walk and see are allowed in the temple.'

David captured the fortress on Mount Zion, then he moved there and named it David's City. He had the city rebuilt, starting with the landfill to the east. David became a great and strong ruler, because the Lord All-Powerful was on his side.

▶ ISAIAH 7.10–14

DAVID AND SONS

2 SAMUEL
6.1–23

THE SACRED CHEST IS TAKEN TO JERUSALEM

Having rebuilt Jerusalem, David wanted to bring the sacred chest with the Ten Commandments in, up to the city and worship God there.

David told her, 'The Lord didn't choose your father or anyone else in your family to be the leader of his people. The Lord chose me, and I was celebrating in honour of him.'

TRAVEL AND TRANSPORT

See also EXODUS 25.10–22

David brought together thirty thousand of Israel's best soldiers and led them to Baalah in Judah, which was also called Kiriath-Jearim. They were going there to get the sacred chest and bring it back to Jerusalem. The throne of the Lord All-Powerful is above the winged creatures on top of this chest, and he is worshipped there.

They put the sacred chest on a new ox cart and started bringing it down the hill from Abinadab's house. Abinadab's sons Uzzah and Ahio were guiding the ox cart, with Ahio walking in front of it. Some of the people of Israel were playing music on small harps and other stringed instruments, and on tambourines, castanets, and cymbals. David and the others were happy, and they danced for the Lord with all their might.

But when they came to Nacon's threshing-floor, the oxen stumbled, so Uzzah reached out and took hold of the sacred chest. The Lord God was very angry with Uzzah for doing this, and he killed Uzzah there beside the chest.

David got angry with God for killing Uzzah. He named that place 'Bursting Out Against Uzzah', and that's what it's still called.

David was afraid of the Lord and thought, 'Should I really take the sacred chest to my city?' He decided not to take it there. Instead, he turned off the road and took it to the home of Obed Edom, who was from Gath.

The chest stayed there for three months, and the Lord greatly blessed Obed Edom, his family, and everything he owned. Then someone told King David, 'The Lord has done this because the sacred chest is in Obed Edom's house.'

Straight away, David went to Obed Edom's house to get the chest and bring it to David's City. Everyone was celebrating. The people carrying the chest walked six steps, then David sacrificed an ox and a choice cow. He was dancing for the Lord with all his might, but he wore only a linen cloth. He and everyone else were celebrating by shouting and blowing horns while the chest was being carried along.

Saul's daughter Michal looked out of her window and watched the chest being brought into David's City. But when she saw David jumping and dancing for the Lord, she was disgusted.

They put the chest inside a tent that David had set up for it. David worshipped the Lord by sacrificing animals and burning them on an altar, then he blessed the people in the name of the Lord All-Powerful. He gave all the men and women in the crowd a small loaf of bread, some meat, and a handful of raisins, and everyone went home.

David went home so he could ask the Lord to bless his family. But Saul's daughter Michal went out and started yelling at him. 'You were really great today!' she said. 'You acted like a dirty old man, dancing around half-naked in front of your servants' slave-girls.'

David told her, 'The Lord didn't choose your father or anyone else in your family to be the leader of his people. The Lord chose me, and I was celebrating in honour of him. I'll show you just how great I can be! I'll even be disgusting to myself. But those slave-girls you talked about will still honour me!'

Michal never had any children.

FROM
2 SAMUEL
11.1–27

DAVID SLEEPS WITH BATHSHEBA

David consolidated his power and God promised that he would be the first king in a long dynasty. But in the end, power went to David's head.

It was now spring, the time when kings go to war. David sent

David sent some messengers to bring her to his palace. She came to him, and he slept with her.

RAPHAEL
DAVID AND
BATHSHEBA
PALAZZI PONTIFICI
THE VATICAN
1519

MARRIAGE AND
FAMILY
VIOLENCE AND
WARFARE

See also
GENESIS 39,
EXODUS 20.14,
EXODUS 20.13

out the whole Israelite army under the command of Joab and his officers. They destroyed the Ammonite army and surrounded the capital city of Rabbah, but David stayed in Jerusalem.

Late one afternoon, David got up from a nap and was walking around on the flat roof of his palace. A beautiful young woman was down below in her courtyard, bathing as her religion required. David happened to see her, and he sent one of his servants to find out who she was.

The servant came back and told David, 'Her name is Bathsheba. She is the daughter of Eliam, and she is the wife of Uriah the Hittite.'

David sent some messengers to bring her to his palace. She came to him, and he slept with her. Then she returned home. But later, when she found out that she was going to have a baby, she sent someone to David with this message: 'I'm pregnant!'

David sent a message to Joab: 'Send Uriah the Hittite to me.'

Joab sent Uriah to David's palace, and David asked him, 'Is Joab well? How is the army doing? And how about the war?' Then David told Uriah, 'Go home and clean up.' Uriah left the king's palace, and David had dinner sent to Uriah's house. But Uriah didn't go home. Instead, he slept outside the entrance to the royal palace, where the king's guards slept.

Someone told David that Uriah had not gone home. So the next morning David asked him, 'Why didn't you go home? Haven't you been away for a long time?'

Uriah answered, 'The sacred chest and the armies of Israel and Judah are camping out somewhere in the fields with our commander Joab and his officers and troops. Do you really think I would go home to eat and drink and sleep with my wife? I swear by your life that I would not!'

Then David said, 'Stay here in Jerusalem today, and I will send you back tomorrow.'

Uriah stayed in Jerusalem that day. Then the next day, David invited him for dinner. Uriah ate with David and drank so much that he got drunk, but he still did not go home. He went out and slept on his mat near the palace guards. Early the next morning, David wrote a letter and told Uriah to deliver it to Joab. The letter said: 'Put Uriah on the front line where the fighting is the worst. Then pull the troops back from him, so that he will be wounded and die.'

Joab had been carefully watching the city of Rabbah, and he put Uriah in a place where he knew there were some of the enemy's best soldiers. When the men of the city came out, they fought and killed some of David's soldiers – Uriah the Hittite was one of them.

When Bathsheba heard that her husband was dead, she mourned for him. Then after the time for mourning was over, David sent someone to bring her to the palace. She became David's wife, and they had a son.

2 SAMUEL
12.1–14

Why did you disobey me and do such a horrible thing? You murdered Uriah the Hittite by letting the Ammonites kill him, so you could take his wife.

REMBRANDT
NATHAN
ADMONISHING
DAVID
METROPOLITAN
MUSEUM OF ART
NEW YORK
1655

DAVID CONDEMNS HIMSELF

The Lord was angry at what David had done, and he sent Nathan the prophet to tell this story to David:

A rich man and a poor man lived in the same town. The rich man owned a lot of sheep and cattle, but the poor man had only one little lamb that he had bought and raised. The lamb became a pet for him and his children. He even let it eat from his plate and drink from his cup and sleep on his lap. The lamb was like one of his own children.

One day someone came to visit the rich man, but the rich man didn't want to kill any of his own sheep or cattle and serve it to the visitor. So he stole the poor man's little lamb and served it instead.

David was furious with the rich man and said to Nathan, 'I swear by the living Lord that the man who did this deserves to die! And because he didn't have any pity on the poor man, he will have to pay four times what the lamb was worth.'

Then Nathan told David:

You are that rich man! Now listen to what the Lord God of

**Birds and
animals
Marriage and
family**

See also
**Matthew 13,
Luke 10.25–37,
Luke 15.11–32,**
Psalm 51.1–19

Israel says to you: 'I chose you to be the king of Israel. I kept you safe from Saul and even gave you his house and his wives. I let you rule Israel and Judah, and if that had not been enough, I would have given you much more. Why did you disobey me and do such a horrible thing? You murdered Uriah the Hittite by letting the Ammonites kill him, so you could take his wife.

'Because you wouldn't obey me and took Uriah's wife for yourself, your family will never live in peace. Someone from your own family will cause you a lot of trouble, and I will take your wives and give them to another man before your very eyes. He will go to bed with them while everyone looks on. What you did was in secret, but I will do this in the open for everyone in Israel to see.'

David said, 'I have disobeyed the Lord.'

'Yes, you have!' Nathan answered. 'You showed you didn't care what the Lord wanted. He has forgiven you, and you won't die. But your newborn son will.'

**2 Samuel
15.1–12**

ABSALOM PLOTS AGAINST THE KING

David's family was torn apart as his sons began to fight each other. Absalom killed his brother Amnon, but David did not punish him for the murder. This made the people think that the king was becoming weak and indecisive.

*Soon everyone in
Israel liked Absalom
better than they
liked David.*

Some time later, Absalom got himself a chariot with horses to pull it, and he had fifty men to run in front. He would get up early each morning and wait by the side of the road that led to the city gate. Anyone who had a complaint to bring to King David would have to go that way, and Absalom would ask each of them, 'Where are you from?'

If they said, 'I'm from a tribe in the north,' Absalom would say, 'You deserve to win your case. But the king doesn't have anyone to hear complaints like yours. I wish someone would make me the judge around here! I would be fair to everyone.'

Whenever anyone would come to Absalom and start bowing down, he would reach out and hug and kiss them. That's how he treated everyone from Israel who brought a complaint to the king. Soon everyone in Israel liked Absalom better than they liked David.

Four years later, Absalom said to David, 'Please, let me go to Hebron. I have to keep a promise that I made to the Lord, when I was living with the Arameans in Geshur. I promised that if the Lord would bring me back to live in Jerusalem, I would worship him in Hebron.'

David gave his permission, and Absalom went to Hebron. He took two hundred men from Jerusalem with him, but they had no idea what he was going to do. Absalom offered sacrifices in Hebron and sent someone to Gilo to tell David's adviser Ahithophel to come.

More and more people were joining Absalom and supporting his plot. Meanwhile, Absalom had secretly sent some messengers to the northern tribes of Israel. The messengers told everyone, 'When you hear the sound of the trumpets, you must shout, "Absalom now rules as king in Hebron!"'

DAVID FLEES JERUSALEM

2 SAMUEL
15.13–23

A messenger came and told David, 'Everyone in Israel is on Absalom's side!'

TRAVEL AND TRANSPORT

A messenger came and told David, 'Everyone in Israel is on Absalom's side!'

David's officials were in Jerusalem with him, and he told them, 'Let's get out of here! We'll have to leave soon, or none of us will escape from Absalom. Hurry! If he moves fast, he could catch us while we're still here. Then he will kill us and everyone else in the city.'

The officials said, 'Your Majesty, we'll do whatever you say.'

David left behind ten of his wives to take care of the palace, but the rest of his family and his officials and soldiers went with him.

They stopped at the last house at the edge of the city. Then David stood there and watched while his regular troops and his bodyguards marched past. The last group was the six hundred soldiers who had followed him from Gath. Their commander was Ittai.

David spoke to Ittai and said, 'You're a foreigner from the town of Gath. You don't have to leave with us. Go back and join the new king! You haven't been with me very long, so why should you have to follow me, when I don't even know where I'm going? Take your soldiers and go back. I pray that the Lord will be kind and faithful to you.'

Ittai answered, 'Your Majesty, just as surely as you and the Lord live, I will go where you go, no matter if it costs me my life.'

'Then come on!' David said.

So Ittai and all his men and their families walked on past David.

The people of Jerusalem were crying and moaning as David and everyone with him passed by. He led them across Kidron Valley and along the road towards the desert.

2 SAMUEL
16.15–23

ABSALOM SETS HIMSELF UP IN JERUSALEM

Ahithophel gave such good advice in those days that both Absalom and David thought it came straight from God.

By this time, Absalom, Ahithophel, and the others had reached Jerusalem. David's friend Hushai came to Absalom and said, 'Long live the king! Long live the king!'

But Absalom asked Hushai, 'Is this how you show loyalty to your friend David? Why didn't you go with him?'

Hushai answered, 'The Lord and the people of Israel have chosen you to be king. I can't leave. I have to stay and serve the one they've chosen. Besides, it seems right for me to serve you, just as I served your father.'

Absalom turned to Ahithophel and said, 'Give us your advice! What should we do?'

Ahithophel answered, 'Some of your father's wives were left

here to take care of the palace. You should have sex with them. Then everyone will find out that you have publicly disgraced your father. This will make you and your followers even more powerful.'

Absalom had a tent set up on the flat roof of the palace, and everyone watched as he went into the tent with his father's wives.

Ahithophel gave such good advice in those days that both Absalom and David thought it came straight from God.

2 SAMUEL
18.1–15

ABSALOM'S REBELLION ENDS IN DISASTER

Absalom's advisor told him to go and fight his father David. So he assembled his army and crossed the river Jordan to engage him in battle.

Absalom was still alive, so Joab took three spears and stuck them through Absalom's chest.

VIOLENCE AND WARFARE

David divided his soldiers into groups of a hundred and groups of a thousand. Then he chose officers to be in command of each group. He sent out one-third of his army under the command of Joab, another third under the command of Abishai the son of Zeruiah, and the rest under the command of Ittai from Gath. He told the soldiers, 'I'm going into battle with you.'

But the soldiers said, 'No, don't go into battle with us! It won't matter to our enemies if they make us all run away, or even if they kill half of us. But you are worth ten thousand of us. It would be better for you to stay in town and send help if we need it.'

David said, 'All right, if you think I should.'

Then in a voice loud enough for everyone to hear, he said, 'Joab! Abishai! Ittai! For my sake, be sure that Absalom comes back unharmed.'

David stood beside the town gate as his army marched past in groups of a hundred and in groups of a thousand.

The war with Israel took place in Ephraim Forest. Battles were being fought all over the forest, and David's soldiers were winning. Twenty thousand soldiers were killed that day, and more of them died from the dangers of the forest than from the fighting itself.

Absalom was riding his mule under a huge tree when his head caught in the branches. The mule ran off and left Absalom hanging in mid-air. Some of David's soldiers happened to pass by, and one of them went and told Joab, 'I saw Absalom hanging in a tree!'

Joab said, 'You saw Absalom? Why didn't you kill him? I would have given you ten pieces of silver and a special belt.'

The man answered, 'Even if you paid me a thousand pieces of silver here and now, I still wouldn't touch the king's son. We all heard King David tell you and Abishai and Ittai not to harm Absalom. He always finds out what's going on. I would have been risking my life to kill Absalom, because you would have let me take the blame.'

Joab said, 'I'm not going to waste any more time on you!'

Absalom was still alive, so Joab took three spears and stuck them through Absalom's chest. Ten of Joab's bodyguards came over and finished him off.

DAVID IS TOLD OF ABSALOM'S DEATH

2 SAMUEL 18.19–33

'My son Absalom! My son, my son Absalom! I wish I could have died instead of you! Absalom, my son, my son!'

Ahimaaz the son of Zadok said, 'Joab, let me run and tell King David that the Lord has rescued him from his enemies.'

Joab answered, 'You're not the one to tell the king that his son is dead. You can take him a message some other time, but not today.'

Someone from Ethiopia was standing there, and Joab told him, 'Go and tell the king what you have seen.' The man knelt down in front of Joab and then got up and started running.

Ahimaaz spoke to Joab again, 'No matter what happens, I still want to run. And besides, the Ethiopian has already left.'

Joab said, 'Why should you run? You won't get a reward for the news you have!'

MICHELANGELO
THE DEATH OF
ABSALOM
THE VATICAN
ROME
1511

'I'll run no matter what!' Ahimaaz insisted.

'All right then, run!' Joab said.

Ahimaaz took the road through the Jordan Valley and outran the Ethiopian.

Meanwhile, David was sitting between the inner and outer gates in the city wall. One of his soldiers was watching from the roof of the gate-tower. He saw a man running towards the town and shouted down to tell David.

David answered, 'If he's alone, he must have some news.'

The runner was getting closer, when the soldier saw someone else running. He shouted down to the gate, 'Look! There's another runner!'

David said, 'He must have some news too.'

The soldier on the roof shouted, 'The first one runs just like Ahimaaz the son of Zadok.'

This time David said, 'He's a good man. He must have some good news.'

Ahimaaz called out, 'We won! We won!' Then he bowed low to David and said, 'Your Majesty, praise the Lord your God! He has given you victory over your enemies.'

'Is my son Absalom all right?' David asked.

Ahimaaz said, 'When Joab sent your personal servant and me, I saw a noisy crowd. But I don't know what it was all about.'

David told him, 'Stand over there and wait.'

Ahimaaz went over and stood there. The Ethiopian came and said, 'Your Majesty, today I have good news! The Lord has rescued you from all your enemies!'

'Is my son Absalom all right?' David asked.

The Ethiopian replied, 'I wish that all Your Majesty's enemies and everyone who tries to harm you would end up like him!'

David started trembling. Then he went up to the room above the city gate to cry. As he went, he kept saying, 'My son Absalom! My son, my son Absalom! I wish I could have died instead of you! Absalom, my son, my son!'

SOLOMON SUCCEEDS DAVID

David reigned for many years and the country grew in strength and standing. When he grew old and frail, one of his sons Adonijah proclaimed himself king, in contradiction to David's command that Solomon should succeed him.

Then he said, 'The living Lord God of Israel has kept me safe. And so today, I will keep the promise I made to you in his name: Solomon will be the next king!'

AGREEMENTS AND PROMISES

When Nathan heard what had happened, he asked Bathsheba, Solomon's mother:

Have you heard that Adonijah the son of Haggith has made himself king? But David doesn't know a thing about it. You and your son Solomon will be killed, unless you do what I tell you. Go and say to David, 'You promised me that Solomon would be the next king. So why is Adonijah now king?'

Meanwhile, David was in his bedroom where Abishag was taking care of him because he was so old. Bathsheba went in and bowed down.

'What can I do for you?' David asked.

Bathsheba answered:

Your Majesty, you promised me in the name of the Lord your God that my son Solomon would be the next king. But Adonijah has already been made king, and you didn't know anything about it.

Then he said, 'The living Lord God of Israel has kept me safe. And so today, I will keep the promise I made to you in his name: Solomon will be the next king!'

Bathsheba bowed with her face to the ground and said, 'Your Majesty, I pray that you will live a long time!'

Then David said, 'Tell Zadok, Nathan, and Benaiah to come here.'

When they arrived, he told them:

Take along some of my officials and let Solomon ride my own mule to Gihon Spring. When you get there, Zadok and Nathan will make Solomon the new king of Israel. Then after the ceremony is over, make someone blow a trumpet and tell everyone to shout, 'Long live King Solomon!' Bring him back here, and he will take my place as king. He is the one I have chosen to rule Israel and Judah.

Benaiah answered, 'We will do it, Your Majesty. I pray that the Lord your God will let it happen. The Lord has always watched over you, and I pray that he will now watch over Solomon. May the Lord help Solomon to be an even greater king than you.'

Zadok, Nathan, and Benaiah left and took along the two groups of David's special bodyguards. Solomon rode on David's mule as they led him to Gihon Spring. Zadok the priest brought some olive oil from the sacred tent and poured it on Solomon's head to show that he was now king. A trumpet was blown and everyone shouted, 'Long live King Solomon!'

SOLOMON'S WISE REQUEST

1 KINGS
3.5–15

*Please make me
wise and teach me
the difference
between right and
wrong. Then I will
know how to rule
your people. If you
don't, there is no
way I could rule this
great nation of
yours.*

AGREEMENTS AND
PROMISES
DREAMS AND
VISIONS

One night while Solomon was in Gibeon, the Lord God appeared to him in a dream and said, 'Solomon, ask for anything you want, and I will give it to you.'

Solomon answered:

My father David, your servant, was honest and did what you commanded. You were always loyal to him, and you gave him a son who is now king. Lord God, I'm your servant, and you've made me king in my father's place. But I'm very young and know so little about being a leader. And now I must rule your chosen people, even though there are too many of them to count.

Please make me wise and teach me the difference between right and wrong. Then I will know how to rule your people. If you don't, there is no way I could rule this great nation of yours.

God said:

Solomon, I'm pleased that you asked for this. You could have asked to live a long time or to be rich. Or you could have asked for your enemies to be destroyed. Instead, you asked

See also
PSALM 51.6,
PSALM 110.10,
PROVERBS,
LUKE 2.52,
ROMANS 11.33,
1 KINGS 4.29–34

for wisdom to make right decisions. So I'll make you wiser than anyone who has ever lived or ever will live.

I'll also give you what you didn't ask for. You'll be rich and respected as long as you live, and you'll be greater than any other king. If you obey me and follow my commands, as your father David did, I'll let you live a long time.

Solomon woke up and realized that God had spoken to him in the dream. He went back to Jerusalem and stood in front of the sacred chest, where he offered sacrifices to please the Lord and sacrifices to ask his blessing. Then Solomon gave a feast for his officials.

SOLOMON'S WISDOM IN ACTION

1 KINGS
3.16–28

Everyone in Israel was amazed when they heard how Solomon had made his decision. They realized that God had given him wisdom to judge fairly.

RAPHAEL
THE JUDGEMENT OF
SOLOMON
THE VATICAN
ROME
1519

One day two women came to King Solomon, and one of them said:

Your Majesty, this woman and I live in the same house. Not long ago my baby was born at home, and three days later her baby was born. Nobody else was there with us.

One night while we were all asleep, she rolled over on her baby, and he died. Then while I was still asleep, she got up and took my son out of my bed. She put him in her bed, then she put her dead baby next to me.

In the morning when I got up to feed my son, I saw that he was dead. But when I looked at him in the light, I knew he wasn't my son.

'No!' the other woman shouted. 'He was your son. My baby is alive!'

'The dead baby is yours,' the first woman yelled. 'Mine is alive!'

They argued back and forth in front of Solomon, until finally he said, 'Both of you say this live baby is yours. Someone bring me a sword.'

A sword was brought, and Solomon ordered, 'Cut the baby in half! That way each of you can have part of him.'

'Please don't kill my son,' the baby's mother screamed. 'Your Majesty, I love him very much, but give him to her. Just don't kill him.'

The other woman shouted, 'Go ahead and cut him in half. Then neither of us will have the baby.'

Solomon said, 'Don't kill the baby.' Then he pointed to the first woman, 'She is his real mother. Give the baby to her.'

Everyone in Israel was amazed when they heard how Solomon had made his decision. They realized that God had given him wisdom to judge fairly.

1 KINGS
5.1–18

SOLOMON PREPARES TO BUILD THE TEMPLE

Although David had wanted to build a temple in Jerusalem, God would not allow him to. Instead that task would fall to Solomon.

The Lord God promised my father that when his son became king, he would build a temple for worshipping the Lord. So I've decided to do that.

See also 2 Samuel 7.5–16

King Hiram of Tyre had always been friends with Solomon's father David. When Hiram learnt that Solomon was king, he sent some of his officials to meet with Solomon.

Solomon sent a message back to Hiram:

Remember how my father David wanted to build a temple where the Lord his God could be worshipped? But enemies kept attacking my father's kingdom, and he never had the chance. Now, thanks to the Lord God, there is peace in my kingdom and no trouble or threat of war anywhere.

The Lord God promised my father that when his son became king, he would build a temple for worshipping the Lord. So I've decided to do that.

I'd like you to send your workers to cut down cedar trees in Lebanon for me. I will pay them whatever you say and will even make my workers help them. We both know that your workers are more experienced than anyone else at cutting timber.

Hiram was so happy when he heard Solomon's request that he said, 'I am grateful that the Lord gave David such a wise son to be king of that great nation!' Then he sent back his answer:

I received your message and will give you all the cedar and pine logs you need. My workers will carry them down from Lebanon to the Mediterranean Sea. They will tie the logs together and float them along the coast to wherever you want them. Then they will untie the logs, and your workers can take them from there.

To pay for the logs, you can provide the grain I need for my household.

Hiram gave Solomon all the cedar and pine logs he needed. In return, Solomon gave Hiram two thousand tonnes of wheat and four hundred thousand litres of pure olive oil each year.

The Lord kept his promise and made Solomon wise. Hiram and Solomon signed a treaty and never went to war against each other.

Solomon ordered thirty thousand people from all over Israel to cut logs for the temple, and he put Adoniram in charge of these workers. Solomon divided them into three groups of ten thousand. Each group worked one month in Lebanon and had two months off at home.

He also had eighty thousand workers to cut stone in the hill country of Israel, seventy thousand workers to carry the stones, and over three thousand assistants to keep track of the work and to supervise the workers. He ordered the workers to cut and shape large blocks of good stone for the foundation of the temple.

Solomon's and Hiram's men worked with men from the city of Gebal, and together they got the stones and logs ready for the temple.

ELIJAH AND ELISHA

1 KINGS
17.1–7

'I'm a servant of the living Lord, the God of Israel. And I swear in his name that it won't rain until I say so. There won't even be any dew on the ground.'

FOOD AND DRINK

See also
DEUTERONOMY
11.17

ELIJAH PROMISES A DROUGHT

After Solomon's death, his kingdom split in two. The northern part, made up of ten tribes, was called Israel, and the southern part, Judah. God sent a series of prophets to speak to both of the newly formed kingdoms. Elijah was the most prominent among them.

Elijah was a prophet from Tishbe in Gilead. One day he went to King Ahab and said, 'I'm a servant of the living Lord, the God of Israel. And I swear in his name that it won't rain until I say so. There won't even be any dew on the ground.'

Later, the Lord said to Elijah, 'Leave and go across the River Jordan so you can hide near Cherith Brook. You can drink water from the brook, and eat the food I've told the ravens to bring you.'

Elijah obeyed the Lord and went to live near Cherith Brook. Ravens brought him bread and meat twice a day, and he drank water from the brook. But after a while, it dried up because there was no rain.

1 KINGS
17.8–16

The Lord kept the promise that his prophet Elijah had made, and she did not run out of flour or oil.

ELIJAH FINDS SHELTER WITH A WIDOW IN ZAREPHATH

The Lord told Elijah, 'Go to the town of Zarephath in Sidon and live there. I've told a widow in that town to give you food.'

When Elijah came near the town gate of Zarephath, he saw a widow gathering sticks for a fire. 'Would you please bring me a cup of water?' he asked. As she left to get it, he asked, 'Would you also please bring me a piece of bread?'

The widow answered, 'In the name of the living Lord your God, I swear that I don't have any bread. All I have is a handful of flour and a little olive oil. I'm on my way home now with these few sticks to cook what I have for my son and me. After that, we will starve to death.'

Elijah said, 'Everything will be fine. Do what you said. Go home and prepare something for yourself and your son. But first, please make a small piece of bread and bring it to me. The Lord God of Israel has promised that your jar of flour won't run out and your bottle of oil won't dry up before he sends rain for the crops.'

The widow went home and did exactly what Elijah had told her. She and Elijah and her family had enough food for a long time. The Lord kept the promise that his prophet Elijah had made, and she did not run out of flour or oil.

FOOD AND DRINK

See also
EXODUS 22.22,
PSALM 68.5,
PSALM 146.9,
JAMES 1.27

FROM 1 KINGS
18.1–39

ELIJAH CONFRONTS THE PROPHETS OF BAAL

For three years no rain fell in Samaria, and there was almost nothing to eat anywhere. The Lord said to Elijah, 'Go and meet with King Ahab. I will soon make it rain.' So Elijah went to see Ahab.

As Obadiah was walking along, he met Elijah. Obadiah recognized him, bowed down, and asked, 'Elijah, is it really you?'

'Yes. Go and tell Ahab I'm here.'

Obadiah left and told Ahab where to find Elijah.

Ahab went to meet Elijah, and when he saw him, Ahab shouted, 'There you are, the biggest troublemaker in Israel!'

Elijah answered: You're the troublemaker – not me! You and your family have disobeyed the Lord's commands by worshipping Baal.

Call together everyone from Israel to meet me on Mount Carmel. Be sure to bring along the four hundred and fifty prophets of Baal and the four hundred prophets of Asherah who eat at Jezebel's table.

Ahab got everyone together, then they went to meet Elijah on Mount Carmel. Elijah stood in front of them and said, 'How

Elijah stood in front of them and said, 'How much longer will you try to have things both ways? If the Lord is God, worship him! But if Baal is God, worship him!'

BIRDS AND ANIMALS
MIRACLES AND WONDERS
VIOLENCE AND WARFARE

much longer will you try to have things both ways? If the Lord is God, worship him! But if Baal is God, worship him!'

The people did not say a word.

Then Elijah continued:

I am the Lord's only prophet, but Baal has four hundred and fifty prophets.

Bring us two bulls. Baal's prophets can take one of them, kill it, and cut it into pieces. Then they can put the meat on the wood without lighting the fire. I will do the same thing with the other bull, and I won't light a fire under it either.

The prophets of Baal will pray to their god, and I will pray to the Lord. The one who answers by starting the fire is God.

'That's a good idea,' everyone agreed.

Elijah said to Baal's prophets, 'There are more of you, so you go first. Pick out a bull and get it ready, but don't light the fire. Then pray to your god.'

They chose their bull, then they got it ready and prayed to Baal all morning, asking him to start the fire. They danced around the altar and shouted, 'Answer us, Baal!' But there was no answer.

At midday, Elijah began making fun of them. 'Pray louder!' he said. 'Baal must be a god. Perhaps he's daydreaming or using the toilet or travelling somewhere. Or perhaps he's asleep, and you have to wake him up.'

The prophets kept shouting louder and louder, and they cut themselves with swords and knives until they were bleeding. This was the way they worshipped, and they kept it up all afternoon. But there was no answer of any kind.

Elijah told everyone to gather around him while he repaired the Lord's altar. Then he used twelve stones to build an altar in honour of the Lord. Each stone stood for one of the tribes of Israel, which was the name the Lord had given to their ancestor Jacob. Elijah dug a ditch around the altar, large enough to hold almost fourteen litres. He placed the wood on the altar, then they cut the bull into pieces and laid the meat on the wood.

He told the people, 'Fill four large jars with water and pour it over the meat and the wood.' After they did this, he told them to do it two more times. They did exactly as he said until finally, the water ran down the altar and filled the ditch.

When it was time for the evening sacrifice, Elijah prayed:
Our Lord, you are the God of Abraham, Isaac, and Israel. Now, prove that you are the God of this nation, and that I, your servant, have done this at your command. Please answer me, so these people will know that you are the Lord God, and that you will turn their hearts back to you.

The Lord immediately sent fire, and it burnt up the sacrifice, the wood, and the stones. It scorched the ground everywhere around the altar and dried up every drop of water in the ditch. When the crowd saw what had happened, they all bowed down and shouted, 'The Lord is God! The Lord is God!'

THE DROUGHT ENDS

1 KINGS
18.41–46

A few minutes later, it got very cloudy and windy, and rain started pouring down.

Elijah told Ahab, 'Get something to eat and drink. I hear a heavy rain coming.'

Ahab left, but Elijah climbed back to the top of Mount Carmel. Then he stooped down with his face almost to the ground and said to his servant, 'Look towards the sea.'

The servant left. And when he came back, he said, 'I looked, but I didn't see anything.' Elijah told him to look seven more times.

After the seventh time the servant replied, 'I see a small cloud coming this way. But it's no bigger than a fist.'

Elijah told him, 'Tell Ahab to get his chariot ready and start home now. Otherwise, the rain will stop him.'

A few minutes later, it got very cloudy and windy, and rain started pouring down. So Elijah wrapped his coat around himself, and the Lord gave him strength to run all the way to Jezreel. Ahab followed him.

ELIJAH'S INNER TURMOIL

1 Kings 19.1–16

'I've had enough. Just let me die! I'm no better off than my ancestors.'

Food and drink
Travel and transport

See also
Exodus 19.20,
Genesis 16.7,
Exodus 23.20,
2 Kings 19.35,
Matthew 1.20,
Luke 1.11,
Luke 1.26,
Acts 12.7

Ahab told his wife Jezebel what Elijah had done and that he had killed the prophets. She sent a message to Elijah: 'You killed my prophets. Now I'm going to kill you! I pray that the gods will punish me even more severely if I don't do it by this time tomorrow.'

Elijah was afraid when he got her message, and he ran to the town of Beersheba in Judah. He left his servant there, then walked another whole day into the desert. Finally, he came to a large bush and sat down in its shade. He begged the Lord, 'I've had enough. Just let me die! I'm no better off than my ancestors.' Then he lay down in the shade and fell asleep.

Suddenly an angel woke him up and said, 'Get up and eat.' Elijah looked around, and by his head was a jar of water and some baked bread. He sat up, ate and drank, then lay down and went back to sleep.

Soon the Lord's angel woke him again and said, 'Get up and eat, or else you'll get too tired to travel.' So Elijah sat up and ate and drank.

The food and water made him strong enough to walk forty more days. At last, he reached Mount Sinai, the mountain of God, and he spent the night there in a cave.

While Elijah was on Mount Sinai, the Lord asked, 'Elijah, why are you here?'

He answered, 'Lord God All-Powerful, I've always done my best to obey you. But your people have broken their solemn promise to you. They have torn down your altars and killed all your prophets, except me. And now they are even trying to kill me!'

'Go out and stand on the mountain,' the Lord replied. 'I want you to see me when I pass by.'

All at once, a strong wind shook the mountain and shattered the rocks. But the Lord was not in the wind. Next, there was an earthquake, but the Lord was not in the earthquake. Then there was a fire, but the Lord was not in the fire.

Finally, there was a gentle breeze, and when Elijah heard it, he covered his face with his coat. He went out and stood at the entrance to the cave.

The Lord asked, 'Elijah, why are you here?'

Elijah answered, 'Lord God All-Powerful, I've always done my best to obey you. But your people have broken their solemn promise to you. They have torn down your altars and killed all your prophets, except me. And now they are even trying to kill me!'

The Lord said:

Elijah, you can go back to the desert near Damascus. And when you get there, appoint Hazael to be king of Syria. Then appoint Jehu son of Nimshi to be king of Israel, and Elisha son of Shaphat to take your place as my prophet.

2 KINGS
2.1–15

ELIJAH'S DRAMATIC FAREWELL

As the kings and the people consistently strayed from God's way, he continued to try to draw them back through his prophets. Yet nothing they did or said appeared to have any long-lasting effect upon the life of the nation.

'I swear by the living Lord and by your own life, that I will stay with you no matter what!' And he went with Elijah to Jericho.

MIRACLES AND WONDERS

Not long before the Lord took Elijah up into heaven in a strong wind, Elijah and Elisha were leaving Gilgal. Elijah said to Elisha, 'The Lord wants me to go to Bethel, but you must stay here.'

Elisha replied, 'I swear by the living Lord and by your own life that I will stay with you no matter what!' And he went with Elijah to Bethel.

A group of prophets who lived there asked Elisha, 'Do you know that today the Lord is going to take away your master?'

'Yes, I do,' Elisha answered. 'But don't remind me of it.'

Elijah then said, 'Elisha, now the Lord wants me to go to Jericho, but you must stay here.'

Elisha replied, 'I swear by the living Lord and by your own life, that I will stay with you no matter what!' And he went with Elijah to Jericho.

A group of prophets who lived there asked Elisha, 'Do you know that today the Lord is going to take away your master?'

'Yes, I do,' Elisha answered. 'But don't remind me of it.'

Elijah then said to Elisha, 'Now the Lord wants me to go to the River Jordan, but you must stay here.'

Elisha replied, 'I swear by the living Lord and by your own life that I will never leave you!' So the two of them walked on together.

Fifty prophets followed Elijah and Elisha from Jericho, then stood at a distance and watched as the two men walked towards the river. When they got there, Elijah took off his coat, then he rolled it up and struck the water with it. At once a path opened up through the river, and the two of them walked across on dry ground.

After they had reached the other side, Elijah said, 'Elisha, the Lord will soon take me away. What can I do for you before that happens?'

Elisha answered, 'Please give me twice as much of your power as you give the other prophets, so I can be the one who takes your place as their leader.'

'It won't be easy,' Elijah answered. 'It can happen only if you see me as I am being taken away.'

Elijah and Elisha were walking along and talking, when suddenly there appeared between them a flaming chariot pulled by fiery horses. Straight away, a strong wind took Elijah up into heaven. Elisha saw this and shouted, 'Israel's cavalry and chariots have taken my master away!' After Elijah had gone, Elisha tore his clothes in sorrow.

Elijah's coat had fallen off, so Elisha picked it up and walked back to the River Jordan. He struck the water with the coat and wondered, 'Will the Lord perform miracles for me as he did for Elijah?' As soon as Elisha did this, a dry path opened up through the water, and he walked across.

When the prophets from Jericho saw what happened, they said to each other, 'Elisha now has Elijah's power.'

A WIDOW'S DEBT

'Perhaps there's something I can do to help,' Elisha said. 'What do you have in your house?' 'Sir, I have nothing but a small bottle of olive oil.'

See also
EXODUS 22.22,
1 KINGS 17.8–16,
PSALM 68.5,
PSALM 146.9,
JAMES 1.27

One day the widow of one of the Lord's prophets said to Elisha, 'You know that before my husband died, he was a follower of yours and a worshipper of the Lord. But he owed a man some money, and now that man is on his way to take my two sons as his slaves.'

'Perhaps there's something I can do to help,' Elisha said. 'What do you have in your house?'

'Sir, I have nothing but a small bottle of olive oil.'

Elisha told her, 'Ask your neighbours for their empty jars. And after you've borrowed as many as you can, go home and shut the door behind you and your sons. Then begin filling the jars with oil and set each one aside as you fill it.'

The woman left.

Later, when she and her sons were back inside their house, the two sons brought her the jars, and she began filling them.

At last, she said to one of her sons, 'Bring me another jar.'

'We don't have any more,' he answered, and the oil stopped flowing from the small bottle.

After she told Elisha what had happened, he said, 'Sell the oil and use part of the money to pay what you owe the man. You and your sons can live on what is left.'

ELISHA REWARDS A HOSPITABLE FAMILY

He walked in, shut the door, and prayed to the Lord.

Once, while Elisha was in the town of Shunem, he met a rich woman who invited him to her home for dinner. After that, whenever he was in Shunem, he would have a meal there with her and her husband.

Some time later the woman said to her husband, 'I'm sure the man who comes here so often is a prophet of God. Why don't we build him a small room on the flat roof of our house? We can put a bed, a table and chair, and an oil lamp in it. Then whenever he comes, he can stay with us.'

AGREEMENTS AND
PROMISES
BIRDS AND
ANIMALS
FARMING AND
PRODUCE
MIRACLES AND
WONDERS
TRAVEL AND
TRANSPORT

See also
MARK 5.21,
JOHN 11.1–44,
MARK 16.1–8

The next time Elisha was in Shunem, he stopped at their house and went up to his room to rest. He said to his servant Gehazi, 'This woman has been very helpful. Ask her to come up here to the roof for a moment.' She came, and Elisha told Gehazi to say to her, 'You've gone to a lot of trouble for us, and we want to help you. Is there something we can request the king or army commander to do?'

The woman answered, 'With my relatives nearby, I have everything I need.'

'Then what can we do for her?' Elisha asked Gehazi.

Gehazi replied, 'I do know that her husband is old, and that she doesn't have a son.'

'Ask her to come here again,' Elisha told his servant. He called for her, and she came and stood in the doorway of Elisha's room.

Elisha said to her, 'Next year at this time, you'll be holding your own baby son in your arms.'

'You're a man of God,' the woman replied. 'Please don't lie to me.'

But a few months later, the woman got pregnant. She gave birth to a son, just as Elisha had promised.

One day while the boy was still young, he was out in the fields with his father, where the workers were harvesting the crops. Suddenly he shouted, 'My head hurts. It hurts a lot!'

'Carry him back to his mother,' the father said to his servant. The servant picked up the boy and carried him to his mother. The boy lay on her lap all morning, and by midday he was dead. She carried him upstairs to Elisha's room and laid him across the bed. Then she walked out and shut the door behind her.

The woman called to her husband, 'I need to see the prophet. Let me use one of the donkeys. Send a servant along with me, and let me leave now, so I can get back quickly.'

'Why do you need to see him today?' her husband asked. 'It's not the Sabbath or time for the New Moon Festival.'

'That's all right,' she answered. She saddled the donkey and said to her servant, 'Let's go. And don't slow down unless I tell you to.' She left at once for Mount Carmel to talk with Elisha.

When Elisha saw her coming, he said, 'Gehazi, look! It's the woman from Shunem. Run and meet her. And ask her if everything is all right with her and her family.'

'Everything is fine,' she answered Gehazi. But as soon as she got to the top of the mountain, she went over and grabbed Elisha by the feet.

Gehazi started towards her to push her away, when Elisha said, 'Leave her alone! Don't you see how sad she is? But the Lord hasn't told me why.'

The woman said, 'Sir, I begged you not to get my hopes up, and I didn't even ask you for a son.'

'Gehazi, get ready and go to her house,' Elisha said. 'Take along my walking stick, and when you get there, lay it on the boy's face. Don't stop to talk to anyone, even if they try to talk to you.'

But the boy's mother said to Elisha, 'I swear by the living Lord and by your own life that I won't leave without you.' So Elisha got up and went with them.

Gehazi ran on ahead and laid Elisha's walking stick on the boy's face, but the boy didn't move or make a sound. Gehazi ran back to Elisha and said, 'The boy didn't wake up.'

Elisha arrived at the woman's house and went straight to his room, where he saw the boy's body on his bed. He walked in, shut the door, and prayed to the Lord. Then he got on the bed and stretched out over the dead body, with his mouth on the boy's mouth, his eyes on his eyes, and his hand on his hands. As he lay there, the boy's body became warm. Elisha got up and walked back and forth in the room, then he went back and leaned over the boy's body. The boy sneezed seven times and opened his eyes.

Elisha called out to Gehazi, 'Ask the boy's mother to come here.' Gehazi did, and when she was at the door, Elisha said, 'You can take your son.'

She came in and bowed down at Elisha's feet. Then she picked up her son and left.

A FOREIGN COMMANDER IS CURED

His servants went over to him and said, 'Sir, if the prophet had told you to do something difficult, you would have done it. So why don't you do what he said? Go and wash and be cured.'

**MIRACLES AND
WONDERS
TRAVEL AND
TRANSPORT**

See also
**EXODUS 4.6,
NUMBERS 12.10,
MATTHEW 11.5,
LUKE 17.12**

Naaman was the commander of the Syrian army. The Lord had helped him and his troops defeat their enemies, so the king of Syria respected Naaman very much. Naaman was a brave soldier, but he had leprosy.

One day while the Syrian troops were raiding Israel, they captured a girl, and she became a servant of Naaman's wife. Some time later the girl said, 'If your husband Naaman would go to the prophet in Samaria, he would be cured of his leprosy.'

When Naaman told the king what the girl had said, the king replied, 'Go ahead! I will give you a letter to take to the king of Israel.'

Naaman left and took along thirty thousand pieces of silver, six thousand pieces of gold, and ten new outfits. He also carried the letter to the king of Israel. It said, 'I am sending my servant Naaman to you. Would you cure him of his leprosy?'

When the king of Israel read the letter, he tore his clothes in fear and shouted, 'That Syrian king believes I can cure this man of leprosy! Does he think I'm God with power over life and death? He must be trying to pick a fight with me.'

As soon as Elisha the prophet heard what had happened, he sent the Israelite king this message: 'Why are you so afraid? Send the man to me, so that he will know there is a prophet in Israel.'

Naaman left with his horses and chariots and stopped at the door of Elisha's house. Elisha sent someone outside to say to him, 'Go and wash seven times in the River Jordan. Then you'll be completely cured.'

But Naaman stormed off, grumbling, 'Why couldn't he come out and talk to me? I thought he would be sure to stand in front of me and pray to the Lord his God, then wave his hand over my skin and cure me. What about the River Abana or the River Pharpar? Those rivers in Damascus are just as good as any river in Israel. I could have washed in them and been cured.'

His servants went over to him and said, 'Sir, if the prophet had told you to do something difficult, you would have done it. So why don't you do what he said? Go and wash and be cured.'

Naaman walked down to the Jordan; he waded out into the water and stooped down in it seven times, just as Elisha had told him. Straight away, he was cured, and his skin became as smooth as a child's.

Exile and return

2 Kings
18.13–37

THE ASSYRIANS AT THE GATES OF JERUSALEM

After many generations of disloyalty to God, the northern kingdom of Israel was attacked by the Assyrians and the people were deported.

In the fourteenth year of Hezekiah's rule in Judah, King Sennacherib of Assyria invaded the country and captured every walled city, except Jerusalem.

VIOLENCE AND WARFARE

See also ISAIAH
36.1–22

In the fourteenth year of Hezekiah's rule in Judah, King Sennacherib of Assyria invaded the country and captured every walled city, except Jerusalem. Hezekiah sent this message to Sennacherib, who was in the town of Lachish: 'I know I am guilty of rebellion. But I will pay you whatever you want, if you stop your attack.'

Sennacherib told Hezekiah to pay ten thousand kilogrammes of silver and a thousand kilogrammes of gold. So Hezekiah collected all the silver from the Lord's temple and the royal treasury. He even stripped the gold that he had used to cover the doors and doorposts in the temple. He gave it all to Sennacherib.

The king of Assyria ordered his three highest military officers to leave Lachish and take a large army to Jerusalem. When they arrived, the officers stood on the road near the cloth makers' shops along the canal from the upper pool. They called out to Hezekiah, and three of his highest officials came out to meet them. One of them was Hilkiah's son Eliakim, who was the prime minister. The other two were Shebna, assistant to the prime minister, and Joah son of Asaph, keeper of the government records.

One of the Assyrian commanders told them:

I have a message for Hezekiah from the great king of Assyria. Ask Hezekiah why he feels so sure of himself. Does he think he can plan and win a war with nothing but words? Who is going to help him, now that he has turned against the king of Assyria? Is he depending on Egypt and its king? That's the same as leaning on a broken stick, and it will go right through his hand.

Is Hezekiah now depending on the Lord your God? Didn't Hezekiah tear down all except one of the Lord's altars and places of worship? Didn't he tell the people of Jerusalem and Judah to worship at that one place?

The king of Assyria wants to make a bet with you people. He will give you two thousand horses, if you have enough troops to ride them. How could you even defeat our lowest ranking officer, when you have to depend on Egypt for chariots and cavalry? Don't forget that it was the Lord who sent me here with orders to destroy your nation!

Eliakim, Shebna, and Joah said, 'Sir, we don't want the people listening from the city wall to understand what you are saying. So please speak to us in Aramaic instead of Hebrew.'

The Assyrian army commander answered, 'My king sent me to speak to everyone, not just to you leaders. These people will soon have to eat their own body waste and drink their own urine! And so will the three of you.'

Then, in a voice loud enough for everyone to hear, he shouted in Hebrew:

Listen to what the great king of Assyria says! Don't be fooled by Hezekiah. He can't save you. Don't trust him when he tells you that the Lord will protect you from the king of Assyria. Stop listening to Hezekiah! Pay attention to my king. Surrender to him. He will let you keep your own vineyards, fig trees, and cisterns for a while. Then he will come and take you away to a country just like yours, where you can plant vineyards, raise your own grain, and have plenty of olive oil and honey. Believe me, you won't starve there.

Hezekiah claims the Lord will save you. But don't be fooled by him. Were any other gods able to defend their land against the king of Assyria? What happened to the gods of Hamath and Arpad? What about the gods of Sepharvaim, Hena, and Ivvah? Were the gods of Samaria able to protect their land against the Assyrian forces? None of these gods kept their people safe from the king of Assyria. Do you think the Lord your God can do any better?

Eliakim, Shebna, and Joah had been warned by King Hezekiah not to answer the Assyrian commander. So they tore their clothes in sorrow and reported to Hezekiah everything the commander had said.

2 KINGS
19.1–19

ISAIAH'S ADVICE IN A TIME OF CRISIS

But you are our Lord and our God! We ask you to keep us safe from the Assyrian king. Then everyone in every kingdom on earth will know that you are the only God.

VIOLENCE AND WARFARE

See also *ISAIAH 37.1–13*

As soon as Hezekiah heard the news, he tore off his clothes in sorrow and put on sackcloth. Then he went into the temple of the Lord. He told Prime Minister Eliakim, Assistant Prime Minister Shebna, and the senior priests to dress in sackcloth and tell the prophet Isaiah:

These are difficult and disgraceful times. Our nation is like a woman too weak to give birth, when it's time for her baby to be born. Please pray for those of us who are left alive. The king of Assyria sent his army commander to insult the living God. Perhaps the Lord heard what he said and will do something, if you will pray.

When these leaders went to Isaiah, he told them that the Lord had this message for Hezekiah:

I am the Lord. Don't worry about the insulting things that have been said about me by these messengers from the king of Assyria. I will upset him with rumours about what's happening in his own country. He will go back, and there I will make him die a violent death.

Meanwhile, the commander of the Assyrian forces heard that his king had left the town of Lachish and was now attacking Libnah. So he went there.

About this same time the king of Assyria learnt that King Tirhakah of Ethiopia was on his way to attack him. Then the king of Assyria sent some messengers with this note for

Hezekiah:

> Don't trust your God or be fooled by his promise to defend Jerusalem against me. You have heard how we Assyrian kings have completely wiped out other nations. What makes you feel so safe? The Assyrian kings before me destroyed the towns of Gozan, Haran, Rezeph, and everyone from Eden who lived in Telassar. What good did their gods do them? The kings of Hamath, Arpad, Sepharvaim, Hena, and Ivvah have all disappeared.

After Hezekiah had read the note from the king of Assyria, he took it to the temple and spread it out for the Lord to see. He prayed:

> Lord God of Israel, your throne is above the winged creatures. You created the heavens and the earth, and you alone rule the kingdoms of this world. But just look how Sennacherib has insulted you, the living God.
>
> It is true, our Lord, that Assyrian kings have turned nations into deserts. They destroyed the idols of wood and stone that the people of those nations had made and worshipped. But you are our Lord and our God! We ask you to keep us safe from the Assyrian king. Then everyone in every kingdom on earth will know that you are the only God.

2 KINGS
22.1–20

THE LONG-LOST BOOK OF THE LAW

After Judah's deliverance, two evil kings reigned for nearly half a century. It was a lawless time when God's ways were forgotten. Eventually, though, a new king came to the throne in Judah, and, despite his youth, proved himself a wise ruler.

Josiah was eight years old when he became king of Judah, and he ruled thirty-one years from Jerusalem. His mother Jedidah was the daughter of Adaiah from Bozkath. Josiah always obeyed the Lord, just as his ancestor David had done.

After Josiah had been king for eighteen years, he told Shaphan, one of his highest officials:

'The Lord must be
furious with me and
everyone else in
Judah, because our
ancestors did not
obey the laws
written in this book.
Go and find out
what the Lord
wants us to do.'

See also
2 CHRONICLES
34,35

Go to the Lord's temple and ask Hilkiah the high priest to collect from the guards all the money that the people have donated. Tell Hilkiah to give it to the men supervising the repairs to the temple. They can use some of the money to pay the workers, and with the rest of it they can buy wood and stone for the repair work. They are honest, so we won't ask them to keep track of the money.

While Shaphan was at the temple, Hilkiah handed him a book and said, 'Look what I found here in the temple – *The Book of God's Law.*'

Shaphan read it, then went back to Josiah and reported, 'Your officials collected the money in the temple and gave it to the men supervising the repairs. But there's something else, Your Majesty. The priest Hilkiah gave me this book.' Then Shaphan read it out loud.

When Josiah heard what was in *The Book of God's Law*, he tore his clothes in sorrow. At once he called together Hilkiah, Shaphan, Ahikam son of Shaphan, Achbor son of Micaiah, and his own servant Asaiah. He said, 'The Lord must be furious with me and everyone else in Judah, because our ancestors did not obey the laws written in this book. Go and find out what the Lord wants us to do.'

The five men left straight away and went to talk with Huldah the prophet. Her husband was Shallum, who was in charge of the king's clothes. Huldah lived in the northern part of Jerusalem, and when they met in her home, she said:

You were sent here by King Josiah, and this is what the Lord God of Israel says to him: 'Josiah, I am the Lord! And I will see to it that this country and everyone living in it will be destroyed. It will happen just as this book says. The people of Judah have rejected me. They have offered sacrifices to foreign gods and have worshipped their own idols. I cannot stand it any longer. I am furious.

'Josiah, listen to what I am going to do. I noticed how sad you were when you read that this country and its people would be completely wiped out. You even tore your clothes in sorrow, and I heard you cry. So I will let you die in peace, before I destroy this place.'

The men left and took Huldah's answer back to Josiah.

before I destroy this place

EZRA 1.1–11

CYRUS COMMANDS THE JEWS TO RETURN

After his people had repeatedly ignored him, the Lord allowed the Babylonians to capture the city of Jerusalem and take its people into exile. God did not abandon his people completely, however, and in due course, some of the exiles began to return home.

I am King Cyrus of Persia. The Lord God of heaven, who is also the God of Israel, has made me the ruler of all nations on earth. And he has chosen me to build a temple for him in Jerusalem, which is in Judah. The Lord God will watch over and encourage any of his people who want to go back to Jerusalem and help build the temple.

TRAVEL AND TRANSPORT

Years ago the Lord sent Jeremiah with a message about a promise for the people of Israel. Then in the first year that Cyrus was king of Persia, the Lord kept his promise by telling Cyrus to send this official message to all parts of his kingdom:

I am King Cyrus of Persia.

The Lord God of heaven, who is also the God of Israel, has made me the ruler of all nations on earth. And he has chosen me to build a temple for him in Jerusalem, which is in Judah. The Lord God will watch over and encourage any of his people who want to go back to Jerusalem and help build the temple.

Everyone else must provide what is needed. They must give money, supplies, and animals, as well as gifts for rebuilding God's temple.

Many people felt that the Lord God wanted them to help rebuild his temple, and they made plans to go to Jerusalem. Among them were priests, Levites, and leaders of the tribes of Judah and Benjamin. The others helped by giving silver articles, gold, personal possessions, cattle, and other valuable gifts, as well as offerings for the temple.

King Cyrus gave back the things that Nebuchadnezzar had taken from the Lord's temple in Jerusalem and had put in the temple of his own gods. Cyrus placed Mithredath, his chief treasurer, in charge of these things. Mithredath counted them and gave a list to Sheshbazzar, the governor of Judah. Included

See also
2 CHRONICLES
36.22–23

among them were: 30 large gold dishes; 1,000 large silver dishes; 29 other dishes; 30 gold bowls; 410 silver bowls; and 1,000 other articles.

Altogether, there were 5,400 gold and silver dishes, bowls, and other articles. Sheshbazzar took them with him when he and the others returned to Jerusalem from Babylonia.

EZRA 3.7–13

They praised the Lord and gave thanks as they took turns singing: 'The Lord is good! His faithful love for Israel will last for ever.' Everyone started shouting and praising the Lord because work on the foundation of the temple had begun.

FOOD AND DRINK

See also 1 KINGS 6,
JOHN 2.12–25,
EXODUS 15.1,
MATTHEW 26.30,
EPHESIANS 5.19,
JAMES 5.13,
NEHEMIAH

LAYING THE FOUNDATIONS OF THE TEMPLE

King Cyrus of Persia had said the Israelites could have cedar trees brought from Lebanon to Joppa by sea. So they sent grain, wine, and olive oil to the cities of Tyre and Sidon as payment for these trees, and they gave money to the stoneworkers and carpenters.

During the second month of the second year after the people had returned from Babylonia, they started rebuilding the Lord's temple. Zerubbabel son of Shealtiel, Joshua son of Jozadak, the priests, the Levites, and everyone else who had returned started working. Every Levite over twenty years of age was put in charge of some part of the work. The Levites in charge of the whole project were Joshua and his sons and relatives and Kadmiel and his sons from the family of Hodaviah. The family of Henadad worked along with them.

When the builders had finished laying the foundation of the temple, the priests put on their robes and blew trumpets in honour of the Lord, while the Levites from the family of Asaph praised God with cymbals. All of them followed the instructions given years before by King David. They praised the Lord and gave thanks as they took turns singing:

'The Lord is good! His faithful love for Israel will last for ever.'

Everyone started shouting and praising the Lord because work on the foundation of the temple had begun. Many of the older priests and Levites and the heads of families cried aloud because they remembered seeing the first temple years before. But others were so happy that they celebrated with joyful shouts. Their shouting and crying were so noisy that it all sounded alike and could be heard a long way off.

NEHEMIAH
1.1–11

WORRYING NEWS FROM JERUSALEM

With some exiles now established back in Jerusalem, news of their troubles there filtered back to the Jews still living in Babylon. This caused great concern and one man, Nehemiah, was particularly disturbed by what he heard.

'Those captives who have come back are having all kinds of troubles. They are terribly disgraced, Jerusalem's walls are broken down, and its gates have been burnt.'

See also EZRA

I am Nehemiah son of Hacaliah, and in this book I tell what I have done.

During the month of Chislev in the twentieth year that Artaxerxes ruled Persia, I was in his fortress city of Susa, when my brother Hanani came with some men from Judah. So I asked them about the Jews who had escaped from being captives in Babylonia. I also asked them about the city of Jerusalem.

They told me, 'Those captives who have come back are having all kinds of troubles. They are terribly disgraced, Jerusalem's walls are broken down, and its gates have been burnt.'

When I heard this, I sat down and cried. Then for several days, I mourned; I went without eating to show my sorrow, and I prayed:

Lord God of heaven, you are great and fearsome. And you faithfully keep your promises to everyone who loves you and obeys your commands. I am your servant, so please have mercy on me and answer the prayer that I make day and night for these people of Israel who serve you. I, my family, and the rest of your people have sinned by choosing to disobey you and the laws and teachings you gave to your servant Moses.

Please remember the promise you made to Moses. You

told him that if we were unfaithful, you would scatter us among foreign nations. But you also said that no matter how far away we were, we could turn to you and start obeying your laws. Then you would bring us back to the place where you have chosen to be worshipped.

Our Lord, I am praying for your servants – those you rescued by your great strength and mighty power. Please answer my prayer and the prayer of your other servants who gladly honour your name. When I serve the king his wine today, make him pleased with me and let him do what I ask.

NEHEMIAH PLEADS HIS CASE

NEHEMIAH
2.1–8

'Sir, if it's all right with you, please send me back to Judah, so that I can rebuild the city where my ancestors are buried.'

FOOD AND DRINK

During the month of Nisan in the twentieth year that Artaxerxes was king, I served him his wine, as I had done before. But this was the first time I had ever looked depressed. So the king said, 'Why do you look so sad? You're not sick. Something must be bothering you.'

Even though I was frightened, I answered, 'Your Majesty, I hope you live for ever! I feel sad because the city where my ancestors are buried is in ruins, and its gates have been burnt down.'

The king asked, 'What do you want me to do?'

I prayed to the God who rules from heaven. Then I told the king, 'Sir, if it's all right with you, please send me back to Judah, so that I can rebuild the city where my ancestors are buried.'

The queen was sitting beside the king when he asked me, 'How long will it take, and when will you be back?' The king agreed to let me go, and I told him when I would return.

Then I asked, 'Your Majesty, would you be willing to give me letters to the governors of the provinces west of the River Euphrates, so that I can travel safely to Judah? I will need timber to rebuild the gates of the fortress near the temple and more timber to construct the city wall and to build a place for me to live. And so, I would appreciate a letter to Asaph, who is in charge of the royal forest.' God was good to me, and the king did everything I asked.

NEHEMIAH CHECKS THE STATE OF THE CITY WALLS

So Nehemiah set off for Jerusalem.

'We are servants of the God who rules from heaven, and he will make our work succeed. So we will start rebuilding Jerusalem, but you have no right to any of its property, because you have had no part in its history.'

BIRDS AND ANIMALS
TRAVEL AND TRANSPORT

The king sent some army officers and cavalry troops along with me, and as I travelled through the Western Provinces, I gave the letters to the governors. But when Sanballat from Horon and Tobiah the Ammonite official heard about what had happened, they became very angry, because they didn't want anyone to help the people of Israel.

Three days after arriving in Jerusalem, I got up during the night and left my house. I took some men with me, without telling anyone what I thought God wanted me to do for the city. The only animal I took was the donkey I rode on. I went through Valley Gate on the west, then south past Dragon Spring, before coming to Rubbish Gate. As I rode along, I took a good look at the crumbled walls of the city and the gates that had been torn down and burnt. On the east side of the city, I headed north to Fountain Gate and King's Pool, but then the path became too narrow for my donkey. So I went down to Kidron Valley and looked at the wall from there. Then before daylight I returned to the city through Valley Gate.

None of the city officials knew what I had in mind. And I had not even told any of the Jews – not the priests, the leaders, the officials, or any other Jews who would be helping in the work. But when I got back, I said to them, 'Jerusalem is truly in a mess! The gates have been torn down and burnt, and everything is in ruins. We must rebuild the city wall so that we can again take pride in our city.'

Then I told them how kind God had been and what the king had said. Immediately, they replied, 'Let's start building now!' So they got everything ready.

When Sanballat, Tobiah, and Geshem the Arab heard about our plans, they started insulting us and saying, 'Just look at you! Do you plan to rebuild the walls of the city and rebel against the king?'

I answered, 'We are servants of the God who rules from heaven, and he will make our work succeed. So we will start rebuilding Jerusalem, but you have no right to any of its property, because you have had no part in its history.'

NEHEMIAH
4.1–23

NEHEMIAH OVERCOMES OPPOSITION

Nehemiah organised the rebuilding of the wall, assigning different sections of its reconstruction to various groups.

'Don't be afraid of your enemies! The Lord is great and fearsome. So think of him and fight for your relatives and children, your wives and homes!'

VIOLENCE AND WARFARE

When Sanballat, the governor of Samaria, heard that we were rebuilding the walls of Jerusalem, he became angry and started insulting our people. In front of his friends and the Samaritan army he said, 'What is this feeble bunch of Jews trying to do? Are they going to rebuild the wall and offer sacrifices all in one day? Do they think they can make something out of this pile of scorched stones?'

Tobiah from Ammon was standing beside Sanballat and said, 'Look at the wall they are building! Why, even a fox could knock over this pile of stones.'

But I prayed, 'Our God, these people hate us and have wished horrible things for us. Please answer our prayers and make their insults fall on them! Let them be the ones to be dragged away as prisoners of war. Don't forgive the mean and evil way they have insulted the builders.'

The people worked hard, and we built the walls of Jerusalem halfway up again. But Sanballat, Tobiah, the Arabs, the Ammonites, and the people from the city of Ashdod saw the walls going up and the holes being repaired. So they became angry and decided to stir up trouble, and to fight against the people of Jerusalem. But we kept on praying to our God, and we also stationed guards day and night.

Meanwhile, the people of Judah were singing a sorrowful song:

'So much rubble for us to haul!

Worn out and weary, will we ever finish this wall?'

Our enemies were saying, 'Before those Jews know what has happened, we will sneak up and kill them and put an end to their work.'

On at least ten different occasions, the Jews living near our enemies warned us against attacks from every side, and so I sent people to guard the wall at its lowest places and where there were still holes in it. I placed them according to families, and they stood guard with swords and spears and with bows and arrows. Then I looked things over and told the leaders, the officials, and the rest of the people, 'Don't be afraid of your enemies! The Lord is great and fearsome. So think of him and fight for your relatives and children, your wives and homes!'

Our enemies found out that we knew about their plot against us, but God kept them from doing what they had planned. So we went back to work on the wall.

From then on, I let half of the young men work while the other half stood guard. They wore armour and had spears and shields, as well as bows and arrows. The leaders helped the workers who were rebuilding the wall. Everyone who hauled building materials kept one hand free to carry a weapon. Even the workers who were rebuilding the wall strapped on a sword. The worker who was to blow the signal trumpet stayed with me.

I told the people and their officials and leaders, 'Our work is so spread out, that we are a long way from one another. If you hear the sound of the trumpet, come quickly and gather around me. Our God will help us fight.'

Every day from dawn to dark, half of the workers rebuilt the walls, while the rest stood guard with their spears.

I asked the men in charge and their workers to stay inside Jerusalem and stand guard at night. So they guarded the city at night and worked during the day. I even slept in my work clothes at night; my children, the workers, and the guards slept in theirs as well. And we always kept our weapons close by.

PLOTS AGAINST NEHEMIAH

Our enemies were trying to frighten us and to keep us from our work. But I asked God to give me strength.

Sanballat, Tobiah, Geshem, and our other enemies learnt that I had completely rebuilt the wall. All I lacked was hanging the doors in the gates. Then Sanballat and Geshem sent a message, asking me to meet with them in one of the villages in Ono Valley. I knew they were planning to harm me in some way. So I sent messengers to tell them, 'My work is too important to stop now and go there. I can't afford to slow down the work just to visit you.' They invited me four times, but each time I refused to go.

Finally, Sanballat sent an official to me with an unsealed letter, which said:

A rumour is going around among the nations that you and the other Jews are rebuilding the wall and planning to rebel, because you want to be their king. And Geshem says it's true! You even have prophets in Jerusalem, claiming you are now the king of Judah. You know the Persian king will hear about this, so let's get together and talk it over.

I sent a message back to Sanballat, saying, 'None of this is true! You are making it all up.'

Our enemies were trying to frighten us and to keep us from our work. But I asked God to give me strength.

One day I went to visit Shemaiah. He was looking very worried, and he said, 'Let's hurry to the holy place of the temple and hide there. We will lock the temple doors, because your enemies are planning to kill you tonight.'

I answered, 'Why should someone like me have to run and hide in the temple to save my life? I won't go!'

Suddenly I realized that God had not given Shemaiah this message. But Tobiah and Sanballat had paid him to trick me and to frighten me into doing something wrong, because they wanted to ruin my good name.

Then I asked God to punish Tobiah and Sanballat for what they had done. I prayed that God would punish the prophet Noadiah and the other prophets who, together with her, had tried to frighten me.

On the twenty-fifth day of the month Elul, the wall was completely rebuilt. It had taken fifty-two days. When our enemies in the surrounding nations learnt that the work was finished, they felt helpless, because they knew that our God had helped us rebuild the wall.

These books express the full range of human emotions. Fantastic expressions of wonder, amazement and love sit alongside anger, self-pity and disappointment. Together they show real people who are sometimes confused, but always confident that whatever they have to say, God will listen.

THE SUFFERINGS OF JOB

JOB 1.1–12

SATAN TESTS JOB

Job was a good man who went through a series of hardships. Throughout his ordeal his love, respect and trust in God never wavered. His story can help anyone seeking answers to the question of why people suffer even when they haven't done anything wrong.

'Try taking away everything he owns, and he will curse you to your face.'

W. BLAKE
SATAN GOING
FORTH FROM THE
PRESENCE OF THE
LORD
FITZWILLIAM
MUSEUM
CAMBRIDGE
1823

Many years ago, a man named Job lived in the land of Uz. He was a truly good person, who respected God and refused to do evil.

Job had seven sons and three daughters. He owned seven thousand sheep, three thousand camels, five hundred pair of oxen, five hundred donkeys, and a large number of servants. He was the richest person in the East.

Job's sons took turns having feasts in their homes, and they always invited their three sisters to join in the eating and drinking. After each feast, Job would send for his children and perform a ceremony, as a way of asking God to forgive them for any wrongs they might have done. He would get up early the next morning and offer a sacrifice for each of them, just in case they had sinned or silently cursed God.

One day, when the angels had gathered around the ord, and

BIRDS AND
ANIMALS
FOOD AND DRINK

See also
MATTHEW 4.1–11,
MATTHEW 6.13,
1 CORINTHIANS
10.13,
JAMES 1.13–14

Satan was there with them, the Lord asked, 'Satan, where have you been?'

Satan replied, 'I have been going all over the earth.'

Then the Lord asked, 'What do you think of my servant Job? No one on earth is like him – he is a truly good person, who respects me and refuses to do evil.'

'Why shouldn't he respect you?' Satan remarked. 'You are like a wall protecting not only him, but his entire family and all his property. You make him successful in whatever he does, and his flocks and herds are everywhere. Try taking away everything he owns, and he will curse you to your face.'

The Lord replied, 'All right, Satan, do what you want with anything that belongs to him, but don't harm Job.'

Then Satan left.

JOB 1.13–22

JOB'S CHILDREN AND WEALTH ARE WIPED OUT

'We bring nothing at birth; we take nothing with us at death. The Lord alone gives and takes. Praise the name of the Lord!'

FOOD AND DRINK
MARRIAGE AND
FAMILY

Job's sons and daughters were having a feast in the home of his eldest son, when someone rushed up to Job and said, 'While your servants were ploughing with your oxen, and your donkeys were nearby eating grass, a gang of Sabeans attacked and stole the oxen and donkeys! Your other servants were killed, and I was the only one who escaped to tell you.'

That servant was still speaking, when a second one came running up and saying, 'God sent down a fire that killed your sheep and your servants. I am the only one who escaped to tell you.'

Before that servant finished speaking, a third one raced up and said, 'Three gangs of Chaldeans attacked and stole your camels! All your other servants were killed, and I am the only one who escaped to tell you.'

That servant was still speaking, when a fourth one dashed up and said, 'Your children were having a feast and drinking wine at the home of your eldest son, when suddenly a storm from the desert blew the house down, crushing all your children. I am the only one who escaped to tell you.'

When Job heard this, he tore his clothes and shaved his head because of his great sorrow. He knelt on the ground, then worshipped God and said:

'We bring nothing at birth; we take nothing with us at death. The Lord alone gives and takes. Praise the name of the Lord!'

In spite of everything, Job did not sin or accuse God of doing wrong.

Job 2.1–10

JOB'S PHYSICAL AGONY

'If we accept blessings from God, we must accept trouble as well.' In all that happened, Job never once said anything against God.

When the angels gathered around the Lord again, Satan was there with them, and the Lord asked, 'Satan, where have you been?'

Satan replied, 'I have been going all over the earth.'

Then the Lord asked, 'What do you think of my servant Job? No one on earth is like him – he is a truly good person, who respects me and refuses to do evil. And he hasn't changed, even though you persuaded me to destroy him for no reason.'

Satan answered, 'There's no pain like your own. People will do anything to stay alive. Try striking Job's own body with pain, and he will curse you to your face.'

'All right!' the Lord replied. 'Make Job suffer as much as you want, but just don't kill him.' Satan left and caused painful sores to break out all over Job's body – from head to toe.

Then Job sat on the ash-heap to show his sorrow. And while he was scraping his sores with a broken piece of pottery, his wife asked, 'Why do you still trust God? Why don't you curse him and die?'

Job replied, 'Don't talk like a fool! If we accept blessings from God, we must accept trouble as well.' In all that happened, Job never once said anything against God.

JOB'S FRIENDS TRY AND HELP

For seven days and nights, they sat silently on the ground beside him, because they realized what terrible pain he was in.

Eliphaz from Teman, Bildad from Shuah, and Zophar from Naamah were three of Job's friends, and they heard about his troubles. So they agreed to visit Job and comfort him. When they came near enough to see Job, they could hardly recognize him. And in their great sorrow, they tore their clothes, then sprinkled dust on their heads and cried bitterly. For seven days and nights, they sat silently on the ground beside him, because they realized what terrible pain he was in.

JOB'S COMPLAINT

I wish I had been born dead and then buried, never to see the light of day.

Finally, Job cursed the day of his birth by saying to God:
Blot out the day of my birth and the night when my parents created a son.
Forget about that day, cover it with darkness, and send thick, gloomy shadows to fill it with dread.
Erase that night from the calendar and conceal it with darkness.
Don't let children be created or joyful shouts be heard ever again in that night.
Let those with magic powers place a curse on that day.
Darken its morning stars and remove all hope of light, because it let me be born into a world of trouble.
Why didn't I die at birth? Why was I accepted and allowed to nurse at my mother's breast?
Now I would be at peace in the silent world below with kings and their advisers whose palaces lie in ruins, and with rulers once rich with silver and gold.
I wish I had been born dead and then buried, never to see the light of day.
In the world of the dead, the wicked and the weary rest without a worry.
Everyone is there – where captives and slaves are free at last.

Why does God let me live when life is miserable and so
   bitter?
I keep longing for death more than I would seek a valuable
   treasure.
Nothing could make me happier than to be in the grave.
Why do I go on living when God has me surrounded, and I
   can't see the road?
Moaning and groaning are my food and drink, and my
   worst fears have all come true
I have no peace or rest – only troubles and worries.

JOB 19.23–27

JOB SEES A GLIMMER OF HOPE

*I know that my
Saviour lives, and at
the end he will
stand on this earth.*

I wish that my words could be written down or chiselled
   into rock.
I know that my Saviour lives, and at the end he will stand
   on this earth.
My flesh may be destroyed, yet from this body I will see
   God.
Yes, I will see him for myself, and I long for that moment.

FROM JOB
32.1–33.13

YOU'RE WRONG, JOB

*Elihu from Buz was
there, and he had
become upset with
Job for blaming God
instead of himself.*

Finally, these three men stopped arguing with Job, because he
refused to admit that he was guilty.

Elihu from Buz was there, and he had become upset with Job
for blaming God instead of himself. He was also angry with
Job's three friends for not being able to prove that Job was
wrong. Elihu was younger than these three, and he let them
speak first.

Job, listen to me! Pay close attention.
I have heard you argue that you are innocent, guilty of
   nothing.
You claim that God has made you his enemy, that he has
   bound your feet and blocked your path.

But, Job, you're wrong – God is greater than any human.
So why do you challenge God to answer you?

JOB 38, 39

GOD SPEAKS AT LAST
At last God intervenes in the argument.

Why do you talk so much when you know so little?

BIRDS AND ANIMALS

See also *GENESIS 1.1–31*

From out of a storm, the Lord said to Job:
Why do you talk so much when you know so little?
Now get ready to face me! Can you answer the questions I
ask?
How did I lay the foundation for the earth?
Were you there?
Doubtless you know who decided its length and width.
What supports the foundation? Who placed the
cornerstone, while morning stars sang, and angels
rejoiced?
When the ocean was born, I set its boundaries and
wrapped it in blankets of thickest fog.
Then I built a wall around it, locked the gates, and said,
'Your powerful waves stop here! They can go no further.'
Did you ever tell the sun to rise? And did it obey?
Did it take hold of the earth and shake out the wicked like
dust from a rug?
Early dawn outlines the hills like stitches on clothing or
sketches on clay.
But its light is too much for those who are evil, and their
power is broken.
Job, have you ever walked on the ocean floor?
Have you seen the gate to the world of the dead? And how
large is the earth? Tell me, if you know!
Where is the home of light, and where does darkness live?
Can you lead them home?
I'm certain you must be able to, since you were already
born when I created everything.
Have you been to the places where I keep snow and hail,
until I use them to punish and conquer nations?

From where does lightning leap, or the east wind blow?
  Who carves out a path for thunderstorms?
Who sends torrents of rain on empty deserts where no one
  lives?
Rain that changes barren land to meadows green with
  grass.
Who is the father of the dew and of the rain?
Who gives birth to the sleet and the frost that fall in winter,
  when streams and lakes freeze solid as a rock?
Can you arrange stars in groups such as Orion and the
  Pleiades?
Do you control the stars or set in place the Great Bear and
  the Little Bear?
Do you know the laws that govern the heavens, and can
  you make them rule the earth?
Can you order the clouds to send a downpour, or will
  lightning flash at your command?
Did you teach birds to know that rain or floods are on their
  way?
Can you count the clouds or pour out their water on the
  dry, lumpy soil?
When lions are hungry, do you help them hunt? Do you
  send an animal into their den?
And when starving young ravens cry out to me for food, do
  you satisfy their hunger?
When do mountain goats and deer give birth? Have you
  been there when their young are born?
How long are they pregnant before they deliver?
Soon their young grow strong and then leave to be on their
  own.
Who set wild donkeys free? I alone help them survive in
  salty desert sand.
They stay far from crowded cities and refuse to be tamed.
  Instead, they roam the hills, searching for pasture land.
Would a wild ox agree to live in your barn and labour for
  you?
Could you force him to plough or to drag a heavy log to

smooth out the soil?

Can you depend on him to use his great strength and do your heavy work?

Can you trust him to harvest your grain or take it to your barn from the threshing place?

An ostrich proudly flaps her wings, but not because she loves her young.

She abandons her eggs and lets the dusty ground keep them warm.

And she doesn't seem to worry that the feet of an animal could crush them all.

She treats her eggs as though they were not her own, unconcerned that her work might be for nothing.

I myself made her foolish and without common sense. But once she starts running, she laughs at a rider on the fastest horse.

Did you give horses their strength and the flowing hair along their necks?

Did you make them able to jump like grasshoppers or to frighten people with their snorting?

Before horses are ridden into battle, they paw at the ground, proud of their strength.

Laughing at fear, they rush towards the fighting, while the weapons of their riders rattle and flash in the sun.

Unable to stand still, they gallop eagerly into battle when trumpets blast.

Stirred by the distant smells and sounds of war, they snort in reply to the trumpet.

Did you teach hawks to fly south for the winter?

Did you train eagles to build their nests on rocky cliffs, where they can look down to spot their next meal? Then their young gather to feast wherever the victim lies.

*The Lord now
blessed Job more
than ever.*

**BIRDS AND
ANIMALS
MARRIAGE AND
FAMILY**

JOB'S FORTUNES RESTORED

The Lord said to Eliphaz:

What my servant Job has said about me is true, but I am angry with you and your two friends for not telling the truth. So I want you to go over to Job and offer seven bulls and seven goats on an altar as a sacrifice to please me. After this, Job will pray, and I will agree not to punish you for your foolishness.

Eliphaz, Bildad, and Zophar obeyed the Lord, and he answered Job's prayer.

After Job had prayed for his three friends, the Lord made Job twice as rich as he had been before. Then Job gave a feast for his brothers and sisters and for his old friends. They expressed their sorrow for the suffering the Lord had brought on him, and they each gave Job some silver and a gold ring.

The Lord now blessed Job more than ever; he gave him fourteen thousand sheep, six thousand camels, a thousand pair of oxen, and a thousand donkeys.

In addition to seven sons, Job had three daughters.

Job lived for another one hundred and forty years – long enough to see his great-grandchildren have children of their own – and when he finally died, he was very old.

Songs and poems to God

Psalm 8.1–9

THE GLORIOUS GOD

The Psalms are a collection of songs written to reflect the full range of emotions and experiences in the lives of those who composed them. They honestly express the joy and sadness, awe and shame felt by those who follow God.

Our Lord and Ruler, your name is wonderful everywhere on earth!

Birds and animals

Our Lord and Ruler, your name is wonderful everywhere on earth!
You let your glory be seen in the heavens above.
With praises from children and from tiny infants, you have built a fortress.
It makes your enemies silent, and all who turn against you are left speechless.
I often think of the heavens your hands have made, and of the moon and stars you put in place.
Then I ask, 'Why do you care about us humans? Why are you concerned for us weaklings?'
You made us a little lower than you yourself, and you have crowned us with glory and honour.
You let us rule everything your hands have made.
And you put all of it under our power – the sheep and the cattle, and every wild animal, the birds in the sky, the fish in the sea, and all ocean creatures.
Our Lord and Ruler, your name is wonderful everywhere on earth!

Psalm 23.1–6

THE LORD OUR SHEPHERD

You, Lord, are my shepherd. I will never be in need.

You, Lord, are my shepherd. I will never be in need. You let me rest in fields of green grass.
You lead me to streams of peaceful water, and you refresh my life.

See also JOHN
10.1–22

You are true to your name, and you lead me along the right
paths.

I may walk through valleys as dark as death, but I won't be
afraid.

You are with me, and your shepherd's rod makes me feel
safe.

You treat me to a feast, while my enemies watch.

You honour me as your guest, and you fill my cup until it
overflows.

Your kindness and love will always be with me each day of
my life, and I will live for ever in your house, Lord.

PSALM
24.1–10

*The earth and
everything on it
belong to the Lord.
The world and its
people belong to
him.*

SALVADOR DALI
*QUIS ASCENDET IN
MENTEM DOMINI?
BIBLIA SACRA*

THE EARTH BELONGS TO GOD

The earth and everything on it belong to the Lord. The
world and its people belong to him.

The Lord placed it all on the oceans and rivers.

Who may climb the Lord's hill or stand in his holy temple?

Only those who do right for the right reasons, and don't
worship idols or tell lies under oath.

The Lord God, who saves them, will bless and reward
them, because they worship and serve the God of
Jacob.

Open the ancient gates, so that the glorious king may
come in. Who is this glorious king? He is our Lord, a
strong and mighty warrior. Open the ancient gates, so
that the glorious king may come in.

Who is this glorious king? He is our Lord, the All-Powerful!

PSALM
46.1–11

GOD IS ON OUR SIDE

God is our mighty fortress, always ready to help in times of
trouble.

And so, we won't be afraid! Let the earth tremble and the
mountains tumble into the deepest sea.

*The Lord All-
Powerful is with us.
The God of Jacob is
our fortress.*

Let the ocean roar and foam, and its raging waves shake
the mountains.

A river and its streams bring joy to the city, which is the
sacred home of God Most High.

God is in that city, and it won't be shaken. He will help it at
dawn.

Nations rage! Kingdoms fall! But at the voice of God the
earth itself melts.

The Lord All-Powerful is with us. The God of Jacob is our
fortress.

Come! See the fearsome things the Lord has done on
earth.

God brings wars to an end all over the world.

He breaks the arrows, shatters the spears, and burns the
shields.

Our God says, 'Calm down, and learn that I am God! All
nations on earth will honour me.'

The Lord All-Powerful is with us. The God of Jacob is our
fortress.

PSALM
51.1–19

A PRAYER FOR MERCY

*You are really the
one I have sinned
against; I have
disobeyed you and
have done wrong.
So it is right and
fair for you to
correct and punish
me.*

You are kind, God! Please have pity on me. You are always
merciful! Please wipe away my sins.

Wash me clean from all of my sin and guilt.

I know about my sins, and I cannot forget my terrible guilt.

You are really the one I have sinned against; I have
disobeyed you and have done wrong.

So it is right and fair for you to correct and punish me.

I have sinned and done wrong since the day I was born.

But you want complete honesty, so teach me true wisdom.

Wash me with hyssop until I am clean and whiter than
snow.

Let me be happy and joyful! You crushed my bones, now
let them celebrate.

Turn your eyes from my sin and cover my guilt.

See also 2 SAMUEL
11.1–17

Create pure thoughts in me and make me faithful again.

Don't chase me away from you or take your Holy Spirit away from me.

Make me as happy as you did when you saved me; make me want to obey!

I will teach sinners your Law, and they will return to you.

Keep me from any deadly sin. Only you can save me! Then I will shout and sing about your power to save.

Help me to speak, and I will praise you, Lord.

Offerings and sacrifices are not what you want.

The way to please you is to feel sorrow deep in our hearts. This is the kind of sacrifice you won't refuse.

Please be willing, Lord, to help the city of Zion and to rebuild its walls.

Then you will be pleased with the proper sacrifices, and we will offer bulls on your altar once again.

GOD'S INCREDIBLE LOVE

Psalm
103.1–22

The Lord is merciful! He is kind and patient, and his love never fails.

With all my heart I praise the Lord, and with all that I am I praise his holy name!

With all my heart I praise the Lord! I will never forget how kind he has been.

The Lord forgives our sins, heals us when we are sick, and protects us from death.

His kindness and love are a crown on our heads.

Each day that we live, he provides for our needs and gives us the strength of a young eagle.

For all who are ill-treated, the Lord brings justice.

He taught his Law to Moses and showed all Israel what he could do.

The Lord is merciful! He is kind and patient, and his love never fails.

The Lord won't always be angry and point out our sins; he doesn't punish us as our sins deserve.

How great is God's love for all who worship him? Greater

than the distance between heaven and earth!

How far has the Lord taken our sins from us? Further than the distance from east to west!

Just as parents are kind to their children, the Lord is kind to all who worship him, because he knows we are made of dust.

We humans are like grass or wild flowers that quickly bloom.

But a scorching wind blows, and they quickly wither to be for ever forgotten.

The Lord is always kind to those who worship him, and he keeps his promises to their descendants who faithfully obey him.

God has set up his kingdom in heaven, and he rules the whole creation.

All you mighty angels, who obey God's commands, come and praise your Lord!

All you thousands who serve and obey God, come and praise your Lord!

All God's creation and all that he rules, come and praise your Lord! With all my heart I praise the Lord!

PSALM
121.1–8

The Lord will protect you and keep you safe from all dangers.

AGREEMENTS AND PROMISES

THE LORD OUR PROTECTOR

I look to the hills! Where will I find help?

It will come from the Lord, who created the heavens and the earth.

The Lord is your protector, and he won't go to sleep or let you stumble.

The protector of Israel doesn't doze or ever get drowsy.

The Lord is your protector, there at your right side to shade you from the sun.

You won't be harmed by the sun during the day or by the moon at night.

The Lord will protect you and keep you safe from all dangers.

The Lord will protect you now and always wherever you go.

All creation, come and praise the name of the Lord. Praise his name alone. The glory of God is greater than heaven and earth.

BIRDS AND ANIMALS

PRAISE THE LORD

Shout praises to the Lord! Shout the Lord's praises in the highest heavens.

All you angels, and all who serve him above, come and offer praise.

Sun and moon, and all you bright stars, come and offer praise.

Highest heavens, and the water above the highest heavens, come and offer praise.

Let all things praise the name of the Lord, because they were created at his command.

He made them to last for ever, and nothing can change what he has done.

All creatures on earth, you obey his commands, so come, praise the Lord!

Sea monsters and the deep sea, fire and hail, snow and frost, and every stormy wind, come, praise the Lord!

All mountains and hills, fruit trees and cedars,

every wild and tame animal, all reptiles and birds, come, praise the Lord!

Every king and every ruler, all nations on earth,

every man and every woman, young people and old, come, praise the Lord!

All creation, come and praise the name of the Lord. Praise his name alone.

The glory of God is greater than heaven and earth.

Like a bull with mighty horns, the Lord protects his faithful nation Israel, because they belong to him.

Shout praises to the Lord!

WHAT'S THE POINT?

The author of Ecclesiastes tried to make sense of life through a range of human activity. In the end, all he discovered was how futile life would be without God.

Nothing makes sense! Everything is nonsense. I have seen it all – nothing makes sense!

See also 1 KINGS 3.5–15

When the son of David was king in Jerusalem, he was known to be very wise, and he said:

Nothing makes sense! Everything is nonsense. I have seen it all – nothing makes sense!

What is there to show for all our hard work here on this earth?

People come, and people go, but still the world never changes.

The sun comes up, the sun goes down; it hurries right back to where it started from.

The wind blows south, the wind blows north; round and round it blows over and over again.

All rivers empty into the sea, but it never spills over; one by one the rivers return to their source.

All of life is far more boring than words could ever say.

Our eyes and our ears are never satisfied with what we see and hear.

Everything that happens has happened before; nothing is new, nothing under the sun.

Someone might say, 'Here is something new!' But it happened before, long before we were born.

No one who lived in the past is remembered any more, and everyone yet to be born will be forgotten too.

I said these things when I lived in Jerusalem as king of Israel. With all my wisdom I tried to understand everything that happens here on earth. And God has made this so hard for us humans to do. I have seen it all, and everything is just as senseless as chasing the wind.

If something is crooked,
it can't be made straight;
if something isn't there,
it can't be counted.

I said to myself, 'You are by far the wisest person who has ever lived in Jerusalem. You are eager to learn, and you have learnt a lot.' Then I decided to find out all I could about wisdom and foolishness. Soon I realized that this too was as senseless as chasing the wind.

> The more you know,
> the more it hurts;
> the more you understand,
> the more you suffer.

ECCLESIASTES
2.11–17

DEATH TREATS EVERYONE THE SAME WAY

Wise or foolish, we all die and are soon forgotten.

Then I thought about everything I had done, including the hard work, and it was simply chasing the wind. Nothing on earth is worth the trouble.

I asked myself, 'What can the next king do that I haven't done?' Then I decided to compare wisdom with foolishness and stupidity. And I discovered that wisdom is better than foolishness, just as light is better than darkness. Wisdom is like having two good eyes; foolishness leaves you in the dark. But wise or foolish, we all end up the same.

Finally, I said to myself, 'Being wise got me nowhere! The same thing will happen to me that happens to fools. Nothing makes sense. Wise or foolish, we all die and are soon forgotten.' This made me hate life. Everything we do is painful; it's just as senseless as chasing the wind.

ECCLESIASTES
3.1–15

EVERYTHING HAS ITS PLACE

> Everything on earth has its own time and its own season.
> There is a time for birth and death, planting and reaping,
> for killing and healing, destroying and building,
> for crying and laughing, weeping and dancing,
> for throwing stones and gathering stones, embracing and

God makes everything happen at the right time. Yet none of us can ever fully understand all he has done, and he puts questions in our minds about the past and the future.

parting.

There is a time for finding and losing, keeping and giving,
for tearing and sewing, listening and speaking.

There is also a time for love and hate, for war and peace.

What do we gain by all our hard work? I have seen what difficult things God demands of us. God makes everything happen at the right time. Yet none of us can ever fully understand all he has done, and he puts questions in our minds about the past and the future. I know the best thing we can do is always to enjoy life, because God's gift to us is the happiness we get from our food and drink and from the work we do. Everything God has done will last for ever; nothing he does can ever be changed. God has done all this, so that we will worship him.

Everything that happens has happened before, and all that
will be has already been – God does everything over and
over again.

PROPHECY

The prophetic books are not simply about telling the future. They actually deal more with what God had already said in the past. God sent many prophets to remind the Israelites of what he expected of them and sometimes to give a glimpse into what was to come.

THE PROPHET ISAIAH

ISAIAH 6.1–8

ISAIAH'S TERRIFYING VISION

Isaiah lived in Jerusalem and prophesied in Judah. He warned the people of the threat posed by Assyria and Babylon as agents of God's judgement, yet he also gave them a series of inspiring messages of hope for the future.

I'm doomed! Everything I say is sinful, and so are the words of everyone around me. Yet I have seen the King, the Lord All-Powerful

DREAMS AND VISIONS

In the year that King Uzziah died, I had a vision of the Lord. He was on his throne high above, and his robe filled the temple. Flaming creatures with six wings each were flying over him. They covered their faces with two of their wings and their bodies with two more. They used the other two wings for flying, as they shouted,

'Holy, holy, holy, Lord All-Powerful! The earth is filled with your glory.'

As they shouted, the doorposts of the temple shook, and the temple was filled with smoke. Then I cried out, 'I'm doomed! Everything I say is sinful, and so are the words of everyone around me. Yet I have seen the King, the Lord All-Powerful.'

One of the flaming creatures flew over to me with a burning coal that it had taken from the altar with a pair of metal tongs. It touched my lips with the hot coal and said, 'This has touched your lips. Your sins are forgiven, and you are no longer guilty.'

After this, I heard the Lord ask, 'Is there anyone I can send? Will someone go for us?'

ISAIAH 6.9–13

TELL THEM NOT TO LISTEN!

'You will listen and listen, but never understand. You will look and look, but never see.'

Then the Lord told me to go and speak this message to the people:
    'You will listen and listen, but never understand.
    You will look and look, but never see.'

The Lord also said,
    'Make these people stubborn!
    Make them stop up their ears, cover their eyes, and fail to understand.
    Don't let them turn to me and be healed.'

Then I asked the Lord, 'How long will this last?'
    The Lord answered:
    Until their towns are destroyed and their homes are deserted, until their fields are empty, and I have sent them far away, leaving their land in ruins. If only a tenth of the people are left, even they will be destroyed. But just as stumps remain after trees have been cut down, some of my chosen ones will be left.

THE VIRGIN'S CHILD

ISAIAH 7.10–14

But the Lord will still give you proof. A virgin is pregnant; she will have a son and will name him Immanuel.

Once again the Lord God spoke to King Ahaz. This time he said, 'Ask me for proof that my promise will come true. Ask for something to happen deep in the world of the dead or high in the heavens above.'
    'No, Lord,' Ahaz answered. 'I won't test you!'
    Then I said:
    Listen, every one of you in the royal family of David. You have already tried my patience. Now you are trying God's

patience by refusing to ask for proof. But the Lord will still give you proof. A virgin is pregnant; she will have a son and will name him Immanuel.

 Isaiah 9.2–7

THE KING TO COME

A child has been born for us.

Agreements and Promises

Those who walked in the dark have seen a bright light. And it shines upon everyone who lives in the land of darkest shadows.

Our Lord, you have made your nation stronger.

Because of you, its people are glad and celebrate like workers at harvest time or like soldiers dividing up what they have taken.

You have broken the power of those who abused and enslaved your people.

You have rescued them just as you saved your people from Midian.

The boots of marching warriors and the blood-stained uniforms have been fed to flames and eaten by fire.

A child has been born for us.

We have been given a son who will be our ruler.

His names will be Wonderful Adviser and Mighty God, Eternal Father and Prince of Peace.

His power will never end; peace will last for ever.

He will rule David's kingdom and make it grow strong.

He will always rule with honesty and justice. The Lord All-Powerful will make certain that all of this is done.

 Isaiah 52.13–53.13

ENEMIES BECOME FRIENDS

*The Spirit of the
Lord will be with
him to give him
understanding,
wisdom, and
insight. He will be
powerful, and he
will know and
honour the Lord.*

**AGREEMENTS AND
PROMISES
BIRDS AND
ANIMALS**

Like a branch that sprouts from a stump, someone from
    David's family will some day be king.
The Spirit of the Lord will be with him to give him
    understanding, wisdom, and insight.
He will be powerful, and he will know and honour the
    Lord.
His greatest joy will be to obey the Lord.
This king won't judge by appearances or listen to rumours.
The poor and the needy will be treated with fairness and
    with justice.
His word will be law everywhere in the land, and criminals
    will be put to death.
Honesty and fairness will be his royal robes.
Leopards will lie down with young goats, and wolves will
    rest with lambs.
Calves and lions will eat together and be cared for by little
    children.
Cows and bears will share the same pasture; their young
    will rest side by side.
Lions and oxen will both eat straw.
Little children will play near snake holes.
They will stick their hands into dens of poisonous snakes
    and never be hurt.
Nothing harmful will take place on the Lord's holy
    mountain.
Just as water fills the sea, the land will be filled with people
    who know and honour the Lord.

**FROM ISAIAH
40**

WHO IS LIKE GOD?

Our God has said:
    'Encourage my people! Give them comfort.
    Speak kindly to Jerusalem and announce:
    Your slavery is past; your punishment is over.

The Lord gives
strength to those
who are weary.

BIRDS AND
ANIMALS

I, the Lord, made you pay double for your sins.'

Someone is shouting: 'Clear a path in the desert! Make a straight road for the Lord our God.

Fill in the valleys; flatten every hill and mountain.

Level the rough and rugged ground.

Then the glory of the Lord will appear for all to see.

The Lord has promised this!'

Someone told me to shout, and I asked, 'What should I shout?'

We humans are merely grass, and we last no longer than wild flowers.

At the Lord's command, flowers and grass disappear, and so do we.

Flowers and grass fade away, but what our God has said will never change.

There is good news for the city of Zion.

Shout it as loud as you can from the highest mountain.

Don't be afraid to shout to the towns of Judah, 'Your God is here!'

Look! The powerful Lord God is coming to rule with his mighty arm.

He brings with him what he has taken in war, and he rewards his people.

The Lord cares for his nation, just as shepherds care for their flocks.

He carries the lambs in his arms, while gently leading the mother sheep.

The Lord gives strength to those who are weary.

Even young people get tired, then stumble and fall.

But those who trust the Lord will find new strength.

They will be strong like eagles soaring upward on wings; they will walk and run without getting tired.

THE LORD'S SERVANT

*Here is my servant!
I have made him
strong. He is my
chosen one; I am
pleased with him. I
have given him my
Spirit, and he will
bring justice to the
nations.*

Here is my servant! I have made him strong.
He is my chosen one; I am pleased with him.
I have given him my Spirit, and he will bring justice to the
nations.
He won't shout or yell or call out in the streets.
He won't break off a bent reed or put out a dying flame,
but he will make sure that justice is done.
He won't stop or give up until he brings justice everywhere
on earth, and people in foreign nations long for his
teaching.
I am the Lord God.
I created the heavens like an open tent above.
I made the earth and everything that grows on it.
I am the source of life for all who live on this earth, so
listen to what I say.
I chose you to bring justice, and I am here at your side.
I selected and sent you to bring light and my promise of
hope to the nations.
You will give sight to the blind; you will set prisoners free
from dark dungeons.
My name is the Lord!
I won't let idols or humans share my glory and praise.
Everything has happened just as I said it would; now I will
announce what will happen next.

ISRAEL WILL SHOW THE WAY

Everyone, listen, even you foreign nations across the sea.
The Lord chose me and gave me a name before I was
born.
He made my words pierce like a sharp sword or a pointed
arrow; he kept me safely hidden in the palm of his hand.
The Lord said to me, 'Israel, you are my servant; and
because of you I will be highly honoured.'

'It isn't enough for
you to be merely my
servant. You must
do more than lead
back survivors from
the tribes of Israel. I
have placed you
here as a light for
other nations; you
must take my
saving power to
everyone on earth.'

I said to myself, 'I'm completely worn out; my time has
been wasted.

But I did it for the Lord God, and he will reward me.'

Even before I was born, the Lord God chose me to serve
him and to lead back the people of Israel.

So the Lord has honoured me and made me strong.

Now the Lord says to me, 'It isn't enough for you to be
merely my servant.

You must do more than lead back survivors from the tribes
of Israel.

I have placed you here as a light for other nations;

you must take my saving power to everyone on earth.'

Israel, I am the holy Lord God, the one who rescues you.

You are slaves of rulers and of a nation who despises you.

Now this is what I promise: kings and rulers will honour
you by kneeling at your feet.

You can trust me! I am your Lord, the holy God of Israel,
and you are my chosen ones.

GOD'S SERVANT SUFFERS

Isaiah
52.13–53.12

By suffering, the
servant will learn
the true meaning of
obeying the Lord.
Although he is
innocent, he will
take the punishment
for the sins of
others, so that
many of them will
no longer be guilty.

The Lord says:

My servant will succeed!

He will be given great praise and the highest honours.

Many were horrified at what happened to him.

But everyone who saw him was even more horrified
because he suffered until he no longer looked human.

My servant will make nations worthy to worship me; kings
will be silent as they bow in wonder.

They will see and think about things they have never seen
or thought about before.

Has anyone believed us or seen the mighty power of the
Lord in action?

Like a young plant or a root that sprouts in dry ground, the
servant grew up obeying the Lord.

Birds and animals

See also
Matthew 26.57–68,
Matthew 27.1–26,
Matthew 27.27–56,
Mark 14.53–65,
Luke 22.63–23.49,
John 18.28–19.16

He wasn't some handsome king.

Nothing about the way he looked made him attractive to us.

He was hated and rejected; his life was filled with sorrow and terrible suffering.

No one wanted to look at him.

We despised him and said, 'He is a nobody!'

He suffered and endured great pain for us, but we thought his suffering was punishment from God.

He was wounded and crushed because of our sins; by taking our punishment, he made us completely well.

All of us were like sheep that had wandered off.

We had each gone our own way, but the Lord gave him the punishment we deserved.

He was painfully abused, but he did not complain.

He was silent like a lamb being led to the butcher, as quiet as a sheep having its wool cut off.

He was condemned to death without a fair trial.

Who could have imagined what would happen to him?

His life was taken away because of the sinful things my people had done.

He wasn't dishonest or violent, but he was buried in a tomb of cruel and rich people.

The Lord decided his servant would suffer as a sacrifice to take away the sin and guilt of others.

Now the servant will live to see his own descendants.

He did everything the Lord had planned.

By suffering, the servant will learn the true meaning of obeying the Lord.

Although he is innocent, he will take the punishment for the sins of others, so that many of them will no longer be guilty.

The Lord will reward him with honour and power for sacrificing his life.

Others thought he was a sinner, but he suffered for our sins and asked God to forgive us.

JEREMIAH 33.14–22

THE LORD'S PASSION FOR ISRAEL

But the Lord your God says, 'I am taking you back!'

See also *HOSEA* 11.1–11

You were like a young wife, broken hearted and crying
  because her husband had divorced her.
But the Lord your God says, 'I am taking you back!
I rejected you for a while, but with love and tenderness I
  will embrace you again.
For a while, I turned away in furious anger.
Now I will have mercy and love you for ever!
I, your protector and Lord, make this promise.'
I once promised Noah that I would never again destroy the
  earth by a flood.
Now I have promised that I will never again get angry and
  punish you.
Every mountain and hill may disappear.
But I will always be kind and merciful to you;
I won't break my agreement to give your nation peace.

MORE WARNINGS FOR JUDAH

THE KING IS COMING

**FROM
JEREMIAH
33.14–22**

*I promise that the
time will come when
I will appoint a king
from the family of
David, a king who
will be honest and
rule with justice.*

**AGREEMENTS AND
PROMISES
DREAMS AND
VISIONS
MARRIAGE AND
FAMILY**

THE KING IS COMING

Jeremiah prophesied in Jerusalem during the final years before Judah was conquered by the Babylonians. His message of turning away from evil largely fell on deaf ears and he suffered a great deal of abuse and humiliation at the hands of his enemies.

The Lord said:
   I promise that the time will come when I will appoint a
      king from the family of David, a king who will be honest
      and rule with justice.
   In those days, Judah will be safe; Jerusalem will have peace
      and will be named, 'The Lord Gives Justice'.

The king of Israel will be one of David's descendants, and there will always be priests from the Levi tribe serving at my altar and offering sacrifices to please me and to give thanks.
   Then the Lord told me:
   I, the Lord, have an agreement with day and night, so they always come at the right time. You can't break the agreement I made with them, and you can't break the agreements I have made with David's family and with the priests from the Levi tribe who serve at my altar. A descendant of David will always rule as king of Israel, and there will be more descendants of David and of the priests from the Levi tribe than stars in the sky or grains of sand on the beach.

HOSEA 11.1–11

34.11–31

THE GOOD SHEPHERD

Ezekiel prophesied before and during Judah's exile to Babylon. His vivid language and startling imagery highlights how seriously the people had strayed from God. Yet he also speaks of a time when the people would return to their homeland with God's blessing.

After that, I will give you a shepherd from the family of my servant King David. All of you, both strong and weak, will have the same shepherd, and he will take good care of you.

PROMISES
BIRDS AND
ANIMALS
FARMING AND
PRODUCE

See also PSALM 23,
ZECHARIAH 11.17,
JOHN 10.11–16,
JOHN 10.1–21

The Lord God then said:

I will look for my sheep and take care of them myself, just as a shepherd looks for lost sheep. My sheep have been lost since that dark and miserable day when they were scattered throughout the nations. But I will rescue them and bring them back from the foreign nations where they now live. I will be their shepherd and will let them graze on Israel's mountains and in the valleys and fertile fields. They will be safe as they feed on grassy meadows and green hills. I promise to take care of them and keep them safe, to look for those that are lost and bring back the ones that wander off, to bandage those that are hurt and protect the ones that are weak. I will also slaughter those that are fat and strong, because I always do right.

The Lord God said to his sheep, the people of Israel:

I will carefully watch each one of you to decide which ones are the strong sheep and which ones are weak. Some of you eat the greenest grass, then trample down what's left when you finish. Others drink clean water, then step in the water to make the rest of it muddy. That means my other sheep have nothing fit to eat or drink.

So I, the Lord God, will separate you strong sheep from the weak. You strong ones have used your powerful horns to chase off those that are weak, but I will rescue them and no longer let them be ill-treated. I will separate the good from the bad.

After that, I will give you a shepherd from the family of my servant King David. All of you, both strong and weak, will have the same shepherd, and he will take good care of you. He will be your leader, and I will be your God. I, the Lord,

PROPHECY   EZEKIEL   **183** have spoken.

The people of Israel are my sheep, and I solemnly promise that they will live in peace. I will chase away every wild animal from the desert and the forest, so my sheep will not be afraid. They will live around my holy mountain, and I will bless them by sending more than enough rain to make their trees produce fruit and their crops grow. I will set them free from slavery and let them live safely in their own land. Then they will know that I am the Lord. Foreign nations will never again rob them, and wild animals will no longer kill and eat them. They will have nothing to fear. I will make their fields produce large amounts of crops, so they will never again go hungry or be laughed at by foreigners. Then everyone will know that I protect my people Israel. I, the Lord, make this promise. They are my sheep; I am their God, and I take care of them.

EZEKIEL
37.1–14

'My Spirit will give you breath, and you will live again. I will bring you home, and you will know that I have kept my promise. I, the Lord, have spoken.'

F. COLLANTES
THE VISION OF ST EZEKIEL
MUSEO DEL PRADO
MADRID
1630

DRY BONES COME TO LIFE

Some time later, I felt the Lord's power take control of me, and his Spirit carried me to a valley full of bones. The Lord showed me all around, and everywhere I looked I saw bones that were dried out. He said, 'Ezekiel, son of man, can these bones come back to life?'

I replied, 'Lord God, only you can answer that.'

He then told me to say:

Dry bones, listen to what the Lord is saying to you, 'I, the Lord God, will put breath in you, and once again you will live. I will wrap you with muscles and skin and breathe life into you. Then you will know that I am the Lord.'

I did what the Lord said, but before I finished speaking, I heard a rattling noise. The bones were coming together! I saw muscles and skin cover the bones, but they had no life in them.

The Lord said:

Ezekiel, now say to the wind, 'The Lord God commands you to blow from every direction and to breathe life into these dead bodies, so they can live again.'

As soon as I said this, the wind blew among the bodies, and they came back to life! They all stood up, and there were enough to make a large army.

The Lord said:

Ezekiel, the people of Israel are like dead bones. They complain that they are dried up and that they have no hope for the future. So tell them, 'I, the Lord God, promise to open your graves and set you free. I will bring you back to Israel, and when that happens, you will realize that I am the Lord. My Spirit will give you breath, and you will live again. I will bring you home, and you will know that I have kept my promise. I, the Lord, have spoken.'

THE LORD RETURNS TO THE TEMPLE

Ezekiel, son of man, this temple is my throne on earth. I will live here among the people of Israel for ever. They and their kings will never again disgrace me by worshipping idols at local shrines or by setting up memorials to their dead kings.

The man took me back to the east gate of the temple, where I saw the brightness of the glory of Israel's God coming from the east. The sound I heard was as loud as ocean waves, and everything around was shining with the dazzling brightness of his glory. This vision was like the one I had seen when God came to destroy Jerusalem and like the one I had seen near the River Chebar.

I immediately bowed with my face to the ground, and the Lord's glory came through the east gate and into the temple. The Lord's Spirit lifted me to my feet and carried me to the inner courtyard, where I saw that the Lord's glory had filled the temple.

The man was standing beside me, and I heard the Lord say from inside the temple:

Ezekiel, son of man, this temple is my throne on earth. I will live here among the people of Israel for ever. They and their kings will never again disgrace me by worshipping idols at local shrines or by setting up memorials to their dead kings.

Israel's kings built their palaces so close to my holy temple that only a wall separated them from me. Then these kings disgraced me with their evil ways, and in my fierce anger I destroyed them. But if the people and their kings stop worshipping other gods and tear down those memorials, I will live among them for ever.

EZEKIEL
47.1–12

The leaves will never dry out, because they will always have water from the stream that flows from the temple, and they will be used for healing people.

THE ENDLESS STREAM

The man took me back to the temple, where I saw a stream flowing from under the entrance. It began in the south part of the temple, where it ran past the altar and continued east through the courtyard.

We walked out of the temple area through the north gate and went around to the east gate. I saw the small stream of water flowing east from the south side of the gate.

The man walked east, then took out his measuring stick and measured five hundred metres downstream. He told me to wade through the stream there, and the water came up to my ankles. Then he measured another five hundred metres downstream, and told me to wade through it there. The water came up to my knees. Another five hundred metres downstream the water came up to my waist. Another five hundred metres downstream, the stream had become a river that could be crossed only by swimming. The man said, 'Ezekiel, son of man, pay attention to what you've seen.'

We walked to the river bank, where I saw dozens of trees on each side. The man said:

This water flows eastwards to the valley of the River Jordan and empties into the Dead Sea, where it turns the salt water into fresh water. Wherever this water flows, there will be all kinds of animals and fish, because it will bring life and fresh water to the Dead Sea. From En-Gedi to Eneglaim, people will fish in the sea and dry their nets along the coast. There will be as many kinds of fish in the Dead Sea as there are in the Mediterranean Sea. But the marshes along the shore will remain salty, so that people can use the salt from them.

Fruit trees will grow all along this river and produce fresh fruit every month. The leaves will never dry out, because they will always have water from the stream that flows from the temple, and they will be used for healing people.

Daniel

Daniel 2.1–13

NEBUCHADNEZZAR'S SECRET DREAM

Daniel was forced into captivity in Babylon where he gave faithful service to a succession of emperors. His experiences, and those of his friends, in a hostile royal court, demonstrate how God looks after those who love and respect him.

'I am disturbed by a dream that I don't understand, and I want you to explain it.'

DREAMS AND VISIONS

See also 2 KINGS 24–25

During the second year that Nebuchadnezzar was king, he had such horrible nightmares that he could not sleep. So he called in his counsellors, advisers, magicians, and wise men, and said, 'I am disturbed by a dream that I don't understand, and I want you to explain it.'

They answered in Aramaic, 'Your Majesty, we hope you live for ever! We are your servants. Please tell us your dream, and we will explain what it means.'

But the king replied, 'No! I have made up my mind. If you don't tell me both the dream and its meaning, you will be chopped to pieces and your houses will be torn down. However, if you do tell me both the dream and its meaning, you will be greatly rewarded and highly honoured. Now tell me the dream and explain what it means.'

'Your Majesty,' they said, 'if you will only tell us your dream, we will interpret it for you.'

The king replied, 'You're just stalling for time, because you know what's going to happen if you don't come up with the answer. You've decided to make up a pack of lies, hoping I might change my mind. Now tell me the dream, and that will prove that you can interpret it.'

His advisers explained, 'Your Majesty, you are demanding the impossible! No king, not even the most famous and powerful, has ever ordered his advisers, magicians, or wise men to do such a thing. It can't be done, except by the gods, and they don't live here on earth.'

This made the king so angry that he gave orders for every wise man in Babylonia to be put to death, including Daniel and his three friends.

DANIEL
2.14–23

THE KING'S DREAM IS NO LONGER A SECRET

'Pray that the God who rules from heaven will be merciful and explain this mystery, so that we and the others won't be put to death.'

DREAMS AND VISIONS

Arioch was the king's official in charge of putting the wise men to death. He was on his way to have it done, when Daniel very wisely went to him and asked, 'Why did the king give such cruel orders?' After Arioch explained what had happened, Daniel rushed off and said to the king, 'If you will just give me some time, I'll explain your dream.'

Daniel returned home and told his three friends. Then he said, 'Pray that the God who rules from heaven will be merciful and explain this mystery, so that we and the others won't be put to death.' In a vision one night, Daniel was shown the dream and its meaning. Then he praised the God who rules from heaven:

'Our God, your name will be praised for ever and for ever.
You are all-powerful, and you know everything.
You control human events – you give rulers their power and take it away, and you are the source of wisdom and knowledge.
'You explain deep mysteries, because even the dark is light to you.
You are the God who was worshipped by my ancestors.
Now I thank you and praise you for making me wise and telling me the king's dream, together with its meaning.'

DANIEL
2.24–49

DANIEL TELLS THE KING HIS DREAM

Daniel went back to Arioch, the official in charge of executing the wise men. Daniel said, 'Don't kill those men! Take me to

'Now I know that your God is above all other gods and kings, because he gave you the power to explain this mystery.'

DREAMS AND VISIONS

the king, and I will explain the meaning of his dream.'

Arioch rushed Daniel to the king and announced, 'Your Majesty, I have found out that one of the men brought here from Judah can explain your dream.'

The king asked Daniel, 'Can you tell me my dream and what it means?'

Daniel answered:

Your Majesty, not even the cleverest person in the world can do what you are demanding. But the God who rules from heaven can explain mysteries. And while you were sleeping, he showed you what will happen in the future. However, you must realize that these mysteries weren't explained to me because I am cleverer than everyone else. Instead, it was done so that you would understand what you have seen.

Your Majesty, what you saw standing in front of you was a huge and terrifying statue, shining brightly. Its head was made of gold, its chest and arms were silver, and from its waist down to its knees, it was bronze. From there to its ankles it was iron, and its feet were a mixture of iron and clay.

As you watched, a stone was cut from a mountain – but not by human hands. The stone struck the feet, completely shattering the iron and clay. Then the iron, the clay, the bronze, the silver, and the gold were crushed and blown away without a trace, like husks of wheat at threshing time. But the stone became a tremendous mountain that covered the entire earth.

That was the dream, and now I'll tell you what it means. Your Majesty, you are the greatest of kings, and God has highly honoured you with power over all humans, animals, and birds. You are the head of gold. After you are gone, another kingdom will rule, but it won't be as strong. Then it will be followed by a kingdom of bronze that will rule the whole world. Next, a kingdom of iron will come to power, crushing and shattering everything.

This fourth kingdom will be divided – it will be both strong and brittle, just as you saw that the feet and toes were a mixture of iron and clay. This kingdom will be the result of a marriage between kingdoms, but it will crumble, just as iron and clay don't stick together.

During the time of those kings, the God who rules from heaven will set up an eternal kingdom that will never fall. It will be like the stone that was cut from the mountain, but not by human hands – the stone that crushed the iron, bronze, clay, silver, and gold. Your Majesty, in your dream the great God has told you what is going to happen, and you can trust this interpretation.

King Nebuchadnezzar bowed low to the ground and worshipped Daniel. Then he gave orders for incense to be burnt and a sacrifice of grain to be offered in honour of Daniel. The king said, 'Now I know that your God is above all other gods and kings, because he gave you the power to explain this mystery.' The king then presented Daniel with a lot of gifts; he promoted him to governor of Babylon Province and put him in charge of the other wise men. At Daniel's request, the king appointed Shadrach, Meshach, and Abednego to high positions in Babylon Province, and he let Daniel stay on as a palace official.

DANIEL 3.1–7

THE GOLD STATUE

When you hear the music, you must bow down and worship the statue that King Nebuchadnezzar has set up. Anyone who refuses will at once be thrown into a flaming furnace.

King Nebuchadnezzar ordered a gold statue to be built twenty-seven metres high and nearly three metres wide. He had it set up in Dura Valley near the city of Babylon, and he commanded his governors, advisers, treasurers, judges, and his other officials to come from everywhere in his kingdom to the dedication of the statue. So all of them came and stood in front of it.

Then an official stood up and announced:

People of every nation and race, now listen to the king's command! Trumpets, flutes, harps, and all other kinds of musical instruments will soon start playing. When you hear the music, you must bow down and worship the statue that King Nebuchadnezzar has set up. Anyone who refuses will at once be thrown into a flaming furnace.

As soon as the people heard the music, they bowed down and worshipped the gold statue that the king had set up.

Daniel 3.8–18

LIVE OR DIE, WE WILL ONLY WORSHIP GOD

'The God we worship can save us from you and your flaming furnace. But even if he doesn't, we still won't worship your gods and the gold statue you have set up.'

See also Exodus 20.4

Some Babylonians used this as a chance to accuse the Jews to King Nebuchadnezzar. They said, 'Your Majesty, we hope you live for ever! You commanded everyone to bow down and worship the gold statue when the music played. And you said that anyone who did not bow down and worship it would be thrown into a flaming furnace. Sir, you appointed three men to high positions in Babylon Province, but they have disobeyed you. Those Jews, Shadrach, Meshach, and Abednego, refuse to worship your gods and the statue you have set up.'

King Nebuchadnezzar was furious. So he sent for the three young men and said, 'I hear that you refuse to worship my gods and the gold statue I have set up. Now I am going to give you one more chance. If you bow down and worship the statue when you hear the music, everything will be all right. But if you don't, you will at once be thrown into a flaming furnace. No god can save you from me.'

The three men replied, 'Your Majesty, we don't need to defend ourselves. The God we worship can save us from you and your flaming furnace. But even if he doesn't, we still won't worship your gods and the gold statue you have set up.'

Daniel 3.19–30

KEPT SAFE IN THE FIRE

'But I see four men walking around in the fire,' the king replied.

Nebuchadnezzar's face twisted with anger at the three men. And he ordered the furnace to be heated seven times hotter than usual. Next, he commanded some of his strongest soldiers to tie up the men and throw them into the flaming furnace.

J.M.W. Turner
Shadrach,
Meshach, and
Abednego in the
burning fiery
furnace
Tate Britain
London
1832

**Miracles and
wonders**

See also **Hebrews**
11.34

The king wanted it done at that very moment. So the soldiers tied up Shadrach, Meshach, and Abednego and threw them into the flaming furnace with all their clothes still on, including their turbans. The fire was so hot that flames leaped out and killed the soldiers.

Suddenly the king jumped up and shouted, 'Weren't only three men tied up and thrown into the fire?'

'But I see four men walking around in the fire,' the king replied. 'None of them is tied up or harmed, and the fourth one looks like a god.'

Nebuchadnezzar went closer to the flaming furnace and said to the three young men, 'You servants of the Most High God, come out at once!

They came out, and the king's high officials, governors, and advisers all crowded around them. The men were not burnt, their hair wasn't scorched, and their clothes didn't even smell like smoke. King Nebuchadnezzar said:

'Praise their God for sending an angel to rescue his servants! They trusted their God and refused to obey my commands. Yes, they chose to die rather than to worship or serve any god except their own. And I won't allow people of any nation or race to say anything against their God. Anyone who does will be chopped up and their houses will be torn down, because no other god has such great power to save.

After this happened, the king appointed Shadrach, Meshach, and Abednego to even higher positions in Babylon Province.

Daniel 5.1–12

THE WRITING ON THE WALL

A new king, Belshazzar, replaced Nebuchadnezzar. It soon became clear that he had not learnt any of the lessons of his predecessor.

Suddenly a human hand was seen writing on the plaster wall of the palace.

One evening, King Belshazzar gave a great banquet for a thousand of his highest officials, and he drank wine with them. He got drunk and ordered his servants to bring in the gold and silver cups his father Nebuchadnezzar had taken from the

W. WALTON
BELSHAZZAR'S
FEAST
1931

DREAMS AND
VISIONS
FOOD AND DRINK

temple in Jerusalem. Belshazzar wanted the cups, so that he and all his wives and officials could drink from them.

When the gold cups were brought in, everyone at the banquet drank from them and praised their idols made of gold, silver, bronze, iron, wood, and stone.

Suddenly a human hand was seen writing on the plaster wall of the palace. The hand was just behind the lampstand, and the king could see it writing. He was so frightened that his face turned pale, his knees started shaking, and his legs became weak.

The king called in his advisers, who claimed they could talk with the spirits of the dead and understand the meanings found in the stars. He told them, 'The man who can read this writing and tell me what it means will become the third most powerful man in my kingdom. He will wear robes of royal purple and a gold chain around his neck.'

All of King Belshazzar's highest officials came in, but not one of them could read the writing or tell what it meant, and they were completely puzzled. Now the king was more afraid than ever before, and his face turned white as a ghost.

When the queen heard the king and his officials talking, she came in and said:

Your Majesty, I hope you live forever! Don't be afraid or look so pale. In your kingdom there is a man who has been given special powers by the holy gods. When your father Nebuchadnezzar was king, this man was known to be as clever, intelligent, and wise as the gods themselves. Your father put him in charge of all who claimed they could talk with the spirits or understand the meanings in the stars or tell about the future. He also changed the man's name from Daniel to Belteshazzar. Not only is he wise and intelligent, but he can explain dreams and riddles and solve difficult problems. Send for Daniel, and he will tell you what the writing means.

DANIEL READS GOD'S WRITING

*God has numbered
the days of your
kingdom and has
brought it to an
end.*

**AGREEMENTS AND
PROMISES**

When Daniel was brought in, the king said:

'So you are Daniel, one of the captives my father brought back from Judah! I was told that the gods have given you special powers and that you are intelligent and very wise. Neither my advisers nor the men who talk with the spirits of the dead could read this writing or tell me what it means. But I have been told that you understand everything and that you can solve difficult problems. Now then, if you can read this writing and tell me what it means, you will become the third most powerful man in my kingdom. You will wear royal purple robes and have a gold chain around your neck.

Daniel answered:

Your Majesty, I will read the writing and tell you what it means. But you may keep your gifts or give them to someone else. Sir, the Most High God made your father a great and powerful man and brought him much honour and glory. God did such great things for him that people of all nations and races shook with fear.

Your father had the power of life and death over everyone, and he could honour or ruin anyone he chose. But when he became proud and stubborn, his glorious kingdom was taken from him. His mind became like that of an animal, and he was forced to stay away from people and live with wild donkeys. Your father ate grass like an ox, and he slept outside where his body was soaked with dew. He was forced to do this until he learnt that the Most High God rules all kingdoms on earth and chooses their kings.

King Belshazzar, you knew all this, but you still refused to honour the Lord who rules from heaven. Instead, you turned against him and ordered the cups from his temple to be brought here, so that you and your wives and officials could drink wine from them. You praised idols made of silver, gold, bronze, iron, wood, and stone, even though they cannot see or hear or think. You refused to worship the God who gives you breath and controls everything you do. That's why he sent the hand to write this message on the wall.

The words written there are *mene*, which means 'numbered', *tekel*, which means 'weighed', and *parsin*, which means 'divided'. God has numbered the days of your kingdom and has brought it to an end. He has weighed you on his balance scales, and you fall short of what it takes to be king. So God has divided your kingdom between the Medes and the Persians.

Belshazzar gave a command for Daniel to be made the third most powerful man in his kingdom and to be given a purple robe and a gold chain.

That same night, the king was killed. Then Darius the Mede, who was sixty-two years old, took over his kingdom.

DANIEL 6.1–23 ## DANIEL'S COURAGE

Daniel kept his important role under the new king, but his position aroused feelings of jealousy in some. They hatched a scheme to bring him to ruin.

'That Jew named Daniel, who was brought here as a captive, refuses to obey you or the law that you ordered to be written. And he still prays to his god three times a day.'

G.L. Bernini
Daniel and the Lion
Rome
1655

Darius divided his kingdom into a hundred and twenty states and placed a governor in charge of each one. In order to make sure that his government was run properly, Darius put three other officials in charge of the governors. One of these officials was Daniel. And he did his work so much better than the other governors and officials that the king decided to let him govern the whole kingdom.

The other men tried to find something wrong with the way Daniel did his work for the king. But they could not accuse him of anything wrong, because he was honest and faithful and did everything he was supposed to do. Finally, they said to one another, 'We will never be able to bring any charge against Daniel, unless it has to do with his religion.'

They all went to the king and said:

Your Majesty, we hope you live forever! All of your officials, leaders, advisers, and governors agree that you should make a law forbidding anyone to pray to any god or human except you for the next thirty days. Everyone who disobeys this law must be thrown into a pit of lions. Order this to be written and then sign it, so it cannot be changed, just as no written law of the Medes and Persians can be changed.'

So King Darius made the law and had it written down.

Daniel heard about the law, but when he returned home, he went upstairs and prayed in front of the window that faced Jerusalem. In the same way that he had always done, he knelt down in prayer three times a day, giving thanks to God.

The men who had spoken to the king watched Daniel and saw him praying to his God for help. They went back to the king and said, 'Didn't you make a law that forbids anyone to pray to any god or human except you for the next thirty days? And doesn't the law say that everyone who disobeys it will be thrown into a pit of lions?'

'Yes, that's the law I made,' the king agreed. 'And just like all written laws of the Medes and Persians, it cannot be changed.'

The men then told the king, 'That Jew named Daniel, who was brought here as a captive, refuses to obey you or the law that you ordered to be written. And he still prays to his god three times a day.' The king was really upset to hear about this, and for the rest of the day he tried to think how he could save Daniel.

At sunset the men returned and said, 'Your Majesty, remember that no written law of the Medes and Persians can be changed, not even by the king.'

So Darius ordered Daniel to be brought out and thrown into a pit of lions. But he said to Daniel, 'You have been faithful to your God, and I pray that he will rescue you.'

A stone was rolled over the pit, and it was sealed. Then Darius and his officials stamped the seal to show that no one should let Daniel out. All night long the king could not sleep. He did not eat anything, and he would not let anyone come in to entertain him.

At daybreak the king got up and ran to the pit. He was anxious and shouted, 'Daniel, you were faithful and served your God. Was he able to save you from the lions?' Daniel answered,

'Your Majesty, I hope you live for ever! My God knew that I was innocent, and he sent an angel to keep the lions from eating me. Your Majesty, I have never done anything to hurt you.'

The king was relieved to hear Daniel's voice, and he gave orders for him to be taken out of the pit. Daniel's faith in his God had kept him from being harmed.

OTHER PROPHETS

HOSEA

11.1–11

LOVE AGAINST ALL ODDS

The prophet Hosea's experiences in his marriage to an unfaithful wife were used by God to illustrate how his love continues even when his people are not interested in following him.

Israel, I can't let you go. I can't give you up. How could I possibly destroy you as I did the towns of Admah and Zeboiim? I just can't do it. My feelings for you are much too strong.

See also *ISAIAH* 54.6–10

When Israel was a child, I loved him, and I called my son
  out of Egypt.
But as the saying goes, 'The more they were called, the
  more they rebelled.'
They never stopped offering incense and sacrifices to the
  idols of Baal.
I took Israel by the arm and taught them to walk.
But they would not admit that I was the one who had
  healed them.
I led them with kindness and with love, not with ropes.
I held them close to me; I bent down to feed them.
But they trusted Egypt instead of returning to me; now
  Assyria will rule them.
War will visit their cities, and their plans will fail.
My people are determined to reject me for a god they
  think is stronger, but he can't help.
Israel, I can't let you go. I can't give you up.
How could I possibly destroy you as I did the towns of
  Admah and Zeboiim? I just can't do it.
My feelings for you are much too strong.
Israel, I won't lose my temper and destroy you again.
I am the Holy God – not merely a human being, and I
  won't stay angry.
I, the Lord, will roar like a lion, and my children will return,
  trembling from the west.
They will come back, fluttering like birds from Egypt or

like doves from Assyria. Then I will bring them back to their homes. I, the Lord, have spoken!

> JOEL 2.28–32

JOEL 2.28–32

GOD'S SPIRIT GIVEN TO EVERYONE

Joel's prophecies came after Judah and Jerusalem had been ravaged by a vast swarm of locusts. His message challenged the people to think beyond the natural disaster and to learn lessons about God's judgement on those who don't follow him.

In those days I will even give my Spirit to my servants, both men and women.

AGREEMENTS AND PROMISES

See also ACTS 2.1–21

Later, I will give my Spirit to everyone. Your sons and
    daughters will prophesy. Your old men will have dreams,
    and your young men will see visions.
In those days I will even give my Spirit to my servants,
    both men and women.
I will work wonders in the sky above and on the earth
    below. There will be blood and fire and clouds of smoke.
The sun will turn dark, and the moon will be as red as
    blood before that great and terrible day when I appear.

Then the Lord will save everyone who faithfully worships him. He has promised there will be survivors on Mount Zion and in Jerusalem, and among them will be his chosen ones.

> MATTHEW 1.18–25

JONAH 1.1–17

JONAH DISOBEYS THE LORD

Jonah's story shows how God expected his people to share his message of love, even with those they considered to be too wicked to pay attention. In the end, God exposes Jonah's prejudice towards others as being irrational and unkind.

But the Lord made a strong wind blow, and such a bad storm came up that the ship was about to be broken to pieces.

GIOTTO
JONAH SWALLOWED
UP BY THE WHALE
CAPPELLA
SCROVEGNI
PADUA
1306

BIRDS AND
ANIMALS
MIRACLES AND
WONDERS
TRAVEL AND
TRANSPORT

One day the Lord told Jonah, the son of Amittai, to go to the great city of Nineveh and say to the people, 'The Lord has seen your terrible sins. You are doomed!'

Instead, Jonah ran from the Lord. He went to the seaport of Joppa and bought a ticket on a ship that was going to Spain. Then he got on the ship and sailed away to escape.

But the Lord made a strong wind blow, and such a bad storm came up that the ship was about to be broken to pieces. The sailors were frightened, and they all started praying to their gods. They even threw the ship's cargo overboard to make the ship lighter.

All this time, Jonah was down below deck, sound asleep. The ship's captain went to him and said, 'How can you sleep at a time like this? Get up and pray to your God! Perhaps he will have pity on us and keep us from drowning.'

Finally, the sailors got together and said, 'Let's ask our gods to show us who caused all this trouble.' It turned out to be Jonah.

They started asking him, 'Are you the one who brought all this trouble on us? What business are you in? Where do you come from? What is your country? Who are your people?'

Jonah answered, 'I'm a Hebrew, and I worship the Lord God of heaven, who made the sea and the dry land.'

When the sailors heard this, they were frightened, because Jonah had already told them he was running from the Lord. Then they said, 'Do you know what you have done?'

The storm kept getting worse, until finally the sailors asked him, 'What should we do with you to make the sea calm down?'

Jonah told them, 'Throw me into the sea, and it will calm down. I'm the cause of this terrible storm.'

The sailors tried their best to row to the shore. But they could not do it, and the storm kept getting worse every minute. So they prayed to the Lord, 'Please don't let us drown for taking this man's life. Don't hold us guilty for killing an innocent man. All this happened because you wanted it to.' Then they threw Jonah overboard, and the sea calmed down. The sailors were so terrified that they offered a sacrifice to the Lord and made all kinds of promises.

The Lord sent a big fish to swallow Jonah, and Jonah was inside the fish for three days and three nights.

Jonah 2.1–10

JONAH'S PRAYER OF DESPERATION

When my life was slipping away, I remembered you – and in your holy temple you heard my prayer.

From inside the fish, Jonah prayed to the Lord his God:

When I was in trouble, Lord, I prayed to you, and you
    listened to me.

From deep in the world of the dead, I begged for your help,
    and you answered my prayer.

You threw me down to the bottom of the sea.

The water was churning all around; I was completely
    covered by your mighty waves.

I thought I was swept away from your sight, never again to
    see your holy temple.

I was almost drowned by the swirling waters that
    surrounded me. Seaweed had wrapped around my head.

I had sunk down below the underwater mountains;

I knew that for ever, I would be a prisoner there.

But, you, Lord God, rescued me from that pit.

When my life was slipping away, I remembered you – and
    in your holy temple you heard my prayer.

All who worship worthless idols turn from the God who
    offers them mercy.

But with shouts of praise, I will offer a sacrifice to you, my
    Lord.

I will keep my promise, because you are the one with
    power to save.

The Lord commanded the fish to vomit up Jonah on the shore. And it did.

JONAH DOES AS HE IS TOLD

*Jonah obeyed the
Lord and went to
Nineveh*

Once again the Lord told Jonah to go to that great city of Nineveh and preach his message of doom.

Jonah obeyed the Lord and went to Nineveh. The city was so big that it took three days just to walk through it. After walking for a day, Jonah warned the people, 'Forty days from now, Nineveh will be destroyed!'

They believed God's message and set a time when they would go without eating to show their sorrow. Then everyone in the city, no matter who they were, dressed in sackcloth.

When the king of Nineveh heard what was happening, he also dressed in sackcloth; he left the royal palace and sat in dust.

Then he and his officials sent out an order for everyone in the city to obey. It said:

None of you or your animals may eat or drink a thing. Each of you must wear sackcloth, and you must even put sackcloth on your animals.

You must also pray to the Lord God with all your heart and stop being sinful and cruel. Perhaps God will change his mind and have mercy on us, so we won't be destroyed.

When God saw that the people had stopped doing evil things, he had pity and did not destroy them as he had planned.

JONAH'S ANGER AT GOD'S MERCY

Jonah was really upset and angry. So he prayed:

Our Lord, I knew from the very beginning that you wouldn't destroy Nineveh. That's why I left my own country and headed for Spain. You are a kind and merciful God, and you are patient. You always show love, and you don't like to punish anyone, not even foreigners.

Now let me die! I'd be better off dead.

In that city of
Nineveh there are
more than a
hundred and twenty
thousand people
who cannot tell
right from wrong,
and many cattle are
also there. Don't
you think I should
be concerned about
that big city?

BIRDS AND
ANIMALS

The Lord replied, 'What right do you have to be angry?'

Jonah then left through the east gate of the city and made a shelter to protect himself from the sun. He sat under the shelter, waiting to see what would happen to Nineveh.

The Lord made a vine grow up to shade Jonah's head and protect him from the sun. Jonah was very happy to have the vine, but early the next morning the Lord sent a worm to chew on the vine, and the vine dried up. During the day the Lord sent a scorching wind, and the sun beat down on Jonah's head, making him feel faint. Jonah was ready to die, and he shouted, 'I wish I were dead!'

But the Lord asked, 'Jonah, do you have the right to be angry about the vine?'

Yes, I do,' he answered, 'and I'm angry enough to die.'

But the Lord said:

You are concerned about a vine that you did not plant or take care of, a vine that grew up in one night and died the next. In that city of Nineveh there are more than a hundred and twenty thousand people who cannot tell right from wrong, and many cattle are also there. Don't you think I should be concerned about that big city?

MICAH 5.1–5

INSIGNIFICANT BETHLEHEM

Micah spoke out against the injustices of his day. He condemned Israel for its sin and called for judgement, yet at the same time he gave powerful prophecies, promising a future of hope and peace.

Bethlehem Ephrath,
you are one of the
smallest towns in
the nation of Judah.
But the Lord will
choose one of your
people.

AGREEMENTS AND
PROMISES

Jerusalem, enemy troops have surrounded you; they have
    struck Israel's ruler in the face with a stick.
Bethlehem Ephrath, you are one of the smallest towns in
    the nation of Judah.
But the Lord will choose one of your people to rule the
    nation – someone whose family goes back to ancient
    times.
The Lord will abandon Israel only until this ruler is born,

See also
MATTHEW 2.1,
LUKE 2.4,
LUKE 2.1–7

and the rest of his family returns to Israel.

Like a shepherd taking care of his sheep, this ruler will lead and care for his people by the power and glorious name of the Lord his God.

His people will live securely, and the whole earth will know his true greatness, because he will bring peace.

ZECHARIAH
9.9–13

THE HUMBLE CONQUEROR

Zechariah encouraged the Jews living in Jerusalem after they had returned from exile. Despite initial progress, they were struggling to overcome resistance. Zechariah's optimistic message of hope drew them away from their own difficulties and pointed to the arrival of a future king.

I will bring peace to nations, and your king will rule from sea to sea. His kingdom will reach from the River Euphrates across the earth.

AGREEMENTS AND
PROMISES
BIRDS AND
ANIMALS

See also
MATTHEW 21.4–9,
MARK 11.7–10,
LUKE 19.35–38,
JOHN 12.12–19

Everyone in Jerusalem, celebrate and shout!

Your king has won a victory, and he is coming to you.

He is humble and rides on a donkey; he comes on the colt of a donkey.

I, the Lord, will take away war chariots and horses from Israel and Jerusalem. Bows that were made for battle will be broken.

I will bring peace to nations, and your king will rule from sea to sea.

His kingdom will reach from the River Euphrates across the earth.

When I made a sacred agreement with you, my people, we sealed it with blood.

Now some of you are captives in waterless pits, but I will come to your rescue and offer you hope.

Return to your fortress, because today I will reward you with twice what you had.

I will use Judah as my bow and Israel as my arrow.

I will take the people of Zion as my sword and attack the Greeks.

THE GOSPELS – THE STORY OF JESUS

The story of Jesus' life, death and resurrection is told by four different writers. Their accounts are called gospels, a word which means 'good news', and while there is a great deal of overlap, each author gives a unique perspective on what happened: Matthew's gospel was written to appeal to a Jewish reader; Mark was especially interested in the power and miraculous things Jesus did; Luke's scholarly approach combines a keen sense of history with a special emphasis upon human nature and John wrote in order to convince his readers that Jesus was sent by God to give true life to men and women. Their accounts are combined here in such a way as to let the story flow easily, but it's obviously worth going back to the originals to see how each stands on its own.

JESUS' BIRTH

JOHN 1.1–14

GOD'S WORD AMONG US

John begins dramatically in a style that echoes the first words of Genesis. This was no accident. He clearly wanted to make the connection between God and Jesus – a link he develops throughout his gospel.

The Word became a human being and lived here with us.

In the beginning was the one who is called the Word.
　　The Word was with God and was truly God.
From the very beginning the Word was with God.
　　And with this Word, God created all things.
Nothing was made without the Word.
　　Everything that was created received its life from him,
　　　　and his life gave light to everyone.

See also
Genesis 1,
Matthew 3.1–12,
Luke 1,
Ephesians 5.8,
1 John 1.1–2.14

dir. George
Stevens
The greatest
story ever told
1965

The light keeps shining in the dark, and darkness has
   never put it out.
God sent a man named John, who came to tell about the
   light and to lead all people to have faith.
John wasn't that light. He came only to tell about the light.
The true light that shines on everyone was coming into the
   world.
The Word was in the world, but no one knew him, though
   God had made the world with his Word.
He came into his own world, but his own nation did not
   welcome him.
Yet some people accepted him and put their faith in him.
   So he gave them the right to be the children of God.
They were not God's children by nature or because of any
   human desires.
God himself was the one who made them his children.
The Word became a human being and lived here with us.
We saw his true glory, the glory of the only Son of the
   Father.
From him all the kindness and all the truth of God have
   come down to us.

Luke 1.5–25

AN UNEXPECTED BABY

Luke's interest in historical detail led him to begin his
account before Jesus was born. He began by recording the
events that surrounded the birth of a child to Elizabeth, the
cousin of Jesus' mother, Mary.

Don't be afraid,
Zechariah! God has
heard your prayers.
Your wife Elizabeth
will have a son, and
you must name him
John.

When Herod was king of Judea, there was a priest called
Zechariah from the priestly group of Abijah. His wife Elizabeth
was from the family of Aaron. Both of them were good people
and pleased the Lord God by obeying all that he had commanded. But they did not have children. Elizabeth could not
have any, and both Zechariah and Elizabeth were already old.
   One day Zechariah's group of priests were on duty, and he
was serving God as a priest. According to the custom of the

priests, he had been chosen to go into the Lord's temple that day and to burn incense, while the people stood outside praying.

All at once an angel from the Lord appeared to Zechariah at the right side of the altar. Zechariah was confused and afraid when he saw the angel. But the angel told him:

Don't be afraid, Zechariah! God has heard your prayers. Your wife Elizabeth will have a son, and you must name him John. His birth will make you very happy, and many people will be glad. Your son will be a great servant of the Lord. He must never drink wine or beer, and the power of the Holy Spirit will be with him from the time he is born.

John will lead many people in Israel to turn back to the Lord their God. He will go ahead of the Lord with the same power and spirit that Elijah had. And because of John, parents will be more thoughtful of their children. And people who now disobey God will begin to think as they ought to. That is how John will get people ready for the Lord.

Zechariah said to the angel, 'How will I know this is going to happen? My wife and I are both very old.'

The angel answered, 'I am Gabriel, God's servant, and I was sent to tell you this good news. You have not believed what I have said. So you will not be able to say a thing until all this happens. But everything will take place when it is supposed to.'

The crowd was waiting for Zechariah and kept wondering why he was staying so long in the temple. When he did come out, he could not speak, and they knew he had seen a vision. He motioned to them with his hands, but did not say a thing.

When Zechariah's time of service in the temple was over, he went home. Soon after that, his wife was expecting a baby, and for five months she did not leave the house. She said to herself, 'What the Lord has done for me will keep people from looking down on me.'

AN ANGEL BRINGS WONDERFUL NEWS

*'Don't be afraid!
God is pleased with
you, and you will
have a son. His
name will be Jesus.'*

PIERO
ANGEL OF THE
ANNUNCIATION
SANSEPOLCRO
1462

AGREEMENTS AND
PROMISES
DREAMS AND
VISIONS

See also
MATTHEW
1.16–25,
MATTHEW 4.13–16

One month later God sent the angel Gabriel to the town of Nazareth in Galilee with a message for a virgin named Mary. She was engaged to Joseph from the family of King David. The angel greeted Mary and said, 'You are truly blessed! The Lord is with you.'

Mary was confused by the angel's words and wondered what they meant. Then the angel told Mary, 'Don't be afraid! God is pleased with you, and you will have a son. His name will be Jesus. He will be great and will be called the Son of God Most High. The Lord God will make him king, as his ancestor David was. He will rule the people of Israel for ever, and his kingdom will never end.'

Mary asked the angel, 'How can this happen? I am not married!'

The angel answered, 'The Holy Spirit will come down to you, and God's power will come over you. So your child will be called the holy Son of God. Your relative Elizabeth is also going to have a son, even though she is old. No one thought she could ever have a baby, but in three months she will have a son. Nothing is impossible for God!'

Mary said, 'I am the Lord's servant! Let it happen as you have said.' And the angel left her.

MARY VISITS ELIZABETH

*God All-Powerful
has done great
things for me, and
his name is holy.*

A short time later Mary hurried to a town in the hill country of Judea. She went into Zechariah's home, where she greeted Elizabeth. When Elizabeth heard Mary's greeting, her baby moved within her.

The Holy Spirit came upon Elizabeth. Then in a loud voice she said to Mary:

God has blessed you more than any other woman! He has also blessed the child you will have. Why should the mother

Pontormo
Visitation
San Michele
Carmignano
Florence
1529

Marriage and family

of my Lord come to me? As soon as I heard your greeting, my baby became happy and moved within me. The Lord has blessed you because you believed that he will keep his promise.

Mary said:
With all my heart I praise the Lord, and I am glad because
    of God my Saviour.
He cares for me, his humble servant.
From now on, all people will say God has blessed me.
God All-Powerful has done great things for me, and his
    name is holy.
He always shows mercy to everyone who worships him.
The Lord has used his powerful arm to scatter those who
    are proud.
He drags strong rulers from their thrones and puts humble
    people in places of power.
God gives the hungry good things to eat, and sends the
    rich away with nothing.
He helps his servant Israel and is always merciful to his
    people.
The Lord made this promise to our ancestors, to Abraham
    and his family for ever!

Mary stayed with Elizabeth about three months. Then she went back home.

Luke 1.57–80

JOHN THE BAPTIST IS BORN

'You, my son, will be called a prophet of God in heaven above. You will go ahead of the Lord to get everything ready for him.'

When Elizabeth's son was born, her neighbours and relatives heard how kind the Lord had been to her, and they too were glad.

Eight days later they did for the child what the Law of Moses commands. They were going to name him Zechariah, after his father. But Elizabeth said, 'No! His name is John.'

The people argued, 'No one in your family has ever been named John.' So they motioned to Zechariah to find out what he wanted to name his son.

Zechariah asked for a writing tablet. Then he wrote, 'His name is John.' Everyone was amazed. Straight away Zechariah started speaking and praising God.

All the neighbours were frightened because of what had happened, and everywhere in the hill country people kept talking about these things. Everyone who heard about this wondered what this child would grow up to be. They knew that the Lord was with him.

The Holy Spirit came upon Zechariah, and he began to speak:

Praise the Lord, the God of Israel!

He has come to save his people.

Our God has given us a mighty Saviour from the family of
    David his servant.

Long ago the Lord promised by the words of his holy
    prophets to save us from our enemies and from
    everyone who hates us.

God said he would be kind to our people and keep his
    sacred promise.

He told our ancestor Abraham that he would rescue us
    from our enemies.

Then we could serve him without fear, by being holy and
    good as long as we live.

You, my son, will be called a prophet of God in heaven
    above.

You will go ahead of the Lord to get everything ready for
    him.

You will tell his people that they can be saved when their
    sins are forgiven.

God's love and kindness will shine upon us like the sun
    that rises in the sky.

On us who live in the dark shadow of death this light will
    shine to guide us into a life of peace.

As John grew up, God's Spirit gave him great power. John lived in the desert until the time he was sent to the people of Israel.

MATTHEW
1.18–25

JOSEPH'S DILEMMA

*Joseph, the baby
that Mary will have
is from the Holy
Spirit. Go ahead
and marry her.*

*DREAMS AND
VISIONS
MARRIAGE AND
FAMILY*

See also LUKE 1.26,
ISAIAH 7.10–14,
MATTHEW 1.23,
LUKE 1.27,
LUKE 2.1–7

This is how Jesus Christ was born. A young woman named Mary was engaged to Joseph from King David's family. But before they were married, she learnt that she was going to have a baby by God's Holy Spirit. Joseph was a good man and did not want to embarrass Mary in front of everyone. So he decided to call off the wedding quietly.

While Joseph was thinking about this, an angel from the Lord came to him in a dream. The angel said, 'Joseph, the baby that Mary will have is from the Holy Spirit. Go ahead and marry her. Then after her baby is born, name him Jesus, because he will save his people from their sins.'

So the Lord's promise came true, just as the prophet had said, 'A virgin will have a baby boy, and he will be called Immanuel,' which means 'God is with us.'

After Joseph woke up, he and Mary were soon married, just as the Lord's angel had told him to do. But they did not sleep together before her baby was born. Then Joseph named him Jesus.

❱ LUKE 2.8–14

■

LUKE 2.8–14

ANGELS ANNOUNCE THE BIRTH OF JESUS

The Roman emperor had ordered that all of his citizens should take part in a census. Everyone had to return to their home town, so Joseph took his heavily pregnant wife, Mary, to Bethlehem.

*'Don't be afraid! I
have good news for
you, which will
make everyone
happy.'*

That night in the fields near Bethlehem some shepherds were guarding their sheep. All at once an angel came down to them from the Lord, and the brightness of the Lord's glory flashed around them. The shepherds were frightened. But the angel said, 'Don't be afraid! I have good news for you, which will make everyone happy. This very day in King David's home town a Saviour was born for you. He is Christ the Lord. You will know who he is, because you will find him dressed in baby clothes and lying on a bed of hay.'

Suddenly many other angels came down from heaven and joined in praising God. They said:

'Praise God in heaven!
Peace on earth to everyone
who pleases God.'

▶ MATTHEW 2.1–12

THE SHEPHERDS FIND THE BABY

LUKE 2.15–20

As the shepherds returned to their sheep, they were praising God and saying wonderful things about him. Everything they had seen and heard was just as the angel had said.

After the angels had left and gone back to heaven, the shepherds said to each other, 'Let's go to Bethlehem and see what the Lord has told us about.' They hurried off and found Mary and Joseph, and they saw the baby lying on a bed of hay.

When the shepherds saw Jesus, they told his parents what the angel had said about him. Everyone listened and was surprised. But Mary kept thinking about all this and wondering what it meant.

As the shepherds returned to their sheep, they were praising God and saying wonderful things about him. Everything they had seen and heard was just as the angel had said.

THE BABY'S FUTURE PREDICTED

LUKE 2.21–38

'Your mighty power is a light for all nations, and it will bring honour to your people Israel.'

Eight days later Jesus' parents did for him what the Law of Moses commands. And they named him Jesus, just as the angel had told Mary when he promised she would have a baby.

The time came for Mary and Joseph to do what the Law of Moses says a mother is supposed to do after her baby is born.

They took Jesus to the temple in Jerusalem and presented him to the Lord, just as the Law of the Lord says, 'Each firstborn baby boy belongs to the Lord.' The Law of the Lord also says that parents have to offer a sacrifice, giving at least a pair of doves or two young pigeons. So that is what Mary and Joseph did.

At this time a man named Simeon was living in Jerusalem. Simeon was a good man. He loved God and was waiting for God to save the people of Israel. God's Spirit came to him and told him that he would not die until he had seen Christ the Lord.

When Mary and Joseph brought Jesus to the temple to do what the Law of Moses says should be done for a new baby, the Spirit told Simeon to go into the temple. Simeon took the baby Jesus in his arms and praised God,

'Lord, I am your servant, and now I can die in peace,
    because you have kept your promise to me.
With my own eyes I have seen what you have done to save
    your people, and foreign nations will also see this.
Your mighty power is a light for all nations, and it will
    bring honour to your people Israel.'

Jesus' parents were surprised at what Simeon had said. Then he blessed them and told Mary, 'This child of yours will cause many people in Israel to fall and others to stand. The child will be like a warning sign. Many people will reject him, and you, Mary, will suffer as though you had been stabbed by a dagger. But all this will show what people are really thinking.'

The prophet Anna was also there in the temple. She was the daughter of Phanuel from the tribe of Asher, and she was very old. In her youth she had been married for seven years, but her husband had died. And now she was eighty-four years old. Night and day she served God in the temple by praying and often going without eating.

At that time Anna came in and praised God. She spoke about the child Jesus to everyone who hoped for Jerusalem to be set free.

VISITORS FROM THE EAST

MATTHEW
2.1–12

*'Bethlehem in the
land of Judea, you
are very important
among the towns of
Judea. From your
town will come a
leader, who will be
like a shepherd for
my people Israel.'*

LEONARDO DA
VINCI
THE ADORATION OF
THE MAGI
FLORENCE
C.1481

DREAMS AND
VISIONS
MIRACLES AND
WONDERS

See also
1 SAMUEL 16.1–13,
RUTH 1.19,
MICAH 5.2,
LUKE 2.4

Some time after Jesus' birth, but while the family was still living in Bethlehem, important foreign visitors came to visit him.

When Jesus was born in the village of Bethlehem in Judea, Herod was king. During this time some wise men from the east came to Jerusalem and said, 'Where is the child born to be king of the Jews? We saw his star in the east and have come to worship him.'

When King Herod heard about this, he was worried, and so was everyone else in Jerusalem. Herod brought together the chief priests and the teachers of the Law of Moses and asked them, 'Where will the Messiah be born?'

They told him, 'He will be born in Bethlehem, just as the prophet wrote,

"Bethlehem in the land of Judea, you are very important
      among the towns of Judea.
From your town will come a leader, who will be like a
      shepherd for my people Israel."'

Herod secretly called in the wise men and asked them when they had first seen the star. He told them, 'Go to Bethlehem and search carefully for the child. As soon as you find him, let me know. I want to go and worship him too.'

The wise men listened to what the king said and then left. And the star they had seen in the east went on ahead of them until it stopped over the place where the child was. They were thrilled and excited to see the star.

When the men went into the house and saw the child with Mary, his mother, they knelt down and worshipped him. They took out their gifts of gold, frankincense, and myrrh and gave them to him. Later they were warned in a dream not to return to Herod, and they went back home by another road.

▶ MATTHEW 3.1–12

EVERY PARENT'S WORRY

The gospel writers were mostly interested in Jesus' adult life. Apart from the stories surrounding his birth, this incident is the only one recorded from his childhood.

'Why did you have to look for me? Didn't you know that I would be in my Father's house?'

MARRIAGE AND FAMILY

See also
JOHN 2.16,
JOHN 14.2,
MATTHEW 4.13,
LUKE 4.16,
JOHN 1.46,
EXODUS 12.21–34,
NUMBERS 9,
MATTHEW 26.26–29,
1 CORINTHIANS 5.7

After Joseph and Mary had done everything that the Law of the Lord commands, they returned home to Nazareth in Galilee. The child Jesus grew. He became strong and wise, and God blessed him.

Every year Jesus' parents went to Jerusalem for Passover. And when Jesus was twelve years old, they all went there as usual for the celebration. After Passover his parents left, but they did not know that Jesus had stayed on in the city. They thought he was travelling with some other people, and they went a whole day before they started looking for him. When they could not find him with their relatives and friends, they went back to Jerusalem and started looking for him there.

Three days later they found Jesus sitting in the temple, listening to the teachers and asking them questions. Everyone who heard him was surprised at how much he knew and at the answers he gave.

When his parents found him, they were amazed. His mother said, 'Son, why have you done this to us? Your father and I have been very worried, and we have been searching for you!'

Jesus answered, 'Why did you have to look for me? Didn't you know that I would be in my Father's house?' But they did not understand what he meant.

Jesus went back to Nazareth with his parents and obeyed them. His mother kept on thinking about all that had happened.

Jesus became wise, and he grew strong. God was pleased with him and so were the people.

THE TEACHINGS AND MIRACLES OF JESUS

GOD'S KINGDOM IS COMING!

MATTHEW
3.1–12

*John was the one
the prophet Isaiah
was talking about,
when he said, 'In
the desert someone
is shouting, "Get the
road ready for the
Lord! Make a
straight path for
him."'*

FOOD AND DRINK

See also
JOHN 1.1–14,
MATTHEW
11.2–19,
MATTHEW
14.1–12, LUKE 1,
MATTHEW 3.16,
ACTS 1.5,
ROMANS 6.3,
MARK 1.1–8,
LUKE 3.1–18,
JOHN 1.19–28

Years later, John the Baptist started preaching in the desert of Judea. He said, 'Turn back to God! The kingdom of heaven will soon be here.'

John was the one the prophet Isaiah was talking about, when he said,

'In the desert someone is shouting,
"Get the road ready for the Lord!
Make a straight path for him."'

John wore clothes made of camel's hair. He had a leather strap around his waist and ate grasshoppers and wild honey.

From Jerusalem and all Judea and from the River Jordan Valley crowds of people went to John. They told how sorry they were for their sins, and he baptized them in the river.

Many Pharisees and Sadducees also came to be baptized. But John said to them:

You snakes! Who warned you to run from the coming judgment? Do something to show that you have really given up your sins. And don't start telling yourselves that you belong to Abraham's family. I tell you that God can turn these stones into children for Abraham. An axe is ready to cut the trees down at their roots. Any tree that doesn't produce good fruit will be chopped down and thrown into a fire.

I baptize you with water so that you will give up your sins. But someone more powerful is going to come, and I am not good enough even to carry his sandals. He will baptize you with the Holy Spirit and with fire. His threshing fork is in his hand, and he is ready to separate the wheat from the husks.

He will store the wheat in a barn and burn the husks in a fire that never goes out.

> MATTHEW 3.13–17

MATTHEW
3.13–17

Then a voice from heaven said, 'This is my own dear Son, and I am pleased with him.'

EL GRECO
THE BAPTISM OF
CHRIST
MODENA
1568

MATTHEW
4.1–11

Jesus answered, 'Go away Satan! The Scriptures say: "Worship the Lord your God and serve only him."'

JESUS IS BAPTISED

Jesus left Galilee and went to the River Jordan to be baptized by John. But John kept objecting and said, 'I ought to be baptized by you. Why have you come to me?'

Jesus answered, 'For now this is how it should be, because we must do all that God wants us to do.' Then John agreed.

So Jesus was baptized. And as soon as he came out of the water, the sky opened, and he saw the Spirit of God coming down on him like a dove. Then a voice from heaven said, 'This is my own dear Son, and I am pleased with him.'

> MATTHEW 4.1–11

THE DEVIL TEMPTS JESUS

The Holy Spirit led Jesus into the desert, so that the devil could test him. After Jesus had gone without eating for forty days and nights, he was very hungry. Then the devil came to him and said, 'If you are God's Son, tell these stones to turn into bread.'

Jesus answered, 'The Scriptures say:

"No one can live only on food.

People need every word that God has spoken."'

Next, the devil took Jesus to the holy city and made him stand on the highest part of the temple. The devil said, 'If you are God's Son, jump off. The Scriptures say:

"God will give his angels orders about you.

BOTTICELLI
THE TEMPTATION OF
CHRIST
ROME
1482

See also
HEBREWS 4.14–16
MARK 1.12,13,
LUKE 4.1–13

They will catch you in their arms,
  and you won't hurt your feet on the stones.'"

Jesus answered, 'The Scriptures also say, "Don't try to test the Lord your God!"'

Finally, the devil took Jesus up on a very high mountain and showed him all the kingdoms on earth and their power. The devil said to him, 'I will give all this to you, if you will bow down and worship me.'

Jesus answered, 'Go away Satan! The Scriptures say:
  "Worship the Lord your God and serve only him."'

Then the devil left Jesus, and angels came to help him.

▶ **MATTHEW 8.1–13**

**MATTHEW
4.12–25**

*Then Jesus started
preaching, 'Turn
back to God! The
kingdom of heaven
will soon be here.'*

JESUS BEGINS HIS WORK

When Jesus heard that John had been put in prison, he went to Galilee. But instead of staying in Nazareth, Jesus moved to Capernaum. This town was beside Lake Galilee in the territory of Zebulun and Naphtali. So God's promise came true, just as the prophet Isaiah had said,

'Listen, lands of Zebulun and Naphtali, lands along the
  road to the sea and east of the Jordan!
Listen Galilee, land of the Gentiles!
Although your people live in darkness, they will see a
  bright light.
Although they live in the shadow of death, a light will shine
  on them.'

Then Jesus started preaching, 'Turn back to God! The kingdom of heaven will soon be here.'

While Jesus was walking along the shore of Lake Galilee, he saw two brothers. One was Simon, also known as Peter, and the other was Andrew. They were fishermen, and they were casting their net into the lake. Jesus said to them, 'Come with

See also
MARK 5.37,
LUKE 18.28,
JOHN 21.1–22,
GALATIANS
2.11–21,
MARK 1.14–20,
LUKE 4.14–15,
LUKE 5.1–11

me! I will teach you how to bring in people instead of fish.' At once the two brothers dropped their nets and went with him.

Jesus walked on until he saw James and John, the sons of Zebedee. They were in a boat with their father, mending their nets. Jesus asked them to come with him too. Straight away they left the boat and their father and went with Jesus.

Jesus went all over Galilee, teaching in the Jewish meeting places and preaching the good news about God's kingdom. He also healed every kind of disease and sickness. News about him spread all over Syria, and people with every kind of sickness or disease were brought to him. Some of them had a lot of demons in them, others were thought to be mad, and still others could not walk. But Jesus healed them all.

Large crowds followed Jesus from Galilee and the region around the ten cities known as Decapolis. They also came from Jerusalem, Judea, and from across the River Jordan.

MARK 2.23–3.6

A CONTROVERSIAL HEALING

'So the Son of Man is Lord over the Sabbath.'

FOOD AND DRINK

See also
EXODUS 20.8,
LUKE 13.10–17,
JOHN 9. 13–25, 1
SAMUEL 21.1–9,
MATTHEW 12.1–14,
MARK 2.23–6,
LUKE 6.1–11

One Sabbath Jesus and his disciples were walking through some wheat fields. His disciples were picking grains of wheat as they went along. Some Pharisees asked Jesus, 'Why are your disciples picking grain on the Sabbath? They are not supposed to do that!'

Jesus answered, 'Haven't you read what David did when he and his followers were hungry and in need? It was during the time of Abiathar the high priest. David went into the house of God and ate the sacred loaves of bread that only priests are allowed to eat. He also gave some to his followers.'

Jesus finished by saying, 'People were not made for the good of the Sabbath. The Sabbath was made for the good of people. So the Son of Man is Lord over the Sabbath.'

The next time that Jesus went into the meeting place, a man with a crippled hand was there. The Pharisees wanted to accuse Jesus of doing something wrong, and they kept watching to see if Jesus would heal him on the Sabbath.

Jesus told the man to stand up where everyone could see him. Then he asked, 'On the Sabbath should we do good deeds or evil deeds? Should we save someone's life or destroy it?' But no one said a word.

Jesus was angry as he looked around at the people. Yet he felt sorry for them because they were so stubborn. Then he told the man, 'Stretch out your hand.' He did, and his bad hand was healed.

The Pharisees left. And straight away they started making plans with Herod's followers to kill Jesus.

MATTHEW
5.3–12

GOD'S BLESSINGS

Jesus travelled throughout the land, teaching about God and the way he expected his people to live. The next few passages are taken from what has become known as 'The Sermon on the Mount'.

*God blesses those
people who depend
only on him.*

AGREEMENTS AND
PROMISES

See also
LUKE 6.20–23

God blesses those people who depend only on him. They belong to the kingdom of heaven!

God blesses those people who grieve. They will find comfort!

God blesses those people who are humble. The earth will belong to them!

God blesses those people who want to obey him more than to eat or drink. They will be given what they want!

God blesses those people who are merciful. They will be treated with mercy!

God blesses those people whose hearts are pure. They will see him!

God blesses those people who make peace. They will be called his children!

God blesses those people who are treated badly for doing right. They belong to the kingdom of heaven.

God will bless you when people insult you, ill-treat you, and tell all kinds of evil lies about you because of me. Be happy and excited! You will have a great reward in heaven. People did these same things to the prophets who lived long ago.

MATTHEW
6.5–18

THE REAL MEANING OF PRAYER

Jesus continued:

When you pray, go into a room alone and close the door. Pray to your Father in private. He knows what is done in private, and he will reward you.

See also LUKE
11.2–4

When you pray, don't be like those show-offs who love to stand up and pray in the meeting places and on the street corners. They do this just to look good. I can assure you that they already have their reward.

When you pray, go into a room alone and close the door. Pray to your Father in private. He knows what is done in private, and he will reward you.

When you pray, don't talk on and on as people do who don't know God. They think God likes to hear long prayers. Don't be like them. Your Father knows what you need before you ask.

You should pray like this:

Our Father in heaven, help us to honour your name.
Come and set up your kingdom, so that everyone on
earth will obey you, as you are obeyed in heaven.
Give us our food for today.
Forgive us for doing wrong, as we forgive others.
Keep us from being tempted and protect us from evil.

If you forgive others for the wrongs they do to you, your Father in heaven will forgive you. But if you don't forgive others, your Father will not forgive your sins.

When you go without eating, don't try to look gloomy as those show-offs do when they go without eating. I can assure you that they already have their reward. Instead, comb your hair and wash your face. Then others won't know that you are going without eating. But your Father sees what is done in private, and he will reward you.

BEING BLIND TO OUR OWN FAULTS

Don't condemn others, and God won't condemn you. God will be as hard on you as you are on others! He will treat you exactly as you treat them.

You can see the speck in your friend's eye, but you don't notice the log in your own eye. How can you say, 'My friend, let me take the speck out of your eye,' when you don't see the log in your own eye? You're nothing but show-offs! First, take the log out of your own eye. Then you can see how to take the speck out of your friend's eye.

THE TWO HOUSE-BUILDERS

Anyone who hears and obeys these teachings of mine is like a wise person who built a house on solid rock. Rain poured down, rivers flooded, and winds beat against that house. But it did not fall, because it was built on solid rock.

Anyone who hears my teachings and doesn't obey them is like a foolish person who built a house on sand. The rain poured down, the rivers flooded, and the winds blew and beat against that house. Finally, it fell with a crash.

When Jesus finished speaking, the crowds were surprised at his teaching. He taught them like someone with authority, and not like their teachers of the Law of Moses.

JESUS THE HEALER

As Jesus came down the mountain, he was followed by large crowds. Suddenly a man with leprosy came and knelt in front of Jesus. He said, 'Lord, you have the power to make me well, if only you wanted to.'

Jesus put his hand on the man and said, 'I want to! Now you

MIRACLES AND WONDERS

See also
EXODUS 3.1–4.16,
NUMBERS 12.10, 2
KINGS 5.1,
LUKE 7.1–10

are well.' At once the man's leprosy disappeared. Jesus told him, 'Don't tell anyone about this, but go and show the priest that you are well. Then take a gift to the temple just as Moses commanded, and everyone will know that you have been healed.'

When Jesus was going into the town of Capernaum, an army officer came up to him and said, 'Lord, my servant is at home in such terrible pain that he can't even move.'

'I will go and heal him,' Jesus replied.

But the officer said, 'Lord, I'm not good enough for you to come into my house. Just give the order, and my servant will get well. I have officers who give orders to me, and I have soldiers who take orders from me. I can say to one of them, "Go!" and he goes. I can say to another, "Come!" and he comes. I can say to my servant, "Do this!" and he will do it.'

When Jesus heard this, he was so surprised that he turned and said to the crowd following him, 'I tell you that in all of Israel I've never found anyone with this much faith! Many people will come from everywhere to enjoy the feast in the kingdom of heaven with Abraham, Isaac, and Jacob. But the ones who should have been in the kingdom will be thrown out into the dark. They will cry and grit their teeth in pain.'

Then Jesus said to the officer, 'You may go home now. Your faith has made it happen.'

At once his servant was healed.

MATTHEW 13.1–23

MATTHEW
11.1–10

'God will bless
everyone who
doesn't reject me
because of what I
do.'

JOHN WONDERS IF HE WAS MISTAKEN

Everywhere he went, Jesus taught the people, and healed those who were unwell. He sent his followers out to heal and help others too.

After Jesus had finished instructing his twelve disciples, he left and began teaching and preaching in the towns.

MIRACLES AND
WONDERS

See also *LUKE*
17.18–35

John was in prison when he heard what Christ was doing. So John sent some of his followers to ask Jesus, 'Are you the one we should be looking for? Or must we wait for someone else?'

Jesus answered, 'Go and tell John what you have heard and seen. The blind are now able to see, and the lame can walk. People with leprosy are being healed, and the deaf can hear. The dead are raised to life, and the poor are hearing the good news. God will bless everyone who doesn't reject me because of what I do.'

As John's followers were going away, Jesus spoke to the crowds about John:

What sort of person did you go out into the desert to see? Was he like tall grass blown about by the wind? What kind of man did you go out to see? Was he someone dressed in fine clothes? People who dress like that live in the king's palace. What did you really go out to see? Was he a prophet? He certainly was. I tell you that he was more than a prophet. In the Scriptures God says about him, 'I am sending my messenger ahead of you to get things ready for you.'

MATTHEW
11.11–19

I tell you that no one ever born on this earth is greater than John the Baptist. But whoever is least in the kingdom of heaven is greater than John.

THE GREATNESS OF JOHN

Jesus continued to talk about John's importance.

I tell you that no one ever born on this earth is greater than John the Baptist. But whoever is least in the kingdom of heaven is greater than John.

From the time of John the Baptist until now, violent people have been trying to take over the kingdom of heaven by force. All the Books of the Prophets and the Law of Moses told what was going to happen up to the time of John. And if you believe them, John is Elijah, the prophet you are waiting for. If you have ears, pay attention!

You people are like children sitting in the market and shouting to each other,

'We played the flute, but you would not dance!
We sang a funeral song, but you would not mourn!'

John the Baptist did not go around eating and drinking, and you said, 'That man has a demon in him!' But the Son of Man goes around eating and drinking, and you say, 'That man eats and drinks too much! He is even a friend of tax collectors and sinners.' Yet Wisdom is shown to be right by what it does.

See also
JOHN 1.1–14,
MATTHEW 3.1–12,
LUKE 1,
Luke 7.18–35

MATTHEW
13.1–8, 18–23

THE SCATTERED SEED

Jesus often explained what God was like and what he expected of people using simple stories called parables such as this one.

The seeds that fell on good ground are the people who hear and understand the message.

SAFTLEVEN
CHRIST TEACHING
FROM ST PETER'S
BOAT
NATIONAL GALLERY
LONDON
1667

BIRDS AND
ANIMALS
FARMING AND
PRODUCE

That same day Jesus left the house and went out beside Lake Galilee, where he sat down to teach. Such large crowds gathered around him that he had to sit in a boat, while the people stood on the shore. Then he taught them many things by using stories. He said:

A farmer went out to scatter seed in a field. While the farmer was scattering the seed, some of it fell along the road and was eaten by birds. Other seeds fell on thin, rocky ground and quickly started growing because the soil wasn't very deep. But when the sun came up, the plants were scorched and dried up, because they did not have enough roots. Some other seeds fell where thorn bushes grew up and choked the plants. But a few seeds did fall on good ground where the plants produced a hundred or sixty or thirty times as much as was scattered.

Now listen to the meaning of the story about the farmer:
The seeds that fell along the road are the people who hear the message about the kingdom, but don't understand it. Then the evil one comes and snatches the message from their hearts. The seeds that fell on rocky ground are the people who gladly hear the message and accept it straight away. But they don't have deep roots, and they don't last very long. As soon as life gets hard or the message gets them in trouble, they give up.

See also

MARK 4.1–20,

LUKE 8.4–15

The seeds that fell among the thorn bushes are also people who hear the message. But they start worrying about the needs of this life and are fooled by the desire to get rich. So the message gets choked out, and they never produce anything. The seeds that fell on good ground are the people who hear and understand the message. They produce as much as a hundred or sixty or thirty times what was planted.

▶ MARK 4.35–41

FROM MATTHEW 13.24–43

SORTING THE WEEDS FROM THE GOOD PLANTS

Jesus then told them this story:

The kingdom of heaven is like what happened when a farmer scattered good seed in a field. But while everyone was sleeping, an enemy came and scattered weeds in the field and then left.

Jesus answered: The one who scattered the good seed is the Son of Man.

FARMING AND PRODUCE

See also

MATTHEW 3.2,

MATTHEW 4.7,

MATTHEW 5–7,

MATTHEW 16.19,

MATTHEW 19.14,

MATTHEW 19.23–24

When the plants came up and began to ripen, the farmer's servants could see the weeds. The servants came and asked, 'Sir, didn't you scatter good seed in your field? Where did these weeds come from?'

'An enemy did this,' he replied. His servants then asked, 'Do you want us to go out and pull up the weeds?'

'No!' he answered. 'You might also pull up the wheat. Leave the weeds alone until harvest time. Then I'll tell my workers to gather the weeds and tie them up and burn them. But I'll order them to store the wheat in my barn.'

After Jesus left the crowd and went inside, his disciples came to him and said, 'Explain to us the story about the weeds in the wheat field.'

Jesus answered:

The one who scattered the good seed is the Son of Man. The field is the world, and the good seeds are the people who belong to the kingdom. The weeds are those who belong to the evil one, and the one who scattered them is the devil. The harvest is the end of time, and angels are the ones who bring in the harvest.

Weeds are gathered and burnt. That's how it will be at the end of time. The Son of Man will send out his angels, and they will gather from his kingdom everyone who does wrong or causes others to sin. Then he will throw them into a flaming furnace, where people will cry and grit their teeth in pain. But everyone who has done right will shine like the sun in their Father's kingdom. If you have ears, pay attention!

Matthew
13.44–52

GOD'S KINGDOM IS LIKE...

The kingdom of heaven is like what happens when someone finds treasure hidden in a field and buries it again. A person like that is happy and goes and sells everything in order to buy that field.

Jesus continued:
The kingdom of heaven is like what happens when someone finds treasure hidden in a field and buries it again. A person like that is happy and goes and sells everything in order to buy that field.

The kingdom of heaven is like what happens when a shop owner is looking for fine pearls. After finding a very valuable one, the owner goes and sells everything in order to buy that pearl.

The kingdom of heaven is like what happens when a net is thrown into a lake and catches all kinds of fish. When the net is full, it is dragged to the shore, and the fishermen sit down to separate the fish. They keep the good ones, but throw the bad ones away. That's how it will be at the end of time. Angels will come and separate the evil people from the ones who have done right. Then those evil people will be thrown into a flaming furnace, where they will cry and grit their teeth in pain.

Jesus asked his disciples if they understood all these things. They said, 'Yes, we do.'

So he told them, 'Every student of the Scriptures who

becomes a disciple in the kingdom of heaven is like someone who brings out new and old treasures from the storeroom.'

MARK 4.35–41

JESUS CALMS A STORM

Now they were more afraid than ever and said to each other, 'Who is this? Even the wind and the waves obey him!'

MIRACLES AND WONDERS

See also
MATTHEW 8.18–23,
LUKE 8.22-25

That evening, Jesus said to his disciples, 'Let's cross to the east side.' So they left the crowd, and his disciples started across the lake with him in the boat. Some other boats followed along. Suddenly a storm struck the lake. Waves started splashing into the boat, and it was about to sink.

Jesus was in the back of the boat with his head on a pillow, and he was asleep. His disciples woke him and said, 'Teacher, don't you care that we're about to drown?'

Jesus got up and ordered the wind and the waves to be quiet. The wind stopped, and everything was calm.

Jesus asked his disciples, 'Why were you afraid? Don't you have any faith?'

Now they were more afraid than ever and said to each other, 'Who is this? Even the wind and the waves obey him!'

▶ MATTHEW 14.24–33

MARK 5.21–43

JESUS IS WAYLAID ON A MISSION OF MERCY

On the other side of the lake Jesus healed a man who had been taken over by an evil spirit. Those living nearby were frightened by Jesus' power and begged him to leave, so he did – but the needy found him wherever he went.

Jesus said to the woman, 'You are now well because of your faith. May God give you peace! You are healed, and you will no longer be in pain.'

Once again Jesus got into the boat and crossed Lake Galilee. Then as he stood on the shore, a large crowd gathered around him. The person in charge of the Jewish meeting place was also there. His name was Jairus, and when he saw Jesus, he went over to him. He knelt at Jesus' feet and started begging

VERONESE
CHRIST AND THE
WOMAN WITH THE
ISSUE OF BLOOD
KUNSTHISTORISCHE
S MUSEUM
VIENNA
1570

MIRACLES AND
WONDERS

See also
MATTHEW 9.18–26,
LUKE 8.41–56

him for help. He said, 'My daughter is about to die! Please come and touch her, so she will get well and live.' Jesus went with Jairus. Many people followed along and kept crowding around.

In the crowd was a woman who had been bleeding for twelve years. She had gone to many doctors, and they had not done anything except cause her a lot of pain. She had paid them all the money she had. But instead of getting better, she only got worse.

The woman had heard about Jesus, so she came up behind him in the crowd and barely touched his clothes. She had said to herself, 'If I can just touch his clothes, I will get well.' As soon as she touched them, her bleeding stopped, and she knew she was well.

At that moment Jesus felt power go out from him. He turned to the crowd and asked, 'Who touched my clothes?'

His disciples said to him, 'Look at all these people crowding around you! How can you ask who touched you?' But Jesus turned to see who had touched him.

The woman knew what had happened to her. She came shaking with fear and knelt down in front of Jesus. Then she told him the whole story.

Jesus said to the woman, 'You are now well because of your faith. May God give you peace! You are healed, and you will no longer be in pain.'

While Jesus was still speaking, some men came from Jairus' home and said, 'Your daughter has died! Why bother the teacher any more?'

Jesus heard what they said, and he said to Jairus, 'Don't worry. Just have faith!'

Jesus did not let anyone go with him except Peter and the two brothers, James and John. They went home with Jairus and saw the people crying and making a lot of noise. Then Jesus went inside and said to them, 'Why are you crying and carrying on like this? The child isn't dead. She is just asleep.' But the people laughed at him.

After Jesus had sent them all out of the house, he took the

girl's father and mother and his three disciples and went to where she was. He took the twelve-year-old girl by the hand and said, 'Talitha, koum!' which means, 'Little girl, get up!' The girl got straight up and started walking around.

Everyone was greatly surprised. But Jesus ordered them not to tell anyone what had happened. Then he said, 'Give her something to eat.'

JOHN 6.1–15

JESUS FEEDS FIVE THOUSAND PEOPLE

Jesus took the bread in his hands and gave thanks to God. Then he passed the bread to the people, and he did the same with the fish, until everyone had plenty to eat.

DÜRER
THE FEEDING OF THE FIVE THOUSAND FROM TWO NUREMBURG PRAYER BOOKS 1503

FOOD AND DRINK
MIRACLES AND WONDERS

Jesus spent considerable time in the area of the Sea of Galilee, and frequently used a boat to get from one side to the other. The crowds, who did not have access to such convenient transport, showed their commitment by catching up with him by walking around the lake.

Jesus crossed Lake Galilee, which was also known as Lake Tiberias. A large crowd had seen him perform miracles to heal the sick, and those people went with him. It was almost time for the Jewish festival of Passover, and Jesus went up on a mountain with his disciples and sat down.

When Jesus saw the large crowd coming towards him, he asked Philip, 'Where will we get enough food to feed all these people?' He said this to test Philip, since he already knew what he was going to do.

Philip answered, 'Don't you know that it would take almost a year's wages just to buy only a little bread for each of these people?'

Andrew, the brother of Simon Peter, was one of the disciples. He spoke up and said, 'There is a boy here who has five small loaves of barley bread and two fish. But what good is that with all these people?'

The ground was covered with grass, and Jesus told his disciples to make everyone sit down. About five thousand men were in the crowd. Jesus took the bread in his hands and gave thanks to God. Then he passed the bread to the people, and he did the same with the fish, until everyone had plenty to eat.

See also
MATTHEW
14.13–21,
MARK 6.32–44,
LUKE 9.10–17

The people ate all they wanted, and Jesus told his disciples to gather up the leftovers, so that nothing would be wasted. The disciples gathered them up and filled twelve large baskets with what was left over from the five barley loaves.

After the people had seen Jesus perform this miracle, they began saying, 'This must be the Prophet who is to come into the world!' Jesus realized that they would try to force him to be their king. So he went up on a mountain, where he could be alone.

JESUS WALKS ON WATER

MATTHEW
14.24–33

Before going off by himself, Jesus had sent his disciples back across the lake in a boat — but he later joined them in dramatic fashion.

A little while before morning, Jesus came walking on the water towards his disciples.

By this time the boat was a long way from the shore. It was going against the wind and was being tossed around by the waves. A little while before morning, Jesus came walking on the water towards his disciples. When they saw him, they thought he was a ghost. They were terrified and started screaming.

SALVADOR DALI
IESUS SUPER MARE
AMBULANS
BIBLIA SACRA
VOLUME 3 PUB.
1969

At once, Jesus said to them, 'Don't worry! I am Jesus. Don't be afraid.'

Peter replied, 'Lord, if it is really you, tell me to come to you on the water.'

'Come on!' Jesus said. Peter then got out of the boat and started walking on the water towards him.

MIRACLES AND
WONDERS

But when Peter saw how strong the wind was, he was afraid and started sinking. 'Save me, Lord!' he shouted.

Straight away, Jesus reached out his hand. He helped Peter up and said, 'You don't have much faith. Why do you doubt?'

See also
MARK 6.45–51,
JOHN 6.15–21

When Jesus and Peter got into the boat, the wind died down. The men in the boat worshipped Jesus and said, 'You really are the Son of God!'

LUKE 9.18–27

LIFE-GIVING BREAD

When the crowds Jesus had fed realised he was gone, they went looking for him.

FOOD AND DRINK

See also *EXODUS
16.1–31*

They found him on the west side of the lake and asked, 'Rabbi, when did you get here?'

Jesus answered, 'I tell you for certain that you are not looking for me because you saw the miracles, but because you ate all the food you wanted. Don't work for food that spoils. Work for food that gives eternal life. The Son of Man will give you this food, because God the Father has given him the right to do so.'

'What exactly does God want us to do?' the people asked.

Jesus answered, 'God wants you to have faith in the one he sent.'

They replied, 'What miracle will you perform, so that we can have faith in you? What will you do? For example, when our ancestors were in the desert, they were given manna to eat. It happened just as the Scriptures say, "God gave them bread from heaven to eat."'

Jesus then told them, 'I tell you for certain that Moses wasn't the one who gave you bread from heaven. My Father is the one who gives you the true bread from heaven. And the bread that God gives is the one who came down from heaven to give life to the world.'

The people said, 'Lord, give us this bread and don't ever stop!'

Jesus replied:

I am the bread that gives life! No one who comes to me will ever be hungry. No one who has faith in me will ever be thirsty.

The people started grumbling because Jesus had said he was the bread that had come down from heaven. They were asking each other, 'Isn't he Jesus, the son of Joseph? Don't we know his father and mother? How can he say that he has come down from heaven?'

Jesus told them:

Stop grumbling! No one can come to me, unless the Father

who sent me makes them want to come. But if they do come, I will raise them to life on the last day. One of the prophets wrote, 'God will teach all of them.' And so everyone who listens to the Father and learns from him will come to me.

The only one who has seen the Father is the one who has come from him. No one else has ever seen the Father. I tell you for certain that everyone who has faith in me has eternal life.

I am the bread that gives life! Your ancestors ate manna in the desert, and later they died. But the bread from heaven has come down, so that no one who eats it will ever die. I am that bread from heaven! Everyone who eats it will live for ever. My flesh is the life-giving bread that I give to the people of this world.

Luke 9.18–27

PETER'S INSPIRED DECLARATION

Jesus led his followers away from the crowds to a place called Caesarea Philippi.

Peter answered, 'You are the Messiah sent from God.'

See also MATTHEW 16.13–28, MARK 8.27–9.1

When Jesus was alone praying, his disciples came to him, and he asked them, 'What do people say about me?'

They answered, 'Some say that you are John the Baptist or Elijah or a prophet from long ago who has come back to life.'

Jesus then asked them, 'But who do you say I am?'

Peter answered, 'You are the Messiah sent from God.'

Jesus strictly warned his disciples not to tell anyone about this.

Jesus told his disciples, 'The nation's leaders, the chief priests, and the teachers of the Law of Moses will make the Son of Man suffer terribly. They will reject him and kill him, but three days later he will rise to life.'

Then Jesus said to all the people:

If any of you want to be my followers, you must forget about yourself. You must take up your cross each day and follow me. If you want to save your life, you will destroy it. But if you give up your life for me, you will save it. What will you gain, if you own the whole world but destroy yourself or waste your life? If you are ashamed of me and my message, the Son of Man will be ashamed of you when he comes in his glory and in the glory of his Father and the holy angels. You can be sure that some of the people standing here will not die before they see God's kingdom.

I Luke 9.28–36

I

Luke 9.28–36

A GLIMPSE OF JESUS' REAL NATURE

They appeared in heavenly glory and talked about all that Jesus' death in Jerusalem would mean.

Raphael
The
Transfiguration
The Vatican
Rome
1520

Dreams and visions

See also Matthew 17.1–8, Mark 9.2–8

About eight days later Jesus took Peter, John, and James with him and went up on a mountain to pray. While he was praying, his face changed, and his clothes became shining white. Suddenly Moses and Elijah were there speaking with him. They appeared in heavenly glory and talked about all that Jesus' death in Jerusalem would mean.

Peter and the other two disciples had been sound asleep. All at once they woke up and saw how glorious Jesus was. They also saw the two men who were with him.

Moses and Elijah were about to leave, when Peter said to Jesus, 'Master, it is good for us to be here! Let us make three shelters, one for you, one for Moses, and one for Elijah.' But Peter did not know what he was talking about.

While Peter was still speaking, a shadow from a cloud passed over them, and they were frightened as the cloud covered them. From the cloud a voice spoke, 'This is my chosen Son. Listen to what he says!'

After the voice had spoken, Peter, John, and James saw only Jesus. For some time they kept quiet and did not say anything about what they had seen.

I John 12.12–19

THE GOOD SAMARITAN

Jesus knew that it was time to make his way to Jerusalem, so he began his journey towards the city. Word of his arrival soon got out, and many came to him to hear what he said or to ask questions.

'Go and do the same!'

An expert in the Law of Moses stood up and asked Jesus a question to see what he would say. 'Teacher,' he asked, 'what must I do to have eternal life?'

Jesus answered, 'What is written in the Scriptures? How do you understand them?'

The man replied, 'The Scriptures say, "Love the Lord your God with all your heart, soul, strength, and mind." They also say, "Love your neighbours as much as you love yourself."'

Jesus said, 'You have given the right answer. If you do this, you will have eternal life.'

But the man wanted to show that he knew what he was talking about. So he asked Jesus, 'Who are my neighbours?'

Jesus replied:

As a man was going down from Jerusalem to Jericho, robbers attacked him and grabbed everything he had. They beat him up and ran off, leaving him half dead.

A priest happened to be going down the same road. But when he saw the man, he walked by on the other side. Later a temple helper came to the same place. But when he saw the man who had been beaten up, he also went by on the other side.

A man from Samaria then came travelling along that road. When he saw the man, he felt sorry for him and went over to him. He treated his wounds with olive oil and wine and bandaged them. Then he put him on his own donkey and took him to an inn, where he took care of him. The next morning he gave the innkeeper two silver coins and said, 'Please take care of the man. If you spend more than this on him, I will pay you when I return.'

Then Jesus asked, 'Which one of these three people was a real neighbour to the man who was beaten up by robbers?'

The teacher answered, 'The one who showed pity.'

Jesus said, 'Go and do the same!'

John 9.1–12

JESUS HEALS A BLIND MAN

As Jesus walked along, he saw a man who had been blind since birth. Jesus' disciples asked, 'Teacher, why was this man born blind? Was it because he or his parents sinned?'

'No, it wasn't!' Jesus answered. 'But because of his blindness, you will see God perform a miracle for him. As long as it is day, we must do what the one who sent me wants me to do. When night comes, no one can work. While I am in the world, I am the light for the world.'

After Jesus said this, he spat on the ground. He made some mud and smeared it on the man's eyes. Then he said, 'Go and wash off the mud in Siloam Pool.' The man went and washed in Siloam, which means 'One who is sent'. When he had washed off the mud, he could see.

The man's neighbours and the people who had seen him begging wondered if he really could be the same man. Some of them said he was the same beggar, while others said he only looked like him. But he told them, 'I am that man.'

'Then how can you see?' they asked.

He answered, 'Someone named Jesus made some mud and smeared it on my eyes. He told me to go and wash it off in Siloam Pool. When I did, I could see.'

'Where is he now?' they asked.

'I don't know,' he answered.

Then he said, 'Go and wash off the mud in Siloam Pool.' The man went and washed in Siloam, which means 'One who is sent'. When he had washed off the mud, he could see.

El Greco
Christ healing the blind
Dresden
1567

Miracles and wonders

John 9.13–25

THE PHARISEES QUESTION THE MAN JESUS HEALED

The day when Jesus made the mud and healed the man was a Sabbath. So the people took the man to the Pharisees. They asked him how he was able to see, and he answered, 'Jesus

'All I know is that I used to be blind, but now I can see!'

made some mud and smeared it on my eyes. Then after I washed it off, I could see.'

Some of the Pharisees said, 'This man Jesus doesn't come from God. If he did, he would not break the law of the Sabbath.'

Others asked, 'How could someone who is a sinner perform such a miracle?'

Since the Pharisees could not agree among themselves, they asked the man, 'What do you say about this one who healed your eyes?'

'He is a prophet!' the man told them.

But the Jewish leaders would not believe that the man had once been blind. They sent for his parents and asked them, 'Is this the son that you said was born blind? How can he now see?'

The man's parents answered, 'We are certain that he is our son, and we know that he was born blind. But we don't know how he got his sight or who gave it to him. Ask him! He is old enough to speak for himself.'

The man's parents said this because they were afraid of the Jewish leaders. The leaders had already agreed that no one was to have anything to do with anyone who said Jesus was the Messiah.

The leaders called the man back and said, 'Swear by God to tell the truth! We know that Jesus is a sinner.'

The man replied, 'I don't know if he is a sinner or not. All I know is that I used to be blind, but now I can see!'

JOHN 9.26–34

THE PHARISEES BAN THE HEALED MAN FROM THEIR MEETING PLACES

'We know that God listens only to people who love and obey him. God doesn't listen to sinners.'

'What did he do to you?' the Jewish leaders asked. 'How did he heal your eyes?'

The man answered, 'I have already told you once, and you refused to listen. Why do you want me to tell you again? Do you also want to become his disciples?'

The leaders insulted the man and said, 'You are his follower! We are followers of Moses. We are sure that God spoke to Moses, but we don't even know where Jesus comes from.'

'How strange!' the man replied. 'He healed my eyes, and yet you don't know where he comes from. We know that God listens only to people who love and obey him. God doesn't listen to sinners. And this is the first time in history that anyone has ever given sight to someone born blind. Jesus could not do anything unless he came from God.'

The leaders told the man, 'You have been a sinner since the day you were born! Do you think you can teach us anything?' Then they said, 'You can never come back into any of our meeting places!'

LUKE 15.1–10

THE LOST SHEEP AND COIN

The Pharisees and religious leaders became increasingly outspoken in their criticism of Jesus. He responded by exposing their self-righteousness and their pride in observing every last detail of the law.

'In the same way there is more happiness in heaven because of one sinner who turns to God than over ninety-nine good people who don't need to.'

BIRDS AND ANIMALS

See also MATTHEW 18.12–14

Tax collectors and sinners were all crowding around to listen to Jesus. So the Pharisees and the teachers of the Law of Moses started grumbling, 'This man is friendly with sinners. He even eats with them.'

Then Jesus told them this story:

If any of you has a hundred sheep, and one of them gets lost, what will you do? Won't you leave the ninety-nine in the field and go and look for the lost sheep until you find it? And when you find it, you will be so glad that you will put it on your shoulder and carry it home. Then you will call in your friends and neighbours and say, 'Let's celebrate! I've found my lost sheep.'

Jesus said, 'In the same way there is more happiness in heaven because of one sinner who turns to God than over ninety-nine good people who don't need to.'

Jesus told the people another story:

What will a woman do if she has ten silver coins and loses one of them? Won't she light a lamp, sweep the floor, and look carefully until she finds it? Then she will call in her friends and neighbours and say, 'Let's celebrate! I've found the coin I lost.'

Jesus said, 'In the same way God's angels are happy when even one person turns to him.'

LUKE 15.11–32

THE LOST SON

'Your brother was dead, but he is now alive. He was lost and has now been found.'

REMBRANDT
THE RETURN OF THE PRODIGAL SON
THE STATE HERMITAGE MUSEUM
ST PETERSBURG
1662

BIRDS AND ANIMALS
MARRIAGE AND FAMILY

Jesus also told them another story:

Once a man had two sons. The younger son said to his father, 'Give me my share of the property.' So the father divided his property between his two sons.

Not long after that, the younger son packed up everything he owned and left for a foreign country, where he wasted all his money in wild living. He had spent everything, when a bad famine spread through that whole land. Soon he had nothing to eat.

He went to work for a man in that country, and the man sent him out to take care of his pigs. He would have been glad to eat what the pigs were eating, but no one gave him a thing.

Finally, he came to his senses and said, 'My father's workers have plenty to eat, and here I am, starving to death! I will go to my father and say to him, "Father, I have sinned against God in heaven and against you. I am no longer good enough to be called your son. Treat me like one of your workers."'

The younger son got up and started back to his father. But when he was still a long way off, his father saw him and felt sorry for him. He ran to his son and hugged and kissed him.

The son said, 'Father, I have sinned against God in heaven and against you. I am no longer good enough to be called your son.'

But his father said to the servants, 'Hurry and bring the best clothes and put them on him. Give him a ring for his finger and sandals for his feet. Get the best calf and prepare it, so we can eat and celebrate. This son of mine was dead, but has now come back to life. He was lost and has now been found.' And they began to celebrate.

The elder son had been out in the field. But when he came near the house, he heard the music and dancing. So he called one of the servants over and asked, 'What's going on here?'

The servant answered, 'Your brother has come home safe and sound, and your father ordered us to kill the best calf.' The elder brother got so angry that he would not even go into the house.

His father came out and begged him to go in. But he said to his father, 'For years I have worked for you like a slave and have always obeyed you. But you have never even given me a little goat, so that I could give a dinner for my friends. This other son of yours wasted your money on prostitutes. And now that he has come home, you ordered the best calf to be killed for a feast.'

His father replied, 'My son, you are always with me, and everything I have is yours. But we should be glad and celebrate! Your brother was dead, but he is now alive. He was lost and has now been found.'

LUKE 16.19–31

THE RICH MAN AND LAZARUS

The Pharisees loved money and the trappings of wealth, so Jesus often challenged them with stories about people who were very well off.

So Abraham said, 'If they won't pay attention to Moses and the prophets, they won't listen even to someone who comes back from the dead.'

There was once a rich man who wore expensive clothes and every day ate the best food. But a poor beggar named Lazarus was brought to the gate of the rich man's house. He was happy just to eat the scraps that fell from the rich man's table. His body was covered with sores, and dogs kept coming up to lick them. The poor man died, and angels took him to the place of honour next to Abraham.

The rich man also died and was buried. He went to hell and was suffering terribly. When he looked up and saw Abraham far off and Lazarus at his side, he said to Abraham, 'Have pity on me! Send Lazarus to dip his finger in water and touch my tongue. I'm suffering terribly in this fire.'

Abraham answered, 'My friend, remember that while you lived, you had everything good, and Lazarus had everything bad. Now he is happy, and you are in pain. And besides, there is a deep ditch between us, and no one from either side can cross over.'

But the rich man said, 'Abraham, then please send Lazarus to my father's home. Let him warn my five brothers, so they won't come to this horrible place.'

Abraham answered, 'Your brothers can read what Moses and the prophets wrote. They should pay attention to that.'

Then the rich man said, 'No, that's not enough! If only someone from the dead would go to them, they would listen and turn to God.'

So Abraham said, 'If they won't pay attention to Moses and the prophets, they won't listen even to someone who comes back from the dead.'

LUKE 18.9–14

THE PHARISEE AND THE TAX COLLECTOR

'When the two men went home, it was the tax collector and not the Pharisee who was pleasing to God. If you put yourself above others, you will be put down. But if you humble yourself, you will be honoured.'

Jesus told a story to some people who thought they were better than others and who looked down on everyone else:

Two men went into the temple to pray. One was a Pharisee and the other a tax collector. The Pharisee stood over by himself and prayed, 'God, I thank you that I am not greedy, dishonest, and unfaithful in marriage like other people. And I am really glad that I am not like that tax collector over there. I go without eating for two days a week, and I give you one tenth of all I earn.'

The tax collector stood off at a distance and did not think

he was good enough even to look up towards heaven. He was so sorry for what he had done that he pounded his chest and prayed, 'God, have pity on me! I am such a sinner.'

Then Jesus said, 'When the two men went home, it was the tax collector and not the Pharisee who was pleasing to God. If you put yourself above others, you will be put down. But if you humble yourself, you will be honoured.'

MATTHEW
19.13–15

JESUS' ATTITUDE TOWARDS CHILDREN

But Jesus said, 'Let the children come to me, and don't try to stop them!'

Some people brought their children to Jesus, so that he could place his hands on them and pray for them. His disciples told the people to stop bothering him. But Jesus said, 'Let the children come to me, and don't try to stop them! People who are like these children belong to God's kingdom.' After Jesus had placed his hands on the children, he left.

LUKE 18.18–30

THE PROBLEM OF WEALTH

'In fact, it's easier for a camel to go through the eye of a needle than for a rich person to get into God's kingdom.'

See also MARK
10.17–30,
LUKE 18.18–30

An important man asked Jesus, 'Good Teacher, what must I do to have eternal life?'

Jesus said, 'Why do you call me good? Only God is good. You know the commandments: "Be faithful in marriage. Do not murder. Do not steal. Do not tell lies about others. Respect your father and mother."'

He told Jesus, 'I have obeyed all these commandments since I was a young man.'

When Jesus heard this, he said, 'There is one thing you still need to do. Go and sell everything you own! Give the money to the poor, and you will have riches in heaven. Then come and be my follower.' When the man heard this, he was sad, because he was very rich.

Jesus saw how sad the man was. So he said, 'It's terribly hard for rich people to get into God's kingdom! In fact, it's easier for a camel to go through the eye of a needle than for a rich person to get into God's kingdom.'

When the crowd heard this, they asked, 'How can anyone ever be saved?'

Jesus replied, 'There are some things that people cannot do, but God can do anything.'

Peter said, 'Remember, we left everything to be your followers!'

Jesus answered, 'You can be sure that anyone who gives up home or wife or brothers or family or children because of God's kingdom will be given much more in this life. And in the future world they will have eternal life.'

MATTHEW
20.24–27

LEADING BY EXAMPLE

As they were walking with Jesus one day, the mother of James and John asked him if her sons could have important positions in his kingdom. The other disciples soon got to hear of her request.

And if you want to be first, you must be the slave of the rest.

See also MARK
10.35–45

When the ten other disciples heard this, they were angry with the two brothers. But Jesus called the disciples together and said:

You know that foreign rulers like to order their people around. And their great leaders have full power over everyone they rule. But don't act like them. If you want to be great, you must be the servant of all the others. And if you want to be first, you must be the slave of the rest.

ZACCHAEUS UNDERGOES A PERSONAL REVOLUTION

'The Son of Man came to look for and to save people who are lost.'

AGREEMENTS AND PROMISES

Jesus was going through Jericho, where a man named Zacchaeus lived. He was in charge of collecting taxes and was very rich. Jesus was heading his way, and Zacchaeus wanted to see what he was like. But Zacchaeus was a short man and could not see over the crowd. So he ran ahead and climbed up into a sycamore tree.

When Jesus got there, he looked up and said, 'Zacchaeus, hurry down! I want to stay with you today.' Zacchaeus hurried down and gladly welcomed Jesus.

Everyone who saw this started grumbling, 'This man Zacchaeus is a sinner! And Jesus is going home to eat with him.'

Later that day Zacchaeus stood up and said to the Lord, 'I will give half of my property to the poor. And I will now pay back four times as much to everyone I have ever cheated.'

Jesus said to Zacchaeus, 'Today you and your family have been saved, because you are a true son of Abraham. The Son of Man came to look for and to save people who are lost.'

Jesus' last week

**Matthew
26.6–13**

JESUS IS ANOINTED AT BETHANY

'You will always
have the poor with
you, but you won't
always have me.'

See also
Mark 14.3–9,
Luke 7.36–50,
John 12.1–8

Jesus was in the town of Bethany, eating at the home of Simon, who had leprosy. A woman came in with a bottle of expensive perfume and poured it on Jesus' head. But when his disciples saw this, they became angry and complained, 'Why such a waste? We could have sold this perfume for a lot of money and given it to the poor.'

Jesus knew what they were thinking, and he said:

Why are you bothering this woman? She has done a beautiful thing for me. You will always have the poor with you, but you won't always have me. She has poured perfume on my body to prepare it for burial. You may be sure that wherever the good news is told all over the world, people will remember what she has done. And they will tell others.

JESUS' TRIUMPHANT ENTRY

**John
12.12–19**

'Hooray! God bless
the one who comes
in the name of the
Lord! God bless the
King of Israel!'

The next day a large crowd was in Jerusalem for Passover. When they heard that Jesus was coming for the festival, they took palm branches and went out to greet him. They shouted,
'Hooray!
God bless the one who comes in the name of the Lord!
God bless the King of Israel!'

Jesus found a donkey and rode on it, just as the Scriptures say,
'People of Jerusalem,
don't be afraid!
Your King is now coming,
and he is riding
on a donkey.'

Giotto
Entry into
Jerusalem
Padua
1306

See also
MATTHEW 21.4–9,
MARK 11.7–10,
LUKE 19.35–38,
ZECHARIAH 9.9–13

At first, Jesus' disciples did not understand. But after he had been given his glory, they remembered all this. Everything had happened exactly as the Scriptures said it would.

A crowd had come to meet Jesus because they had seen him call Lazarus out of the tomb. They kept talking about him and this miracle. But the Pharisees said to each other, 'There is nothing that can be done! Everyone in the world is following Jesus.'

▶ MATTHEW 26.1–16

FROM MARK
11.15–19

*Everything you ask
for in prayer will be
yours, if you only
have faith.*

See also 1 KINGS 6,
EZRA 3.7–13,
JOHN 2.12–25,
MATTHEW
21.12–16,
LUKE 19.45–47,
JOHN 2.13–16

JESUS CAUSES HAVOC AT THE TEMPLE

After Jesus and his disciples reached Jerusalem, he went into the temple and began chasing out everyone who was selling and buying. He turned over the tables of the moneychangers and the benches of those who were selling doves. Jesus would not let anyone carry things through the temple. Then he taught the people and said, 'The Scriptures say, "My house should be called a place of worship for all nations." But you have made it a place where robbers hide!'

The chief priests and the teachers of the Law of Moses heard what Jesus said, and they started looking for a way to kill him. They were afraid of him, because the crowds were completely amazed at his teaching.

That evening, Jesus and the disciples went outside the city.

MATTHEW
21.28–32

JESUS CRITICISES THE PHARISEES

Jesus stayed at Mary and Martha's house just outside Jerusalem, but returned each day to teach to the crowds in the city, and to answer his critics among the religious leaders.

You can be sure
that tax collectors
and prostitutes will
get into the
kingdom of God
before you ever will!

MARRIAGE AND
FAMILY

Jesus said:

I will tell you a story about a man who had two sons. Then you can tell me what you think. The father went to the elder son and said, 'Go and work in the vineyard today!' His son told him that he would not do it, but later he changed his mind and went. The man then told his younger son to go and work in the vineyard. The boy said he would, but he didn't go. Which one of the sons obeyed his father?

'The elder one,' the chief priests and leaders answered.

Then Jesus told them:

You can be sure that tax collectors and prostitutes will get into the kingdom of God before you ever will! When John the Baptist showed you how to do right, you would not believe him. But these evil people did believe. And even when you saw what they did, you still would not change your minds and believe.

MATTHEW
21.33–46

*I tell you that God's
kingdom will be
taken from you and
given to people who
will do what he
demands.*

FARMING AND
PRODUCE

See also
MARK 12.1–12,
LUKE 20.9–19

THE UNGRATEFUL TENANTS

Jesus told the chief priests and leaders to listen to this story:

A land owner once planted a vineyard. He built a wall around it and dug a pit to crush the grapes in. He also built a lookout tower. Then he let his vineyard and left the country.

When it was harvest time, the owner sent some servants to get his share of the grapes. But the tenants grabbed those servants. They beat up one, killed one, and stoned one of them to death. He then sent more servants than he did the first time. But the tenants treated them in the same way.

Finally, the owner sent his own son to the tenants, because he thought they would respect him. But when they saw the man's son, they said, 'Some day he will own the vineyard. Let's kill him! Then we can have it all for ourselves.' So they grabbed him, threw him out of the vineyard, and killed him.

Jesus asked, 'When the owner of that vineyard comes, what do you suppose he will do to those tenants?'

The chief priests and leaders answered, 'He will kill them in some horrible way. Then he will let his vineyard to people who will give him his share of grapes at harvest time.'

Jesus replied, 'Surely you know that the Scriptures say,

"The stone that the builders tossed aside is now the most important stone of all.

This is something the Lord has done, and it is amazing to us."

I tell you that God's kingdom will be taken from you and given to people who will do what he demands. Anyone who stumbles over this stone will be crushed, and anyone it falls on will be smashed to pieces.'

When the chief priests and the Pharisees heard these stories, they knew that Jesus was talking about them. So they looked for a way to arrest Jesus. But they were afraid to, because the people thought he was a prophet.

CONSPIRACY

FROM
MATTHEW
26.1–16

They secretly planned to have Jesus arrested and put to death.

See also
MARK 14.1–2,
LUKE 22.1–2

When Jesus had finished teaching, he told his disciples, 'You know that two days from now will be Passover. That is when the Son of Man will be handed over to his enemies and nailed to a cross.'

At that time the chief priests and the nation's leaders were meeting at the home of Caiaphas the high priest. They secretly planned to have Jesus arrested and put to death. But they said, 'We must not do it during Passover, because the people will riot.'

Judas Iscariot was one of the twelve disciples. He went to the chief priests and asked, 'How much will you give me if I help you arrest Jesus?' They paid Judas thirty silver coins, and from then on he started looking for a good chance to betray Jesus.

MATTHEW 26.26–29

JESUS WASHES HIS DISCIPLES' FEET

I have set the example, and you should do for each other exactly what I have done for you

DUCCIO
THE WASHING OF THE FEET
SIENA
1311

FOOD AND DRINK

It was before Passover, and Jesus knew that the time had come for him to leave this world and to return to the Father. He had always loved his followers in this world, and he loved them to the very end.

Even before the evening meal started, the devil had made Judas, the son of Simon Iscariot, decide to betray Jesus.

Jesus knew that he had come from God and would go back to God. He also knew that the Father had given him complete power. So during the meal Jesus got up, removed his outer garment, and wrapped a towel around his waist. He put some water into a large bowl. Then he began washing his disciples' feet and drying them with the towel he was wearing.

But when he came to Simon Peter, that disciple asked, 'Lord, are you going to wash my feet?'

Jesus answered, 'You don't really know what I am doing, but later you will understand.'

'You will never wash my feet!' Peter replied.

'If I don't wash you,' Jesus told him, 'you don't really belong to me.'

Peter said, 'Lord, don't wash just my feet. Wash my hands and my head.'

Jesus answered, 'People who have bathed and are clean all over need to wash just their feet. And you, my disciples, are clean, except for one of you.' Jesus knew who would betray him. That is why he said, 'except for one of you.'

After Jesus had washed his disciples' feet and had put his outer garment back on, he sat down again. Then he said:

Do you understand what I have done? You call me your teacher and Lord, and you should, because that is who I am. And if your Lord and teacher has washed your feet, you should do the same for each other. I have set the example, and you should do for each other exactly what I have done for you.

JESUS' FINAL MEAL

MATTHEW
26.26–29

This is my blood, and with it God makes his agreement with you.

LEONARDO DA VINCI
THE LAST SUPPER
MILAN
1498

Jesus told some of his followers to prepare the Passover meal in Jerusalem. They went ahead to do this and then, later that evening, they all gathered to eat it in each others' company.

During the meal Jesus took some bread in his hands. He blessed the bread and broke it. Then he gave it to his disciples and said, 'Take this and eat it. This is my body.'

Jesus picked up a cup of wine and gave thanks to God. He then gave it to his disciples and said, 'Take this and drink it. This is my blood, and with it God makes his agreement with you. It will be poured out, so that many people will have their sins forgiven. From now on I am not going to drink any wine, until I drink new wine with you in my Father's kingdom.'

MATTHEW 26.47–56

JESUS ENCOURAGES HIS DISCIPLES

JOHN 14.1–26

'I am the way, the truth, and the life!' Jesus answered. 'Without me, no one can go to the Father.'

AGREEMENTS AND PROMISES

While they ate, Jesus shared some of his innermost thoughts.

Jesus said to his disciples, 'Don't be worried! Have faith in God and have faith in me. There are many rooms in my Father's house. I wouldn't tell you this, unless it was true. I am going there to prepare a place for each of you. After I have done this, I will come back and take you with me. Then we will be together. You know the way to where I am going.'

Thomas said, 'Lord, we don't even know where you are going! How can we know the way?'

'I am the way, the truth, and the life!' Jesus answered. 'Without me, no one can go to the Father. If you had known me, you would have known the Father. But from now on, you do know him, and you have seen him.'

Philip said, 'Lord, show us the Father. That is all we need.'

Jesus replied:

See also **Exodus**
12.21–34,
Mark 14.13–25,
Luke 22.7–20,
1 Corinthians
11.23–25

Philip, I have been with you for a long time. Don't you know who I am? If you have seen me, you have seen the Father. How can you ask me to show you the Father? Don't you believe that I am one with the Father and that the Father is one with me? What I say isn't said on my own. The Father who lives in me does these things.

Have faith in me when I say that the Father is one with me and that I am one with the Father. Or else have faith in me simply because of the things I do. I tell you for certain that if you have faith in me, you will do the same things that I am doing. You will do even greater things, now that I am going back to the Father. Ask me, and I will do whatever you ask. This way the Son will bring honour to the Father. I will do whatever you ask me to do.

Jesus said to his disciples:

If you love me, you will do as I command. Then I will ask the Father to send you the Holy Spirit who will help you and always be with you. The Spirit will show you what is true. The people of this world cannot accept the Spirit, because they don't see or know him. But you know the Spirit, who is with you and will keep on living in you.

I won't leave you like orphans. I will come back to you. In a little while the people of this world won't be able to see me, but you will see me. And because I live, you will live. Then you will know that I am one with the Father. You will know that you are one with me, and I am one with you. If you love me, you will do what I have said, and my Father will love you. I will also love you and show you what I am like.

The other Judas, not Judas Iscariot, then spoke up and asked, 'Lord, what do you mean by saying that you will show us what you are like, but you will not show the people of this world?'

Jesus replied:

If anyone loves me, they will obey me. Then my Father will love them, and we will come to them and live in them. But anyone who doesn't love me, won't obey me. What they have heard me say doesn't really come from me, but from the Father who sent me.

I have told you these things while I am still with you. But the Holy Spirit will come and help you, because the Father will send the Spirit to take my place. The Spirit will teach you everything and will remind you of what I said while I was with you.

MATTHEW
26.31–35

JESUS PREDICTS THAT PETER WILL DENY KNOWING HIM

Jesus replied, 'I promise you that before a cock crows tonight, you will say three times that you don't know me.'

See also MARK
14.27–3,
LUKE 22.31–34

Jesus said to his disciples, 'During this very night, all of you will reject me, as the Scriptures say,

"I will strike down the shepherd, and the sheep will be scattered."

But after I am raised to life, I will go to Galilee ahead of you.'

Peter spoke up, 'Even if all the others reject you, I never will!'

Jesus replied, 'I promise you that before a cock crows tonight, you will say three times that you don't know me.' But Peter said, 'Even if I have to die with you, I will never say I don't know you.'

All the others said the same thing.

MATTHEW
26.36–46

A PAINFUL PRAYER

'My Father, if it is possible, don't make me suffer by making me drink from this cup. But do what you want, and not what I want.'

Jesus went with his disciples to a place called Gethsemane. When they got there, he told them, 'Sit here while I go over there and pray.'

Jesus took along Peter and the two brothers, James and John. He was very sad and troubled, and he said to them, 'I am so sad that I feel as if I am dying. Stay here and keep awake with me.'

Jesus walked on a little way. Then he knelt with his face to the ground and prayed, 'My Father, if it is possible, don't make me suffer by making me drink from this cup. But do what you want, and not what I want.'

DONATELLO
AGONY IN THE
GARDEN
FLORENCE
1465

See also MARK
14.32–42,
LUKE 22.40–46

He came back and found his disciples sleeping. So he said to Peter, 'Can't any of you stay awake with me for just one hour? Stay awake and pray that you won't be tested. You want to do what is right, but you are weak.'

Again Jesus went to pray and said, 'My Father, if there is no other way, and I must suffer, I will still do what you want.'

Jesus came back and found them sleeping again. They simply could not keep their eyes open. He left them and prayed the same prayer once more.

Finally, Jesus returned to his disciples and said, 'Are you still sleeping and resting? The time has come for the Son of Man to be handed over to sinners. Get up! Let's go. The one who will betray me is already here.'

MATTHEW
26.47–56

Judas had told them beforehand, 'Arrest the man I greet with a kiss.'

FRA ANGELICO
BETRAYAL OF JUDAS
FLORENCE
1450

See also
MATTHEW 10.4,
JOHN 6.70,71,
JOHN 13.2, 18–30,
ACTS 1.16–25,
MARK 14.43–50,
LUKE 22.47–53

☒ JESUS IS ARRESTED

Jesus was still speaking, when Judas the betrayer came up. He was one of the twelve disciples, and a large mob armed with swords and clubs was with him. They had been sent by the chief priests and the nation's leaders. Judas had told them beforehand, 'Arrest the man I greet with a kiss.'

Judas walked right up to Jesus and said, 'Hello, teacher.' Then Judas kissed him.

Jesus replied, 'My friend, why are you here?'

The men grabbed Jesus and arrested him. One of Jesus' followers pulled out a sword. He struck the servant of the high priest and cut off his ear.

But Jesus told him, 'Put your sword away. Anyone who lives by fighting will die by fighting. Don't you know that I could ask my Father, and straight away he would send me more than twelve armies of angels? But then, how could the words of the Scriptures come true, which say that this must happen?'

Jesus said to the mob, 'Why do you come with swords and clubs to arrest me like a criminal? Day after day I sat and taught in the temple, and you didn't arrest me. But all this happened, so that what the prophets wrote would come true.'

All Jesus' disciples left him and ran away.

▶ MATTHEW 27.27–44

MARK
14.53–65

The chief priests and the whole council tried to find someone to accuse Jesus of a crime, so they could put him to death. But they could not find anyone to accuse him.

VIOLENCE AND
WARFARE

See also
MATTHEW
26.57–68,
LUKE 22.7–71,
JOHN 18.12–24

JESUS IS PUT ON TRIAL

Jesus was led off to the high priest. Then the chief priests, the nation's leaders, and the teachers of the Law of Moses all met together. Peter had followed at a distance. And when he reached the courtyard of the high priest's house, he sat down with the guards to warm himself beside a fire.

The chief priests and the whole council tried to find someone to accuse Jesus of a crime, so they could put him to death. But they could not find anyone to accuse him. Many people did tell lies against Jesus, but they did not agree on what they said. Finally, some men stood up and lied about him. They said, 'We heard him say he would tear down this temple that we built. He also claimed that in three days he would build another one without any help.' But even then they did not agree on what they said.

The high priest stood up in the council and asked Jesus, 'Why don't you say something in your own defence? Don't you hear the charges they are making against you?' But Jesus kept quiet and did not say a word. The high priest asked him another question, 'Are you the Messiah, the Son of the glorious God?'

'Yes, I am!' Jesus answered.

'Soon you will see the Son of Man
    sitting at the right side of God All-Powerful,
and coming with the clouds of heaven.'

At once the high priest ripped his robe apart and shouted, 'Why do we need more witnesses? You heard him claim to be God! What is your decision?' They all agreed that he should be put to death.

Some of the people started spitting on Jesus. They blind-folded him, hit him with their fists, and said, 'Tell us who hit you!' Then the guards took charge of Jesus and beat him.

PETER DENIES JESUS

MATTHEW
26.69–75

Peter remembered that Jesus had said, 'Before a cock crows, you will say three times that you don't know me.' Then Peter went out and cried hard.

See also MARK
14.66–72,
LUKE 22.55–62,
JOHN 18.16–27

While Peter was sitting out in the courtyard, a servant girl came up to him and said, 'You were with Jesus from Galilee.'

But in front of everyone Peter said, 'That isn't so! I don't know what you are talking about!'

When Peter had gone out to the gate, another servant girl saw him and said to some people there, 'This man was with Jesus from Nazareth.'

Again Peter denied it, and this time he swore, 'I don't even know that man!'

A little while later some people standing there walked over to Peter and said, 'We know that you are one of them. We can tell it because you talk like someone from Galilee.'

Peter began to curse and swear, 'I don't know that man!'

At once a cock crowed, and Peter remembered that Jesus had said, 'Before a cock crows, you will say three times that you don't know me.' Then Peter went out and cried hard.

JESUS BEFORE PILATE

MARK 15.1–15

Jesus' enemies wanted to have him executed, but they didn't have the authority to order his death. The best way of achieving their aim was to convince the Roman authorities that Jesus was a threat to their rule.

Pilate wanted to please the crowd. So he set Barabbas free. Then he ordered his soldiers to beat Jesus with a whip and nail him to a cross.

Early the next morning the chief priests, the nation's leaders, and the teachers of the Law of Moses met together with the whole Jewish council. They tied up Jesus and led him off to Pilate.

He asked Jesus, 'Are you the king of the Jews?'

'Those are your words,' Jesus answered.

CORREGGIO
CHRIST PRESENTED
TO THE PEOPLE
THE NATIONAL
GALLERY
LONDON
1530

VIOLENCE AND
WARFARE

See also
MATTHEW
27.11–26,
LUKE 23.18–25,
JOHN 18.29–19.16

The chief priests brought many charges against Jesus. Then Pilate questioned him again, 'Don't you have anything to say? Don't you hear what crimes they say you have done?' But Jesus did not answer, and Pilate was amazed.

During Passover, Pilate always freed one prisoner chosen by the people. And at that time there was a prisoner named Barabbas. He and some others had been arrested for murder during a riot. The crowd now came and asked Pilate to set a prisoner free, just as he usually did.

Pilate asked them, 'Do you want me to free the king of the Jews?' Pilate knew that the chief priests had brought Jesus to him because they were jealous.

But the chief priests told the crowd to ask Pilate to free Barabbas.

Then Pilate asked the crowd, 'What do you want me to do with this man you say is the king of the Jews?'

They yelled, 'Nail him to a cross!'

Pilate asked, 'But what crime has he done?'

'Nail him to a cross!' they yelled even louder.

Pilate wanted to please the crowd. So he set Barabbas free. Then he ordered his soldiers to beat Jesus with a whip and nail him to a cross.

MATTHEW
27.27–44

Above his head they
put a sign that told
why he was nailed
there. It read, 'This
is Jesus, the King of
the Jews.'

JESUS IS EXECUTED

The governor's soldiers led Jesus into the fortress and brought together the rest of the troops. They stripped off Jesus' clothes and put a scarlet robe on him. They made a crown out of thorn branches and placed it on his head, and they put a stick in his right hand. The soldiers knelt down and pretended to worship him. They made fun of him and shouted, 'Hey, you king of the Jews!' Then they spat on him. They took the stick from him and beat him on the head with it.

When the soldiers had finished making fun of Jesus, they took off the robe. They put his own clothes back on him and

VIOLENCE AND WARFARE

See also
MARK 15.16–32,
LUKE 23.33–43,
JOHN 9.17–24

led him off to be nailed to a cross. On the way they met a man from Cyrene named Simon, and they forced him to carry Jesus' cross.

They came to a place named Golgotha, which means 'Place of a Skull'. There they gave Jesus some wine mixed with a drug to ease the pain. But when Jesus tasted what it was, he refused to drink it.

The soldiers nailed Jesus to a cross and gambled to see who would get his clothes. Then they sat down to guard him. Above his head they put a sign that told why he was nailed there. It read, 'This is Jesus, the King of the Jews.' The soldiers also nailed two criminals on crosses, one to the right of Jesus and the other to his left.

People who passed by said terrible things about Jesus. They shook their heads and shouted, 'So you're the one who claimed you could tear down the temple and build it again in three days! If you are God's Son, save yourself and come down from the cross!'

The chief priests, the leaders, and the teachers of the Law of Moses also made fun of Jesus. They said, 'He saved others, but he can't save himself. If he is the king of Israel, he should come down from the cross! Then we will believe him. He trusted God, so let God save him, if he wants to. He even said he was God's Son.' The two criminals also said cruel things to Jesus.

MATTHEW 27.45–56

THE DEATH OF JESUS

MATTHEW
27.45–56

The officer and the soldiers guarding Jesus felt the earthquake and saw everything else that

At midday the sky turned dark and stayed that way until three o'clock. Then about that time Jesus shouted, 'Eli, Eli, lema sabachthani?' which means, 'My God, my God, why have you deserted me?'

Some of the people standing there heard Jesus and said, 'He's calling for Elijah.' One of them at once ran and grabbed

happened. They
were frightened and
said, 'This man
really was God's
Son!'

**MIRACLES AND
WONDERS
VIOLENCE AND
WARFARE**

See also PSALM 22,
MARK 15.33–41,
LUKE 23.44–49

a sponge. He soaked it in wine, then put it on a stick and held it up to Jesus.

Others said, 'Wait! Let's see if Elijah will come and save him.' Once again Jesus shouted, and then he died.

At once the curtain in the temple was torn in two from top to bottom. The earth shook, and rocks split apart. Graves opened, and many of God's people were raised to life. Then after Jesus had risen to life, they came out of their graves and went into the holy city, where they were seen by many people.

The officer and the soldiers guarding Jesus felt the earthquake and saw everything else that happened. They were frightened and said, 'This man really was God's Son!'

Many women had come with Jesus from Galilee to be of help to him, and they were there, looking on at a distance. Mary Magdalene, Mary the mother of James and Joseph, and the mother of James and John were some of these women.

▶ MARK 16.1–8

JOHN
19.31–42

JESUS' BODY IS PLACED IN A TOMB

It was a desolate and frightening time for all the disciples, but even so, some were brave enough to risk further trouble by trying to restore some measure of dignity to their dead leader.

Joseph from
Arimathea was one
of Jesus' disciples . . .
He asked Pilate to
let him have Jesus'
body. Pilate gave
him permission, and
Joseph took it down
from the cross.

The next day would be both a Sabbath and the Passover. It was a special day for the Jewish people, and they did not want the bodies to stay on the crosses during that day. So they asked Pilate to break the men's legs and take their bodies down. The soldiers first broke the legs of the other two men who were nailed there. But when they came to Jesus, they saw that he was already dead, and they did not break his legs.

One of the soldiers stuck his spear into Jesus' side, and blood and water came out. We know this is true, because it was told by someone who saw it happen. Now you can have faith too. All this happened so that the Scriptures would come true,

BUSATI
THE ENTOMBMENT
THE NATIONAL
GALLERY
LONDON
1512

See also
MATTHEW
27.57–61,
MARK 15.42–47,
LUKE 23.50–56

which say, 'No bone of his body will be broken' and, 'They will see the one in whose side they stuck a spear.'

Joseph from Arimathea was one of Jesus' disciples. He had kept it secret though, because he was afraid of the Jewish leaders. But now he asked Pilate to let him have Jesus' body. Pilate gave him permission, and Joseph took it down from the cross.

Nicodemus also came with about thirty kilogrammes of spices made from myrrh and aloes. This was the same Nicodemus who had visited Jesus one night. The two men wrapped the body in a linen cloth, together with the spices, which was how the Jewish people buried their dead. In the place where Jesus had been nailed to a cross, there was a garden with a tomb that had never been used. The tomb was nearby, and since it was the time to prepare for the Sabbath, they were in a hurry to put Jesus' body there.

Jesus' resurrection

MARK 16.1–8

CONFUSION IN THE EARLY MORNING

'You are looking for Jesus from Nazareth, who was nailed to a cross. God has raised him to life, and he isn't here.'

MOORE
THE THREE MARIES
1981

MIRACLES AND WONDERS

See also MATTHEW 28.1–8,
LUKE 24.1–10,
JOHN 20.1–18

After the Sabbath, Mary Magdalene, Salome, and Mary the mother of James bought some spices to put on Jesus' body. Very early on Sunday morning, just as the sun was coming up, they went to the tomb. On their way, they were asking one another, 'Who will roll the stone away from the entrance for us?' But when they looked, they saw that the stone had already been rolled away. And it was a huge stone!

The women went into the tomb, and on the right side they saw a young man in a white robe sitting there. They were alarmed.

The man said, 'Don't be alarmed! You are looking for Jesus from Nazareth, who was nailed to a cross. God has raised him to life, and he isn't here. You can see the place where they put his body. Now go and tell his disciples, and especially Peter, that he will go ahead of you to Galilee. You will see him there, just as he told you.'

When the women ran from the tomb, they were confused and shaking all over. They were too afraid to tell anyone what had happened.

 MATTHEW 28.16–20

JOHN 20.1–18

THE EMPTY TOMB

Jesus told her, 'Don't hold on to me! I have not yet gone to the Father.

On Sunday morning while it was still dark, Mary Magdalene went to the tomb and saw that the stone had been rolled away from the entrance. She ran to Simon Peter and to Jesus' favourite disciple and said, 'They have taken the Lord from the

But tell my disciples that I am going to the one who is my Father and my God, as well as your Father and your God.'

GIOTTO
NOLI ME TANGERE
CAPPELLA
SCROVEGNI
PADUA
1306

MIRACLES AND WONDERS

See also
MATTHEW 28.1–8,
MARK 16.1–8,
LUKE 24.1–10

tomb! We don't know where they have put him.'

Peter and the other disciple set off for the tomb. They ran side by side, until the other disciple ran faster than Peter and got there first. He bent over and saw the strips of linen cloth lying inside the tomb, but he did not go in.

When Simon Peter got there, he went into the tomb and saw the strips of cloth. He also saw the piece of cloth that had been used to cover Jesus' face. It was rolled up and in a place by itself. The disciple who got there first then went into the tomb, and when he saw it, he believed. At that time Peter and the other disciple did not know that the Scriptures said Jesus would rise to life. So the two of them went back to the other disciples.

Mary Magdalene stood crying outside the tomb. She was still weeping, when she stooped down and saw two angels inside. They were dressed in white and were sitting where Jesus' body had been. One was at the head and the other was at the foot. The angels asked Mary, 'Why are you crying?'

She answered, 'They have taken away my Lord's body! I don't know where they have put him.'

As soon as Mary said this, she turned around and saw Jesus standing there. But she did not know who he was. Jesus asked her, 'Why are you crying? Who are you looking for?'

She thought he was the gardener and said, 'Sir, if you have taken his body away, please tell me, so I can go and get him.'

Then Jesus said to her, 'Mary!'

She turned and said to him, 'Rabboni.' The Aramaic word 'Rabboni' means 'Teacher'.

Jesus told her, 'Don't hold on to me! I have not yet gone to the Father. But tell my disciples that I am going to the one who is my Father and my God, as well as your Father and your God.' Mary Magdalene then went and told the disciples that she had seen the Lord. She also told them what he had said to her.

*They said to the
soldiers, 'Tell
everyone that Jesus'
disciples came
during the night
and stole his body
while you were
asleep.'*

THE GUARD'S REPORT

While the women were on their way, some soldiers who had been guarding the tomb went into the city. They told the chief priests everything that had happened. So the chief priests met with the leaders and decided to bribe the soldiers with a lot of money. They said to the soldiers, 'Tell everyone that Jesus' disciples came during the night and stole his body while you were asleep. If the governor hears about this, we will talk to him. You won't have anything to worry about.' The soldiers took the money and did what they were told. Some of the Jewish people still tell each other this story.

JOHN
20.24–29

*'First, I must see the
nail scars in his
hands and touch
them with my
finger... I won't
believe unless I do
this!'*

MIRACLES AND
WONDERS

THOMAS MEETS THE RISEN JESUS

Although Thomas the Twin was one of the twelve disciples, he wasn't with the others when Jesus appeared to them. So they told him, 'We have seen the Lord!'

But Thomas said, 'First, I must see the nail scars in his hands and touch them with my finger. I must put my hand where the spear went into his side. I won't believe unless I do this!'

A week later the disciples were together again. This time, Thomas was with them. Jesus came in while the doors were still locked and stood in the middle of the group. He greeted his disciples and said to Thomas, 'Put your finger here and look at my hands! Put your hand into my side. Stop doubting and have faith!'

Thomas replied, 'You are my Lord and my God!'

Jesus said, 'Thomas, do you have faith because you have seen me? The people who have faith in me without seeing me are the ones who are really blessed!'

A SURPRISE MEETING

Jesus then explained
everything written
about himself in the
Scriptures,
beginning with the
Law of Moses and
the Books of the
Prophets.

ORSI
ON THE WAY TO
EMMAUS
NATIONAL GALLERY
LONDON
1575

FOOD AND DRINK
MIRACLES AND
WONDERS

That same day two of Jesus' disciples were going to the village of Emmaus, which was about eleven kilometres from Jerusalem. As they were talking and thinking about what had happened, Jesus came near and started walking along beside them. But they did not know who he was.

Jesus asked them, 'What were you talking about as you walked along?'

The two of them stood there looking sad and gloomy. Then the one named Cleopas asked Jesus, 'Are you the only person from Jerusalem who didn't know what was happening there these last few days?'

'What do you mean?' Jesus asked.

They answered:

Those things that happened to Jesus from Nazareth. By what he did and said he showed that he was a powerful prophet, who pleased God and all the people. Then the chief priests and our leaders had him arrested and sentenced to die on a cross. We had hoped that he would be the one to set Israel free! But it has already been three days since all this happened.

Some women in our group surprised us. They had gone to the tomb early in the morning, but did not find the body of Jesus. They came back, saying that they had seen a vision of angels who told them that he is alive. Some men from our group went to the tomb and found it just as the women had said. But they didn't see Jesus either.

Then Jesus asked the two disciples, 'Why can't you understand? How can you be so slow to believe all that the prophets said? Didn't you know that the Messiah would have to suffer before he was given his glory?' Jesus then explained everything written about himself in the Scriptures, beginning with the Law of Moses and the Books of the Prophets.

When the two of them came near the village where they were going, Jesus seemed to be going further. They begged him, 'Stay with us! It's already late, and the sun is going down.'

So Jesus went into the house to stay with them.

After Jesus sat down to eat, he took some bread. He blessed it and broke it. Then he gave it to them. At once they knew who he was, but he disappeared. They said to each other, 'When he talked with us along the road and explained the Scriptures to us, didn't it warm our hearts?' So they got up at once and returned to Jerusalem.

The two disciples found the eleven apostles and the others gathered together. And they learnt from the group that the Lord was really alive and had appeared to Peter. Then the disciples from Emmaus told what happened on the road and how they knew he was the Lord when he broke the bread.

JOHN 21.1–14

DOWN BY THE LAKE

Early the next morning Jesus stood on the shore, but the disciples did not realize who he was.

BIRDS AND ANIMALS
FOOD AND DRINK

Jesus later appeared to his disciples along the shore of Lake Tiberias. Simon Peter, Thomas the Twin, Nathanael from Cana in Galilee, and the brothers James and John, were there, together with two other disciples. Simon Peter said, 'I'm going fishing!'

The others said, 'We will go with you.' They went out in their boat. But they didn't catch a thing that night.

Early the next morning Jesus stood on the shore, but the disciples did not realize who he was. Jesus shouted, 'Friends, have you caught anything?'

'No!' they answered.

So he told them, 'Let your net down on the right side of your boat, and you will catch some fish.'

They did, and the net was so full of fish that they could not drag it up into the boat.

Jesus' favourite disciple told Peter, 'It's the Lord!' When Simon heard that it was the Lord, he put on the clothes that he had taken off while he was working. Then he jumped into the water. The boat was only about a hundred metres from shore. So the other disciples stayed in the boat and dragged in the net full of fish.

When the disciples got out of the boat, they saw some bread and a charcoal fire with fish on it. Jesus told his disciples, 'Bring some of the fish you have just caught.' Simon Peter got back into the boat and dragged the net to shore. In it were one hundred and fifty-three large fish, but still the net did not rip.

Jesus said, 'Come and eat!' But none of the disciples dared ask who he was. They knew he was the Lord. Jesus took the bread in his hands and gave some of it to his disciples. He did the same with the fish. This was the third time that Jesus appeared to his disciples after he was raised from death.

PETER'S SECOND CHANCE

JOHN
21.15–22

Peter and some of the disciples went fishing. In the morning, after they had passed the night without catching a single fish, Jesus appeared and told them to cast their nets once more. This time they caught lots of fish. When they reached the shore Jesus had prepared breakfast for them all.

Jesus answered, 'What is it to you, if I want him to live until I return? You must follow me.'

RUBENS
CHRIST'S CHARGE
TO PETER
WALLACE
COLLECTION
LONDON
1616

FOOD AND DRINK

When Jesus and his disciples had finished eating, he asked, 'Simon son of John, do you love me more than the others do?'

Simon Peter answered, 'Yes, Lord, you know I do!'

'Then feed my lambs,' Jesus said. Jesus asked a second time, 'Simon son of John, do you love me?'

Peter answered, 'Yes, Lord, you know I love you!'

'Then take care of my sheep,' Jesus told him.

Jesus asked a third time, 'Simon son of John, do you love me?'

Peter was hurt because Jesus had asked him three times if he loved him. So he told Jesus, 'Lord, you know everything. You know I love you.'

Jesus replied, 'Feed my sheep. I tell you for certain that when you were a young man, you dressed yourself and went wherever you wanted to go. But when you are old, you will hold out your hands. Then others will tie your belt around you and lead you where you don't want to go.'

Jesus said this to tell how Peter would die and bring honour to God. Then he said to Peter, 'Follow me!'

Peter turned and saw Jesus' favourite disciple following them. He was the same one who had sat next to Jesus at the meal and had asked, 'Lord, who is going to betray you?' When Peter saw that disciple, he asked Jesus, 'Lord, what about him?'

Jesus answered, 'What is it to you, if I want him to live until I return? You must follow me.'

JESUS SAYS GOODBYE TO HIS DISCIPLES

Matthew
28.16–20

I have been given all
authority in heaven
and on earth!

Vrelant
The apostolic
mission
J. *Paul Getty*
Museum
Los Angeles
c. 1460

Agreements and
Promises

Jesus' eleven disciples went to a mountain in Galilee, where Jesus had told them to meet him. They saw him and worshipped him, but some of them doubted.

Jesus came to them and said:

I have been given all authority in heaven and on earth! Go to the people of all nations and make them my disciples. Baptize them in the name of the Father, the Son, and the Holy Spirit, and teach them to do everything I have told you. I will be with you always, even until the end of the world.

▶ Acts 1.4–11

THE GOSPELS   JESUS' RESURRECTION   **267**

THE EARLY CHURCH

After he came back to life, Jesus appeared to his disciples on a number of occasions, and he told them to share the story of his life with everyone in the world. The book of Acts shows how this enormous task got started.

THE GOOD NEWS SPREADS

Acts 1.4–11

JESUS IS TAKEN UP TO HEAVEN

But the Holy Spirit will come upon you and give you power.

W Blake
The Ascension
California
1805

Agreements and Promises

See also **Matthew 3.11, John 14.26, Acts 2.1–21, 11.16–17, Romans 8, Matthew 28.16–20**

While he was still with them, he said:

Don't leave Jerusalem yet. Wait here for the Father to give you the Holy Spirit, just as I told you he has promised to do. John baptized with water, but in a few days you will be baptized with the Holy Spirit.

While the apostles were still with Jesus, they asked him, 'Lord, are you now going to give Israel its own king again?'

Jesus said to them, 'You don't need to know the time of those events that only the Father controls. But the Holy Spirit will come upon you and give you power. Then you will tell everyone about me in Jerusalem, in all Judea, in Samaria, and everywhere in the world.' After Jesus had said this and while they were watching, he was taken up into a cloud. They could not see him, but as he went up, they kept looking up into the sky.

Suddenly two men dressed in white clothes were standing there beside them. They said, 'Why are you men from Galilee standing here and looking up into the sky? Jesus has been taken to heaven. But he will come back in the same way that you have seen him go.'

Acts 2.1–21

THE HOLY SPIRIT TAKES CONTROL

When Jesus left them, the disciples returned to Jerusalem, where they prayed and waited for the Holy Spirit to come.

'When the last days come, I will give my Spirit to everyone.'

VAN DYCK
THE DESCENT OF THE HOLY SPIRIT
SANSSOUCI,
POTSDAM
1620

AGREEMENTS AND PROMISES
MIRACLES AND WONDERS

See also **JOHN** 14.26;
ACTS 1.4–11; 4.31;
11.16,17;
ROMANS 8;
GALATIANS 5.22–25

On the day of Pentecost all the Lord's followers were together in one place. Suddenly there was a noise from heaven like the sound of a mighty wind! It filled the house where they were meeting. Then they saw what looked like fiery tongues moving in all directions, and a tongue came and settled on each person there. The Holy Spirit took control of everyone, and they began speaking whatever languages the Spirit let them speak.

Many religious Jews from every country in the world were living in Jerusalem. And when they heard this noise, a crowd gathered. But they were surprised, because they were hearing everything in their own languages. They were excited and amazed, and said:

Don't all these who are speaking come from Galilee? Then why do we hear them speaking our very own languages? Some of us are from Parthia, Media, and Elam. Others are from Mesopotamia, Judea, Cappadocia, Pontus, Asia, Phrygia, Pamphylia, Egypt, parts of Libya near Cyrene, Rome, Crete, and Arabia. Some of us were born Jews, and others of us have chosen to be Jews. Yet we all hear them using our own languages to tell the wonderful things God has done.

Everyone was excited and confused. Some of them even kept asking each other, 'What does all this mean?'

Others made fun of the Lord's followers and said, 'They are drunk.'

Peter stood with the eleven apostles and spoke in a loud and clear voice to the crowd:

Friends and everyone else living in Jerusalem, listen carefully to what I have to say! You are wrong to think that these people are drunk. After all, it is only nine o'clock in

the morning. But this is what God led the prophet Joel to
say,

'When the last days come, I will give my Spirit to everyone.
Your sons and daughters will prophesy.

Your young men will see visions, and your old men will
have dreams. In those days I will give my Spirit to my
servants, both men and women, and they will prophesy.

I will perform miracles in the sky above and wonders on
the earth below.

There will be blood and fire and clouds of smoke.

The sun will turn dark, and the moon will be as red as
blood before the great and wonderful day of the Lord
appears.

Then the Lord will save everyone who asks for his help.'

> ACTS 2.22–35

PETER'S FIRST MESSAGE

*'Jesus was taken up
to sit at the right
side of God, and he
was given the Holy
Spirit, just as the
Father had
promised. Jesus is
also the one who
has given the Spirit
to us, and that is
what you are now
seeing and hearing.'*

Now, listen to what I have to say about Jesus from Nazareth.
God proved that he sent Jesus to you by having him perform
miracles, wonders, and signs. All of you know this. God had
already planned and decided that Jesus would be handed
over to you. So you took him and had evil men put him to
death on a cross. But God set him free from death and raised
him to life. Death could not hold him in its power. What
David said are really the words of Jesus,

'I always see the Lord near me, and I will not be afraid
with him at my right side.

Because of this, my words will be joyful, my heart will be
glad, and I will live in hope.

The Lord won't leave me in the grave. I am his holy one,
and he won't let my body decay.

He has shown me the path to life, and he makes me glad
by being near me.'

My friends, it is right for me to speak to you about our ancestor David. He died and was buried, and his tomb is still here. But David was a prophet, and he knew that God had made a promise he would not break. He had told David that someone from his own family would some day be king.

David knew this would happen, and so he told us that Christ would be raised to life. He said that God would not leave him in the grave or let his body decay. All of us can tell you that God has raised Jesus to life!

Jesus was taken up to sit at the right side of God, and he was given the Holy Spirit, just as the Father had promised. Jesus is also the one who has given the Spirit to us, and that is what you are now seeing and hearing.

David didn't go up to heaven. So he wasn't talking about himself when he said, 'The Lord told my Lord to sit at his right side, until he made my Lord's enemies into a footstool for him.'

⟩ Acts 2.36–47

Acts 2.36–47

'Turn back to God! Be baptized in the name of Jesus Christ, so that your sins will be forgiven. Then you will be given the Holy Spirit.'

Food and drink
Miracles and
wonders

LIFE IN THE EARLY CHURCH

'Everyone in Israel should then know for certain that God has made Jesus both Lord and Christ, even though you put him to death on a cross.'

When the people heard this, they were very upset. They asked Peter and the other apostles, 'Friends, what shall we do?'

Peter said, 'Turn back to God! Be baptized in the name of Jesus Christ, so that your sins will be forgiven. Then you will be given the Holy Spirit. This promise is for you and your children. It is for everyone our Lord God will choose, no matter where they live.'

Peter told them many other things as well. Then he said, 'I beg you to save yourselves from what will happen to all these evil people.' On that day about three thousand believed his message and were baptized. They spent their time learning from the apostles, and they were like family to each other. They also broke bread and prayed together.

Everyone was amazed by the many miracles and wonders that the apostles performed. All the Lord's followers often met together, and they shared everything they had. They would sell their property and possessions and give the money to whoever needed it. Day after day they met together in the temple. They broke bread together in different homes and shared their food happily and freely, while praising God. Everyone liked them, and each day the Lord added to their group others who were being saved.

▶ REVELATION 21 AND 22

ACTS 3.1–10

HEALTH IS BETTER THAN MONEY

'In the name of Jesus Christ from Nazareth, get up and start walking.'

POUSSIN
ST PETER AND ST JAMES CURE THE LAME MAN
METROPOLITAN MUSEUM OF ART
NEW YORK
1655

MIRACLES AND WONDERS

The time of prayer was about three o'clock in the afternoon, and Peter and John were going into the temple. A man who had been born lame was being carried to the temple door. Each day he was placed beside this door, known as the Beautiful Gate. He sat there and begged from the people who were going in.

The man saw Peter and John entering the temple, and he asked them for money. But they looked straight at him and said, 'Look up at us!'

The man stared at them and thought he was going to get something. But Peter said, 'I don't have any silver or gold! But I will give you what I do have. In the name of Jesus Christ from Nazareth, get up and start walking.' Peter then took him by the right hand and helped him up.

At once the man's feet and ankles became strong, and he jumped up and started walking. He went with Peter and John into the temple, walking and jumping and praising God. Everyone saw him walking around and praising God. They knew that he was the beggar who had been lying beside the Beautiful Gate, and they were completely surprised. They could not imagine what had happened to the man.

PETER AND JOHN EXPLAIN THEIR ACTIONS

'This man is standing here completely well because of the power of Jesus Christ from Nazareth.'

See also
MATTHEW 3.11,
MATTHEW 4.1,
LUKE 4.18,
JOHN 14.26,
ACTS 1.4–11,
2.1–21, 11.16,17,
ROMANS 8,
GALATIANS
5.22–25,
MARK 14.53–65

The apostles were still talking to the people, when some priests, the captain of the temple guard, and some Sadducees arrived. These men were angry because the apostles were teaching the people that the dead would be raised from death, just as Jesus had been raised from death. It was already late in the afternoon, and they arrested Peter and John and put them in jail for the night. But a lot of people who had heard the message believed it. So by now there were about five thousand followers of the Lord.

The next morning the leaders, the elders, and the teachers of the Law of Moses met in Jerusalem. The high priest Annas was there, as well as Caiaphas, John, Alexander, and other members of the high priest's family. They brought in Peter and John and made them stand in the middle while they questioned them. They asked, 'By what power and in whose name have you done this?'

Peter was filled with the Holy Spirit and told the nation's leaders and the elders:

You are questioning us today about a kind deed in which a crippled man was healed. But there is something we must tell you and everyone else in Israel. This man is standing here completely well because of the power of Jesus Christ from Nazareth. You put Jesus to death on a cross, but God raised him to life. He is the stone that you builders thought was worthless, and now he is the most important stone of all. Only Jesus has the power to save! His name is the only one in all the world that can save anyone.

The officials were amazed to see how brave Peter and John were, and they knew that these two apostles were only ordinary men and not well educated. The officials were certain that these men had been with Jesus. But they could not deny what had happened. The man who had been healed was standing there with the apostles.

The officials commanded them to leave the council room. Then the officials said to each other, 'What can we do with these men? Everyone in Jerusalem knows about this miracle, and we cannot say it didn't happen. But to keep this thing from spreading, we will warn them never again to speak to anyone about the name of Jesus.' So they called the two apostles back in and told them that they must never, for any reason, teach anything about the name of Jesus.

Peter and John answered, 'Do you think God wants us to obey you or to obey him? We cannot keep quiet about what we have seen and heard.'

The officials could not find any reason to punish Peter and John. So they threatened them and let them go. The man who was healed by this miracle was more than forty years old, and everyone was praising God for what had happened.

ACTS 4.32–37

THE DISCIPLES SHARE THEIR POSSESSIONS

The group of followers all felt the same way about everything. None of them claimed that their possessions were their own, and they shared everything they had with each other.

The group of followers all felt the same way about everything. None of them claimed that their possessions were their own, and they shared everything they had with each other. In a powerful way the apostles told everyone that the Lord Jesus was now alive. God greatly blessed his followers, and no one went in need of anything. Everyone who owned land or houses would sell them and bring the money to the apostles. Then they would give the money to anyone who needed it.

Joseph was one of the followers who had sold a piece of property and brought the money to the apostles. He was a Levite from Cyprus, and the apostles called him Barnabas, which means 'one who encourages others'.

UNDER ARREST

The apostles performed many miracles and wonders among the people.

MARRIAGE AND FAMILY
MIRACLES AND WONDERS

The apostles performed many miracles and wonders among the people. All the Lord's followers often met in the part of the temple known as Solomon's Porch. No one outside their group dared join them, even though everyone liked them very much.

Many men and women started having faith in the Lord. Then sick people were brought out to the road and placed on stretchers and mats. It was hoped that Peter would walk by, and his shadow would fall on them and heal them. A lot of people living in the towns near Jerusalem brought those who were sick or troubled by evil spirits, and they were all healed.

The high priest and all the other Sadducees who were with him became jealous. They arrested the apostles and put them in the city jail. But that night an angel from the Lord opened the doors of the jail and led the apostles out. The angel said, 'Go to the temple and tell the people everything about this new life.' So they went into the temple before sunrise and started teaching.

The high priest and his men called together their council, which included all Israel's leaders. Then they ordered the apostles to be brought to them from the jail. The temple police who were sent to the jail did not find the apostles. They returned and said, 'We found the jail locked tight and the guards standing at the doors. But when we opened the doors and went in, we didn't find anyone there.' The captain of the temple police and the chief priests listened to their report, but they did not know what to think about it.

Just then someone came in and said, 'Now those men you put in jail are in the temple, teaching the people!' The captain went with some of the temple police and brought the apostles back. But they did not use force. They were afraid that the people might start throwing stones at them.

RESOLVING PRACTICAL PROBLEMS

The high priest and the council questioned the apostles. Some of the leaders wanted to execute them, but a wise adviser spoke against this. In the end they decided to release them, but not before they had given them a severe beating and warned them to stop talking about Jesus. Despite this, the disciples carried on speaking about him.

God's message spread, and many more people in Jerusalem became followers. Even a large number of priests put their faith in the Lord.

A lot of people were now becoming followers of the Lord. But some of the ones who spoke Greek started complaining about the ones who spoke Aramaic. They complained that the Greek-speaking widows were not given their share when the food supplies were handed out each day.

The twelve apostles called the whole group of followers together and said, 'We should not give up preaching God's message in order to serve at tables. My friends, choose seven men who are respected and wise and filled with God's Spirit. We will put them in charge of these things. We can spend our time praying and serving God by preaching.'

This suggestion pleased everyone, and they began by choosing Stephen. He had great faith and was filled with the Holy Spirit. Then they chose Philip, Prochorus, Nicanor, Timon, Parmenas, and also Nicolaus, who worshipped with the Jewish people in Antioch. These men were brought to the apostles. Then the apostles prayed and placed their hands on the men to show that they had been chosen to do this work. God's message spread, and many more people in Jerusalem became followers. Even a large number of priests put their faith in the Lord.

STEPHEN IS STONED TO DEATH

God gave Stephen the power to perform great miracles and wonders among the people. But some Jews from Cyrene and Alexandria were members of a group who called themselves 'Free Men'. They started arguing with Stephen. Some others from Cilicia and Asia also argued with him.

They turned the people and their leaders and the teachers of the Law of Moses against Stephen. Then they all grabbed Stephen and dragged him in front of the council.

The high priest asked Stephen, 'Are they telling the truth about you?'

Stephen answered:

Friends, listen to me. Our glorious God appeared to our ancestor Abraham while he was still in Mesopotamia, before he had moved to Haran. God told him, 'Leave your country and your relatives and go to a land that I will show you.' Then Abraham left the land of the Chaldeans and settled in Haran.

After his father died, Abraham came and settled in this land where you now live. God didn't give him any part of it, not even a square metre. But God did promise to give it to him and his family for ever, even though Abraham didn't have any children.

God said that Abraham's descendants would live for a while in a foreign land. There they would be slaves and would be ill-treated four hundred years. But he also said, 'I will punish the nation that makes them slaves. Then later they will come and worship me in this place.' God said to Abraham, 'Every son in each family must be circumcised to show that you have kept your agreement with me.' So when Isaac was eight days old, Abraham circumcised him. Later, Isaac circumcised his son Jacob, and Jacob circumcised his twelve sons. These men were our ancestors.

Joseph was also one of our famous ancestors. His brothers were jealous of him and sold him as a slave to be taken to Egypt. But God was with him and rescued him from all his troubles. God made him so wise that the Egyptian king Pharaoh thought highly of him. Pharaoh even made Joseph governor over Egypt and put him in charge of everything he owned.

Joseph sent for his father and his relatives. In all, there were seventy-five of them. His father went to Egypt and died there, just as our ancestors did.

Finally, the time came for God to do what he had promised Abraham. By then the number of our people in Egypt had greatly increased.

During this time Moses was born. He was a very beautiful child, and for three months his parents took care of him in their home.

Moses is the one who told the people of Israel, 'God will choose one of your people to be a prophet, just as he chose me.'

But our ancestors refused to obey Moses. They rejected him and wanted to go back to Egypt.

God turned his back on his people and left them. Then they worshipped the stars in the sky, just as it says in the Book of the Prophets, 'People of Israel, you didn't offer sacrifices and offerings to me during those forty years in the desert. Instead, you carried the tent where the god Molech is worshipped, and you took along the star of your god Rephan. You made those idols and worshipped them. So now I will have you carried off beyond Babylonia.'

You stubborn and hardheaded people! You are always fighting against the Holy Spirit, just as your ancestors did.

When the council members heard Stephen's speech, they were angry and furious. But Stephen was filled with the Holy Spirit. He looked towards heaven, where he saw our glorious God and Jesus standing at his right side. Then Stephen said, 'I see heaven open and the Son of Man standing at the right side of God!'

The council members shouted and covered their ears. At once they all attacked Stephen and dragged him out of the city. Then they started throwing stones at him. The men who had brought charges against him put their coats at the feet of a young man named Saul.

As Stephen was being stoned to death, he called out, 'Lord Jesus, please welcome me!' He knelt down and shouted, 'Lord, don't blame them for what they have done.' Then he died.

Saul approved the stoning of Stephen. Some faithful

followers of the Lord buried Stephen and mourned very much for him.

At that time the church in Jerusalem suffered terribly. All the Lord's followers, except the apostles, were scattered everywhere in Judea and Samaria.

ACTS 8.26–40

ENCOUNTER IN THE DESERT

One of those who left Jerusalem was a man called Philip who went to Samaria, telling people about Jesus, healing them and performing miracles. Some of the Samaritans accepted his message and received God's Holy Spirit.

So Philip began at this place in the Scriptures and explained the good news about Jesus.

MIRACLES AND
WONDERS
TRAVEL AND
TRANSPORT

The Lord's angel said to Philip, 'Go south along the desert road that leads from Jerusalem to Gaza.' So Philip left.

An important Ethiopian official happened to be going along that road in his chariot. He was the chief treasurer for Candace, the Queen of Ethiopia. The official had gone to Jerusalem to worship and was now on his way home. He was sitting in his chariot, reading the book of the prophet Isaiah.

The Spirit told Philip to catch up with the chariot. Philip ran up close and heard the man reading aloud from the book of Isaiah. Philip asked him, 'Do you understand what you are reading?' The official answered, 'How can I understand unless someone helps me?' He then invited Philip to come up and sit beside him.

The man was reading the passage that said,
'He was led like a sheep on its way to be killed.
He was silent as a lamb whose wool is being cut off, and he did not say a word.
He was treated like a nobody and did not receive a fair trial.
How can he have children, if his life is snatched away?'

The official said to Philip, 'Tell me, was the prophet talking about himself or about someone else?'

So Philip began at this place in the Scriptures and explained the good news about Jesus. As they were going along the road, they came to a place where there was some water. The official said, 'Look! Here is some water. Why can't I be baptized?' He ordered the chariot to stop. Then they both went down into the water, and Philip baptized him.

After they had come out of the water, the Lord's Spirit took Philip away. The official never saw him again, but he was very happy as he went on his way.

Philip later appeared in Azotus. He went from town to town, all the way to Caesarea, telling people about Jesus.

ACTS 9.1–9

SAUL'S DRAMATIC MEETING WITH JESUS

The followers of Jesus had many enemies, but none was more aggressive than a Pharisee called Saul. He seemed to be on a one man mission to destroy the new religion.

He fell to the ground and heard a voice that said, 'Saul! Saul! Why are you so cruel to me?'

CARAVAGGIO
CONVERSION OF ST
PAUL
ROME
1600

DREAMS AND
VISIONS
TRAVEL AND
TRANSPORT

Saul kept on threatening to kill the Lord's followers. He even went to the high priest and asked for letters to the Jewish leaders in Damascus. He did this because he wanted to arrest and take to Jerusalem any man or woman who had accepted the Lord's Way. When Saul had almost reached Damascus, a bright light from heaven suddenly flashed around him. He fell to the ground and heard a voice that said, 'Saul! Saul! Why are you so cruel to me?'

'Who are you?' Saul asked.

'I am Jesus,' the Lord answered. 'I am the one you are so cruel to. Now get up and go into the city, where you will be told what to do.'

The men with Saul stood there speechless. They had heard the voice, but they had not seen anyone. Saul got up from the ground, and when he opened his eyes, he could not see a thing. Someone then led him by the hand to Damascus, and for three days he was blind and did not eat or drink.

ANANIAS HELPS AN ENEMY

The Lord said to Ananias, 'Go! I have chosen him to tell foreigners, kings, and the people of Israel about me.'

A follower named Ananias lived in Damascus, and the Lord spoke to him in a vision. Ananias answered, 'Lord, here I am.'

The Lord said to him, 'Get up and go to the house of Judas in Straight Street. When you get there, you will find a man named Saul from the city of Tarsus. Saul is praying, and he has seen a vision. He saw a man named Ananias coming to him and putting his hands on him, so that he could see again.'

Ananias replied, 'Lord, a lot of people have told me about the terrible things this man has done to your followers in Jerusalem. Now the chief priests have given him the power to come here and arrest anyone who worships in your name.'

The Lord said to Ananias, 'Go! I have chosen him to tell foreigners, kings, and the people of Israel about me. I will show him how much he must suffer for worshipping in my name.'

Ananias left and went into the house where Saul was staying. Ananias placed his hands on him and said, 'Saul, the Lord Jesus has sent me. He is the same one who appeared to you along the road. He wants you to be able to see and to be filled with the Holy Spirit.'

Suddenly something like fish scales fell from Saul's eyes, and he could see. He got up and was baptized. Then he ate and felt much better.

For several days Saul stayed with the Lord's followers in Damascus.

SAUL IN JERUSALEM

Saul joined the other followers at their meetings. He surprised everyone by now agreeing with them that Jesus was God's special messenger. Soon his words aroused opposition among the Jews, and he was forced to escape from the city and travel back to Jerusalem.

When Saul arrived in Jerusalem, he tried to join the followers. But they were all afraid of him, because they did not believe he

Saul moved about
freely with the
followers in
Jerusalem and told
everyone about the
Lord.

was a true follower. Then Barnabas helped him by taking him to the apostles. He explained how Saul had seen the Lord and how the Lord had spoken to him. Barnabas also said that when Saul was in Damascus, he had spoken bravely in the name of Jesus.

Saul moved about freely with the followers in Jerusalem and told everyone about the Lord. He was always arguing with the Jews who spoke Greek, and so they tried to kill him. But the followers found out about this and took Saul to Caesarea. From there they sent him to the city of Tarsus.

The church in Judea, Galilee, and Samaria now had a time of peace and kept on worshipping the Lord. The church became stronger, as the Holy Spirit encouraged it and helped it grow.

FROM ACTS
10.1–48

PETER TAKES HIS MESSAGE TO THE GENTILES

The church grew and grew. Peter travelled from place to place, encouraging the new believers and healing people. On one such journey his travels took him to Joppa, where he was the guest of a man called Simon, himself a follower of Jesus.

'These Gentiles have
been given the Holy
Spirit, just as we
have! I am certain
that no one would
dare stop us from
baptizing them.'

In Caesarea there was a man named Cornelius, who was the captain of a group of soldiers called 'The Italian Unit'. Cornelius was a very religious man. He worshipped God, and so did everyone else who lived in his house. He had given a lot of money to the poor and was always praying to God.

One afternoon at about three o'clock, Cornelius had a vision. He saw an angel from God coming to him and calling him by name. Cornelius was surprised and stared at the angel. Then he asked, 'What is this all about?'

CAVALLINO
ST PETER AND
CORNELIUS THE
CENTURION
ROME
C. 1640

The angel answered, 'God has heard your prayers and knows about your gifts to the poor. Now send some men to Joppa for a man named Simon Peter. After saying this, the angel left.

Cornelius called in two of his servants and one of his soldiers who worshipped God. He explained everything to them and sent them off to Joppa.

The next day about midday these men were coming near Joppa. Peter went up on the roof of the house to pray and became very hungry. While the food was being prepared, he fell sound asleep and had a vision. He saw heaven open, and something came down like a huge sheet held up by its four corners. In it were all kinds of animals, snakes, and birds. A voice said to him, 'Peter, get up! Kill these and eat them.'

But Peter said, 'Lord, I can't do that! I've never eaten anything that is unclean and not fit to eat.'

The voice spoke to him again, 'When God says that something can be used for food, don't say it isn't fit to eat.'

This happened three times before the sheet was suddenly taken back to heaven.

Peter was still wondering what all this meant, when the men sent by Cornelius came and stood at the gate. They had found their way to Simon's house and were asking if Simon Peter was staying there.

While Peter was still thinking about the vision, the Holy Spirit said to him, 'Three men are here looking for you. Hurry down and go with them. Don't worry, I sent them.'

Peter invited them to spend the night.

The next morning, Peter and some of the Lord's followers in Joppa left with the men who had come from Cornelius.

When Peter arrived, Cornelius greeted him. Then he knelt at Peter's feet and started worshipping him. But Peter took hold of him and said, 'Stand up! I am nothing more than a human.'

As Peter entered the house, he was still talking with Cornelius. Many people were there, and Peter said to them, 'You know that we Jews are not allowed to have anything to do with other people. But God has shown me that he doesn't think anyone is unclean or unfit. I agreed to come here, but I want to know why you sent for me.'

Cornelius answered:

Four days ago at about three o'clock in the afternoon I was praying at home. Suddenly a man in bright clothes stood in front of me. He said, 'Cornelius, God has heard your prayers, and he knows about your gifts to the poor. Now send to

Joppa for Simon Peter. He is staying in the home of Simon the leather maker, who lives near the sea.'

I sent for you straight away, and you have been good enough to come. All of us are here in the presence of the Lord God, so that we can hear what he has to say.

Peter then said:

Now I am certain that God treats all people alike.

While Peter was still speaking, the Holy Spirit took control of everyone who was listening. Some Jewish followers of the Lord had come with Peter, and they were surprised that the Holy Spirit had been given to Gentiles. Now they were hearing Gentiles speaking unknown languages and praising God.

Peter said, 'These Gentiles have been given the Holy Spirit, just as we have! I am certain that no one would dare stop us from baptizing them.' Peter ordered them to be baptized in the name of Jesus Christ, and they asked him to stay on for a few days.

ACTS 12.1–19 ## PETER'S ESCAPE FROM PRISON

Peter returned to Jerusalem, where he passed on the thrilling news that the Holy Spirit had also been given to the Gentiles. The church was expanding throughout the Roman world, but in Jerusalem and its surroundings, life was hard.

Peter now realized what had happened, and he said, 'I am certain that the Lord sent his angel to rescue me from Herod and from everything the Jewish leaders planned to do to me.'

At that time King Herod caused terrible suffering for some members of the church. He ordered soldiers to cut off the head of James, the brother of John. When Herod saw that this pleased the Jewish people, he had Peter arrested during the Festival of Thin Bread. He put Peter in jail and ordered four squads of soldiers to guard him. Herod planned to put him on trial in public after the festival.

While Peter was being kept in jail, the church never stopped praying to God for him.

The night before Peter was to be put on trial, he was asleep and bound by two chains. A soldier was guarding him on each side, and two other soldiers were guarding the entrance to the jail. Suddenly an angel from the Lord appeared, and light flashed around in the cell. The angel poked Peter in the side and woke him up. Then he said, 'Quick! Get up!'

The chains fell off his hands, and the angel said, 'Get dressed and put on your sandals.' Peter did what he was told. Then the angel said, 'Now put on your coat and follow me.' Peter left with the angel, but he thought everything was only a dream. They went past the two groups of soldiers, and when they came to the iron gate to the city, it opened by itself. They went out and were going along the street, when all at once the angel disappeared.

Peter now realized what had happened, and he said, 'I am certain that the Lord sent his angel to rescue me from Herod and from everything the Jewish leaders planned to do to me.' Then Peter went to the house of Mary the mother of John whose other name was Mark. Many of the Lord's followers had come together there and were praying.

Peter knocked on the gate, and a servant named Rhoda came to answer. When she heard Peter's voice, she was too excited to open the gate. She ran back into the house and said that Peter was standing there.

'You are mad!' everyone told her. But she kept saying that it was Peter. Then they said, 'It must be his angel.' But Peter kept on knocking, until finally they opened the gate. They saw him and were completely amazed.

Peter motioned for them to keep quiet. Then he told how the Lord had led him out of jail. He also said, 'Tell James and the others what has happened.' After that, he left and went somewhere else.

The next morning the soldiers who had been on guard were terribly worried and wondered what had happened to Peter. Herod ordered his own soldiers to search for him, but they could not find him. Then he questioned the guards and had them put to death. After this, Herod left Judea to stay in Caesarea for a while.

RESOLVING PROBLEMS

Saul was sent by the Christians living in Antioch to take the message about Jesus to other locations. At this point he became known by his Greek name, Paul. Together with Barnabas, he sailed to the island of Cyprus. Then they travelled to many other places before going back to report on their travels.

And so, my friends, I don't think we should place burdens on the Gentiles who are turning to God.

After arriving in Antioch, they called the church together. They told the people what God had helped them do and how he had made it possible for the Gentiles to believe. Then they stayed there with the followers for a long time.

Some people came from Judea and started teaching the Lord's followers that they could not be saved, unless they were circumcised as Moses had taught. This caused trouble, and Paul and Barnabas argued with them about this teaching. So it was decided to send Paul and Barnabas and a few others to Jerusalem to discuss this problem with the apostles and the church leaders.

The men who were sent by the church went through Phoenicia and Samaria, telling how the Gentiles had turned to God. This news made the Lord's followers very happy. When the men arrived in Jerusalem, they were welcomed by the church, including the apostles and the leaders. They told them everything God had helped them do. But some Pharisees had become followers of the Lord. They stood up and said, 'Gentiles who have faith in the Lord must be circumcised and told to obey the Law of Moses.'

The apostles and church leaders met to discuss this problem about Gentiles. They had talked it over for a long time, when Peter got up and said:

My friends, you know that God decided long ago to let me be the one from your group to preach the good news to the Gentiles. God did this so that they would hear and obey him. He knows what is in everyone's heart. And he showed that he had chosen the Gentiles, when he gave them the Holy Spirit, just as he had given his Spirit to us. God treated them in the same way that he treated us. They put their faith in him, and he made their hearts pure.

Now why are you trying to make God angry by placing a heavy burden on these followers? This burden was too heavy for us or our ancestors. But our Lord Jesus was kind to us, and we are saved by faith in him, just as the Gentiles are.

Everyone kept quiet and listened as Barnabas and Paul told how God had given them the power to perform a lot of miracles and wonders for the Gentiles.

After they had finished speaking, James said:

My friends, listen to me! Simon Peter has told how God first came to the Gentiles and made some of them his own people. This agrees with what the prophets wrote,

'I, the Lord, will return and rebuild David's fallen house.

I will build it from its ruins and set it up again.

Then other nations will turn to me and be my chosen ones.

I, the Lord, say this. I promised it long ago.'

And so, my friends, I don't think we should place burdens on the Gentiles who are turning to God. We should simply write and tell them not to eat anything that has been offered to idols. They should be told not to eat the meat of any animal that has been strangled or that still has blood in it. They must also not commit any terrible sexual sins.

We must remember that the Law of Moses has been preached in city after city for many years, and every Sabbath it is read when we Jews meet.

ACTS 16.16–24 **PAUL AND SILAS IN PRISON**

Paul set off to revisit the places he had been to. While on this journey he had a vision of a man asking him to go to Macedonia. Immediately he left for the capital city of that region, a town called Philippi.

One day on our way to the place of prayer, we were met by a

slave girl. She had a spirit in her that gave her the power to tell the future. By doing this she made a lot of money for her owners. The girl followed Paul and the rest of us and kept yelling, 'These men are servants of the Most High God! They are telling you how to be saved.'

This went on for several days. Finally, Paul got so upset that he turned and said to the spirit, 'In the name of Jesus Christ, I order you to leave this girl alone!' At once the evil spirit left her.

When the girl's owners realized that they had lost all chances for making more money, they grabbed Paul and Silas and dragged them into court. They told the officials, 'These Jews are upsetting our city! They are telling us to do things we Romans are not allowed to do.'

The crowd joined in the attack on Paul and Silas. Then the officials tore the clothes off the two men and ordered them to be beaten with a whip. After they had been badly beaten, they were put in jail, and the jailer was told to guard them carefully. The jailer did as he was told. He put them deep inside the jail and chained their feet to heavy blocks of wood.

The crowd joined in the attack on Paul and Silas. Then the officials tore the clothes off the two men and ordered them to be beaten with a whip.

VIOLENCE AND WARFARE

ACTS 16.25–34

A TERRIFIED JAILER IS SAVED

'Have faith in the Lord Jesus and you will be saved! This is also true for everyone who lives in your home.'

MIRACLES AND WONDERS

About midnight Paul and Silas were praying and singing praises to God, while the other prisoners listened. Suddenly a strong earthquake shook the jail to its foundations. The doors opened, and the chains fell from all the prisoners.

When the jailer woke up and saw that the doors were open, he thought that the prisoners had escaped. He pulled out his sword and was about to kill himself. But Paul shouted, 'Don't harm yourself! No one has escaped.'

The jailer asked for a torch and went into the jail. He was shaking all over as he knelt down in front of Paul and Silas. After he had led them out of the jail, he asked, 'What must I do to be saved?'

They replied, 'Have faith in the Lord Jesus and you will be saved! This is also true for everyone who lives in your home.'

Then Paul and Silas told him and everyone else in his house about the Lord. While it was still night, the jailer took them to a place where he could wash their cuts and bruises. Then he and everyone in his home were baptized. They were very glad that they had put their faith in God. After this, the jailer took Paul and Silas to his home and gave them something to eat.

ACTS 22.17–29

PAUL STIRS UP A CROWD

Paul continued on his journey, experiencing times of joy but also of great personal suffering. Finally he went to Jerusalem to give a report on his mission. Once, when he was at the temple, he was explaining to a group of hostile Jews his personal reasons for following Jesus.

The men who were about to beat and question Paul quickly backed off. And the commander himself was frightened when he realized that he had put a Roman citizen in chains.

DREAMS AND VISIONS
VIOLENCE AND WARFARE

After this I returned to Jerusalem and went to the temple to pray. There I had a vision of the Lord who said to me, 'Hurry and leave Jerusalem! The people won't listen to what you say about me.'

I replied, 'Lord, they know that in many of our meeting places I arrested and beat people who had faith in you. Stephen was killed because he spoke for you, and I stood there and cheered them on. I even guarded the clothes of the men who murdered him.'

But the Lord told me to go, and he promised to send me far away to the Gentiles.

The crowd listened until Paul said this. Then they started shouting, 'Get rid of this man! He doesn't deserve to live.' They kept shouting. They waved their clothes around and threw dust into the air.

The Roman commander ordered Paul to be taken into the fortress and beaten with a whip. He did this to find out why the people were screaming at Paul.

While the soldiers were tying Paul up to be beaten, he asked the officer standing there, 'Is it legal to beat a Roman citizen before he has been tried in court?'

When the officer heard this, he went to the commander and said, 'What are you doing? This man is a Roman citizen!'

The commander went to Paul and asked, 'Tell me, are you a Roman citizen?'

'Yes,' Paul answered.

The commander then said, 'I paid a lot of money to become a Roman citizen.'

But Paul replied, 'I was born a Roman citizen.'

The men who were about to beat and question Paul quickly backed off. And the commander himself was frightened when he realized that he had put a Roman citizen in chains.

Acts
22.30–23.11

*'My friends, I am a
Pharisee and the
son of a Pharisee. I
am on trial simply
because I believe
that the dead will be
raised to life.'*

VIOLENCE AND
WARFARE

PAUL IS QUESTIONED

The next day the commander wanted to know the real reason why the Jewish leaders had brought charges against Paul. So he had Paul's chains removed, and he ordered the chief priests and the whole council to meet. Then he had Paul led in and made him stand in front of them.

Paul looked straight at the council members and said, 'My friends, to this day I have served God with a clear conscience!'

Then Ananias the high priest ordered the men standing beside Paul to hit him on the mouth. Paul turned to the high priest and said, 'You whitewashed wall! God will hit you. You sit there to judge me by the Law of Moses. But at the same time you order men to break the Law by hitting me.'

The men standing beside Paul asked, 'Don't you know you are insulting God's high priest?'

Paul replied, 'Oh! I didn't know he was the high priest. The Scriptures do tell us not to speak evil about a leader of our people.'

When Paul saw that some of the council members were Sadducees and others were Pharisees, he shouted, 'My friends, I am a Pharisee and the son of a Pharisee. I am on trial simply because I believe that the dead will be raised to life.'

As soon as Paul said this, the Pharisees and the Sadducees

got into a big argument, and the council members started taking sides. The Sadducees do not believe in angels or spirits or that the dead will rise to life. But the Pharisees believe in all these, and so there was a lot of shouting. Some of the teachers of the Law of Moses were Pharisees. Finally, they became angry and said, 'We don't find anything wrong with this man. Perhaps a spirit or an angel really did speak to him.'

The argument became fierce, and the commander was afraid that Paul would be pulled apart. So he ordered the soldiers to go in and rescue Paul. Then they took him back into the fortress.

That night the Lord stood beside Paul and said, 'Don't worry! Just as you have told others about me in Jerusalem, you must also tell about me in Rome.'

ACTS 23.23–35

PAUL IS ESCORTED TO THE GOVERNOR IN CAESAREA

'This man isn't guilty of anything for which he should die or even be put in jail.'

TRAVEL AND TRANSPORT

The commander called in two of his officers and told them, 'By nine o'clock tonight have two hundred soldiers ready to go to Caesarea. Take along seventy men on horseback and two hundred foot soldiers with spears. Get a horse ready for Paul and make sure that he gets safely through to Felix the governor.'

The commander wrote a letter that said:

Greetings from Claudius Lysias to the Honourable Governor Felix:

Some Jews grabbed this man and were about to kill him. But when I found out that he was a Roman citizen, I took some soldiers and rescued him.

I wanted to find out what they had against him. So I brought him before their council and learnt that the charges concern only their religious laws. This man isn't guilty of anything for which he should die or even be put in jail.

As soon as I learnt that there was a plot against him, I sent him to you and told their leaders to bring charges against him in your court.

The soldiers obeyed the commander's orders, and that same night they took Paul to the city of Antipatris. The next day the foot soldiers returned to the fortress and let the soldiers on horseback take him the rest of the way. When they came to Caesarea, they gave the letter to the governor and handed Paul over to him.

The governor read the letter. Then he asked Paul and found out that he was from Cilicia. The governor said, 'I will listen to your case as soon as the people come to bring their charges against you.' After saying this, he gave orders for Paul to be kept as a prisoner in Herod's palace.

PAUL APPEALS TO THE EMPEROR

The high priest then came from Jerusalem with accusations against Paul. After a brief trial, the proceedings were adjourned, but Felix kept Paul under guard for two years and was then succeeded by Porcius Festus.

Paul replied, 'I am on trial in the Emperor's court, and that's where I should be tried. You know very well that I have not done anything to harm the Jewish nation.'

Three days after Festus had become governor, he went from Caesarea to Jerusalem. There the chief priests and some Jewish leaders told him about their charges against Paul. They also asked Festus if he would be willing to bring Paul to Jerusalem. They begged him to do this because they were planning to attack and kill Paul on the way. But Festus told them, 'Paul will be kept in Caesarea, and I am soon going there myself. If he has done anything wrong, let your leaders go with me and bring charges against him there.'

Festus stayed in Jerusalem for eight or ten more days before going to Caesarea. Then the next day he took his place as judge and had Paul brought into court. As soon as Paul came in, the Jewish leaders from Jerusalem crowded around him and said he was guilty of many serious crimes. But they could not prove anything. Then Paul spoke in his own defence, 'I have not broken the Law of my people. And I have not done anything against either the temple or the Emperor.'

Festus wanted to please the leaders. So he asked Paul, 'Are

you willing to go to Jerusalem and be tried by me on these charges?'

Paul replied, 'I am on trial in the Emperor's court, and that's where I should be tried. You know very well that I have not done anything to harm the Jewish nation. If I had done something deserving death, I would not ask to escape the death penalty. But I am not guilty of any of these crimes, and no one has the right to hand me over to these people. I now ask to be tried by the Emperor himself.'

After Festus had talked this over with members of his council, he told Paul, 'You have asked to be tried by the Emperor, and to the Emperor you will go!'

Acts
27.9–28.1

A STORM AT SEA

When the time came for Paul to travel to the Emperor in Rome, he set sail from Caesarea. The ship hugged the coast before crossing open sea to Crete. They reached the island safely, but progress had been slow.

Paul, don't be afraid! You will stand trial before the Emperor. And because of you, God will save the lives of everyone on the ship.

FOOD AND DRINK
MIRACLES AND
WONDERS
TRAVEL AND
TRANSPORT

By now we had already lost a lot of time, and sailing was no longer safe. In fact, even the Great Day of Forgiveness was past. Then Paul spoke to the crew of the ship, 'Men, listen to me! If we sail now, our ship and its cargo will be badly damaged, and many lives will be lost.' But Julius listened to the captain of the ship and its owner, rather than to Paul.

The harbour at Fair Havens wasn't a good place to spend the winter. Because of this, almost everyone agreed that we should at least try to sail along the coast of Crete as far as Phoenix. It had a harbour that opened towards the south-west and north-west, and we could spend the winter there.

When a gentle wind from the south started blowing, the men thought it was a good time to do what they had planned. So they pulled up the anchor, and we sailed along the coast of Crete. But soon a strong wind called 'The North-easter' blew against us from the island. The wind struck the ship, and we could not sail against it. So we let the wind carry the ship.

We went along the island of Cauda on the side that was protected from the wind. We had a hard time holding the lifeboat in place, but finally we got it where it belonged. Then the sailors tied ropes around the ship to hold it together. They lowered the sail and let the ship drift along, because they were afraid it might hit the sandbanks in the gulf of Syrtis.

The storm was so fierce that the next day they threw some of the ship's cargo overboard. Then on the third day, with their bare hands they threw overboard some of the ship's gear. For several days we could not see either the sun or the stars. A strong wind kept blowing, and we finally gave up all hope of being saved.

Since none of us had eaten anything for a long time, Paul stood up and told the men:

You should have listened to me! If you had stayed on in Crete, you would not have had this damage and loss. But now I beg you to cheer up, because you will be safe. Only the ship will be lost.

I belong to God, and I worship him. Last night he sent an angel to tell me, 'Paul, don't be afraid! You will stand trial before the Emperor. And because of you, God will save the lives of everyone on the ship.' Cheer up! I am sure that God will do exactly what he promised. But we will first be shipwrecked on some island.

For fourteen days and nights we had been blown around over the Mediterranean Sea. But about midnight the sailors realized that we were getting near land. They measured and found that the water was about forty metres deep. A little later they measured again and found it was only about thirty metres. The sailors were afraid that we might hit some rocks, and they let down four anchors from the back of the ship. Then they prayed for daylight.

The sailors wanted to escape from the ship. So they lowered the lifeboat into the water, pretending that they were letting down an anchor from the front of the ship. But Paul said to Captain Julius and the soldiers, 'If the sailors don't stay on the ship, you won't have any chance to save your lives.' The soldiers then cut the ropes that held the lifeboat and let it fall into the sea.

Just before daylight Paul begged the people to eat something. He told them, 'For fourteen days you have been so worried that you haven't eaten a thing. I beg you to eat something. Your lives depend on it. Do this and not one of you will be hurt.'

After Paul had said this, he took a piece of bread and gave thanks to God. Then in front of everyone, he broke the bread and ate some. They all felt encouraged, and each of them ate something. There were 276 people on the ship, and after everyone had eaten, they threw the cargo of wheat into the sea to make the ship lighter.

Morning came, and the ship's crew saw a coast that they did not recognize. But they did see a cove with a beach. So they decided to try to run the ship aground on the beach. They cut the anchors loose and let them sink into the sea. At the same time they untied the ropes that were holding the rudders. Next, they raised the sail at the front of the ship and let the wind carry the ship towards the beach. But it ran aground on a sandbank. The front of the ship stuck firmly in the sand, and the rear was being smashed by the force of the waves.

The soldiers decided to kill the prisoners to keep them from swimming away and escaping. But Captain Julius wanted to save Paul's life, and he did not let the soldiers do what they had planned. Instead, he ordered everyone who could swim to dive into the water and head for shore. Then he told the others to hold on to planks of wood or parts of the ship. At last, everyone safely reached shore.

When we came ashore, we learnt that the island was called Malta.

Paul spent the winter on the island and when the weather improved he and his companions caught up a ship that sailed up the Italian coast to the Bay of Naples. From here they walked to Rome where Paul, despite being placed under house arrest, continued to tell everyone about Jesus.

Advice to the first churches

In addition to his travelling ministry, Paul wrote many letters to his friends and the churches he'd been involved with, further explaining the Christian message and encouraging them to live in a way that pleased God.

Romans
8.28–39

GOD'S PROTECTING LOVE

This letter is a powerful explanation of the fundamentals of the Christian faith, in which Paul explains why people need help and how Jesus is the solution God has provided.

What can we say about all this? If God is on our side, can anyone be against us?

Agreements and Promises

See also *Hosea* 11.1–11

We know that God is always at work for the good of everyone who loves him. They are the ones God has chosen for his purpose, and he has always known who his chosen ones would be. He had decided to let them become like his own Son, so that his Son would be the first of many children. God then accepted the people he had already decided to choose, and he has shared his glory with them.

What can we say about all this? If God is on our side, can anyone be against us? God did not keep back his own Son, but he gave him for us. If God did this, won't he freely give us everything else? If God says his chosen ones are acceptable to him, can anyone bring charges against them? Or can anyone condemn them? No indeed! Christ died and was raised to life, and now he is at God's right side, speaking to him for us. Can anything separate us from the love of Christ? Can trouble, suffering, and hard times, or hunger and nakedness, or danger and death? It is exactly as the Scriptures say,

'For you we face death all day long.

We are like sheep on their way to be butchered.'

In everything we have won more than a victory because of Christ who loves us. I am sure that nothing can separate us from God's love – not life or death, not angels or spirits, not the present or the future, and not powers above or powers below. Nothing in all creation can separate us from God's love for us in Christ Jesus our Lord!

1 CORINTHIANS
11.17–33

REMEMBERING JESUS' DEATH

Although Paul loved the Christians at Corinth, there were serious problems in the church. Sexual immorality, a lack of unity and incorrect teaching are all addressed in this passionate letter, which underlines that love is the key to living as God wants.

But if you eat the bread and drink the wine in a way that isn't worthy of the Lord, you sin against his body and blood.

AGREEMENTS AND PROMISES
FOOD AND DRINK

See also MATTHEW
26.26–30

Your worship services do you more harm than good. I am certainly not going to praise you for this. I am told that you can't get along with each other when you worship, and I am sure that some of what I have heard is true. You are bound to argue with each other, but it is easy to see which of you have God's approval.

When you meet together, you don't really celebrate the Lord's Supper. You even start eating before everyone gets to the meeting, and some of you go hungry, while others get drunk. Don't you have homes where you can eat and drink? Do you hate God's church? Do you want to embarrass people who don't have anything? What can I say to you? I certainly cannot praise you.

I have already told you what the Lord Jesus did on the night he was betrayed. And it came from the Lord himself.

He took some bread in his hands. Then after he had given thanks, he broke it and said, 'This is my body, which is given for you. Eat this and remember me.'

After the meal, Jesus took a cup of wine in his hands and

said, 'This is my blood, and with it God makes his new agreement with you. Drink this and remember me.'

The Lord meant that when you eat this bread and drink from this cup, you tell about his death until he comes.

But if you eat the bread and drink the wine in a way that isn't worthy of the Lord, you sin against his body and blood. That's why you must examine the way you eat and drink. If you fail to understand that you are the body of the Lord, you will condemn yourselves by the way you eat and drink. That's why many of you are sick and weak and why a lot of others have died. If we carefully judge ourselves, we won't be punished. But when the Lord judges and punishes us, he does it to keep us from being condemned with the rest of the world.

My dear friends, you should wait until everyone gets there before you start eating.

1 CORINTHIANS
12.12–27

ONE BODY WITH MANY PARTS

Together you are the body of Christ. Each one of you is part of his body.

The body of Christ has many different parts, just as any other body does. Some of us are Jews, and others are Gentiles. Some of us are slaves, and others are free. But God's Spirit baptized each of us and made us part of the body of Christ. Now we each drink from that same Spirit.

Our bodies don't have just one part. They have many parts. Suppose a foot says, 'I'm not a hand, and so I'm not part of the body.' Wouldn't the foot still belong to the body? Or suppose an ear says, 'I'm not an eye, and so I'm not part of the body.' Wouldn't the ear still belong to the body? If our bodies were only an eye, we couldn't hear a thing. And if they were only an ear, we couldn't smell a thing. But God has put all parts of our body together in the way that he decided is best.

A body isn't really a body, unless there is more than one part. It takes many parts to make a single body. That's why the eyes cannot say they don't need the hands. That's also why the head cannot say it doesn't need the feet. In fact, we cannot get along without the parts of the body that seem to be the weakest. We take special care to dress up some parts of our bodies. We are modest about our personal parts, but we don't have to be modest about other parts.

God put our bodies together in such a way that even the parts that seem the least important are valuable. He did this to make all parts of the body work together smoothly, with each part caring about the others. If one part of our body hurts, we hurt all over. If one part of our body is honoured, the whole body will be happy.

Together you are the body of Christ. Each one of you is part of his body.

FROM
1 CORINTHIANS
15.1–58

I told you the most important part of the message exactly as it was told to me. That part is: Christ died for our sins, as the Scriptures say. He was buried, and three days later he was raised to life, as the Scriptures say.

See also MARK
16.1–8

THE IMPORTANCE OF THE RESURRECTION

My friends, I want you to remember the message that I preached and that you believed and trusted. You will be saved by this message, if you hold firmly to it. But if you don't, your faith was all for nothing.

I told you the most important part of the message exactly as it was told to me. That part is:

Christ died for our sins, as the Scriptures say.

He was buried, and three days later he was raised to life, as the Scriptures say.

Christ appeared to Peter, then to the twelve.

After this, he appeared to more than five hundred other followers.

Most of them are still alive, but some have died.

If we preach that Christ was raised from death, how can some of you say that the dead will not be raised to life? If they won't be raised to life, Christ himself wasn't raised to life. And if Christ wasn't raised to life, our message is worthless, and so is your faith.

But Christ has been raised to life! And he makes us certain

that others will also be raised to life. Just as we will die because of Adam, we will be raised to life because of Christ. Adam brought death to all of us, and Christ will bring life to all of us.

Some of you have asked, 'How will the dead be raised to life? What kind of bodies will they have?' Don't be foolish. A seed must die before it can sprout from the ground. Wheat seeds and all other seeds look different from the sprouts that come up.

Everyone on earth has a body like the body of the one who was made from the dust of the earth. And everyone in heaven has a body like the body of the one who came from heaven. Just as we are like the one who was made out of earth, we will be like the one who came from heaven.

My friends, I want you to know that our bodies of flesh and blood will decay. This means that they cannot share in God's kingdom, which lasts for ever. I will explain a mystery to you. Not every one of us will die, but we will all be changed. It will happen suddenly, quicker than the blink of an eye. At the sound of the last trumpet the dead will be raised. We will all be changed, so that we will never die again. Our dead and decaying bodies will be changed into bodies that won't die or decay. The bodies we now have are weak and can die. But they will be changed into bodies that are eternal. Then the Scriptures will come true,

'Death has lost the battle!
Where is its victory?
Where is its sting?'

Sin is what gives death its sting, and the Law is the power behind sin. But thank God for letting our Lord Jesus Christ give us the victory!

My dear friends, stand firm and don't be shaken. Always keep busy working for the Lord. You know that everything you do for him is worthwhile.

DOWN, BUT NOT OUT

Paul followed up his first letter to the church at Corinth with this intensely personal one. Stung by criticisms of his conduct, he highlights his role as an apostle of Jesus, as well as the authority that comes with it.

We are not preaching about ourselves. Our message is that Jesus Christ is Lord. He also sent us to be your servants.

God has been kind enough to trust us with this work. That's why we never give up. We don't do shameful things that must be kept secret. And we don't try to fool anyone or twist God's message around. God is our witness that we speak only the truth, so others will be sure that we can be trusted. If there is anything hidden about our message, it is hidden only to someone who is lost.

The god who rules this world has blinded the minds of unbelievers. They cannot see the light, which is the good news about our glorious Christ, who shows what God is like. We are not preaching about ourselves. Our message is that Jesus Christ is Lord. He also sent us to be your servants.

We are like clay jars in which this treasure is stored. The real power comes from God and not from us. We often suffer, but we are never crushed. Even when we don't know what to do, we never give up. In times of trouble, God is with us, and when we are knocked down, we get up again. We face death every day because of Jesus. Our bodies show what his death was like, so that his life can also be seen in us.

We never give up. Our bodies are gradually dying, but we ourselves are being made stronger each day. These little troubles are getting us ready for an eternal glory that will make all our troubles seem like nothing. Things that are seen don't last for ever, but things that are not seen are eternal. That's why we keep our minds on the things that cannot be seen.

We know what it means to respect the Lord, and we encourage everyone to turn to him. God himself knows what we are like, and I hope you also know what kind of people we are. We are not trying once more to boast about ourselves. But we want you to be proud of us, when you are with those who are not sincere and boast about what others think of them.

If we seem out of our minds, it is between God and us. But if we are in our right minds, it is for your good. We are ruled by Christ's love for us. We are certain that if one person died for everyone else, then all of us have died. And Christ did die for all of us. He died so we would no longer live for ourselves, but for the one who died and was raised to life for us.

We are careful not to judge people by what they seem to be, though we once judged Christ in that way. Anyone who belongs to Christ is a new person. The past is forgotten, and everything is new. God has done it all! He sent Christ to make peace between himself and us, and he has given us the work of making peace between himself and others.

What we mean is that God was in Christ, offering peace and forgiveness to the people of this world. And he has given us the work of sharing his message about peace. We were sent to speak for Christ, and God is begging you to listen to our message. We speak for Christ and sincerely ask you to make peace with God. Christ never sinned! But God treated him as a sinner, so that Christ could make us acceptable to God.

We work together with God, and we beg you to make good use of God's kindness to you. In the Scriptures God says,

'When the time came, I listened to you, and when you needed help, I came to save you.'

GALATIANS
5.1–23

TRUE FREEDOM

One branch of the early church was teaching that in order to be real Christians, everyone had to be circumcised according to the Jewish practice. Paul responded to this attempt by making clear that all that mattered was faith in Jesus.

Christ has set us free! This means we are really free. Now hold on to your freedom and don't ever become slaves of the Law again.

I, Paul, promise you that Christ won't do you any good if you get circumcised. If you do, you must obey the whole Law. And if you try to please God by obeying the Law, you have cut

My friends, you were chosen to be free. So don't use your freedom as an excuse to do anything you want. Use it as an opportunity to serve each other with love.

See also
GENESIS 17.11,
ACTS 11. 1–18,
ACTS 1.4–11, 2.4,
4.31,
ROMANS 8,
JOHN 8.31–41

yourself off from Christ and his wonderful kindness. But the Spirit makes us sure that God will accept us because of our faith in Christ. If you are a follower of Christ Jesus, it makes no difference whether you are circumcised or not. All that matters is your faith that makes you love others.

You were doing so well until someone made you turn from the truth. And that person was certainly not sent by the one who chose you. A little yeast can change a whole batch of dough, but you belong to the Lord. That makes me certain that you will do what I say, instead of what someone else tells you to do. Whoever is causing trouble for you will be punished.

My friends, if I still preach that people need to be circumcised, why am I in so much trouble? The message about the cross would no longer be a problem, if I told people to be circumcised. I wish that everyone who is upsetting you would not only get circumcised, but would cut off much more!

My friends, you were chosen to be free. So don't use your freedom as an excuse to do anything you want. Use it as an opportunity to serve each other with love. All that the Law says can be summed up in the command to love others as much as you love yourself. But if you keep attacking each other like wild animals, you had better watch out or you will destroy yourselves.

If you are guided by the Spirit, you won't obey your selfish desires. The Spirit and your desires are enemies of each other. They are always fighting each other and keeping you from doing what you feel you should. But if you obey the Spirit, the Law of Moses has no control over you.

People's desires make them give in to immoral ways, filthy thoughts, and shameful deeds. They worship idols, practise witchcraft, hate others, and are hard to get along with. People become jealous, angry, and selfish. They not only argue and cause trouble, but they are envious. They get drunk, carry on at wild parties, and do other evil things as well. I told you before, and I am telling you again: no one who does these things will share in the blessings of God's kingdom.

God's Spirit makes us loving, happy, peaceful, patient, kind, good, faithful, gentle, and self-controlled. There is no law against behaving in any of these ways.

EPHESIANS
2.1–10

LIFE IN CHRIST

In this letter Paul teaches how God's great love, shown in Jesus, breaks down all barriers and unites all those who follow him. It emphasises the practical outworking of faith in the battle against evil.

You were saved by faith in God, who treats us much better than we deserve. This is God's gift to you, and not anything you have done on your own.

In the past you were dead because you sinned and fought against God. You followed the ways of this world and obeyed the devil. He rules the world, and his spirit has power over everyone who doesn't obey God. Once we were also ruled by the selfish desires of our bodies and minds. We had made God angry, and we were going to be punished like everyone else.

But God was merciful! We were dead because of our sins, but God loved us so much that he made us alive with Christ, and God's wonderful kindness is what saves you. God raised us from death to life with Christ Jesus, and he has given us a place beside Christ in heaven. God did this so that in the future world he could show how truly good and kind he is to us because of what Christ Jesus has done. You were saved by faith in God, who treats us much better than we deserve. This is God's gift to you, and not anything you have done on your own. It isn't something you have earned, so there is nothing you can boast about. God planned for us to do good things and to live as he has always wanted us to live. That's why he sent Christ to make us what we are.

EPHESIANS
5.1–33

GUIDELINES FOR CHRISTIAN LIVING

Honour Christ and put others first.

Do as God does. After all, you are his dear children. Let love be your guide. Christ loved us and offered his life for us as a sacrifice that pleases God.

MARRIAGE AND FAMILY

See also
EXODUS 15.1,
EZRA 3.7–13,
PSALMS,
MATTHEW 26.30,
JAMES 5.13

You are God's people, so don't let it be said that any of you are immoral or indecent or greedy. Don't use dirty or foolish or filthy words. Instead, say how thankful you are. Being greedy, indecent, or immoral is just another way of worshipping idols. You can be sure that people who behave in this way will never be part of the kingdom that belongs to Christ and to God.

Don't let anyone trick you with foolish talk. God punishes everyone who disobeys him and says foolish things. So don't have anything to do with anyone like that.

You used to be like people living in the dark, but now you are people of the light because you belong to the Lord. So act like people of the light and make your light shine. Be good and honest and truthful, as you try to please the Lord. Don't take part in doing those worthless things that are done in the dark. Instead, show how wrong they are. It is disgusting even to talk about what is done in the dark. But the light will show what these things are really like. Light shows up everything, just as the Scriptures say,

'Wake up from your sleep
and rise from death.
Then Christ will shine on you.'

Act like people with good sense and not like fools. These are evil times, so make every minute count. Don't be stupid. Instead, find out what the Lord wants you to do. Don't destroy yourself by getting drunk, but let the Spirit fill your life. When you meet together, sing psalms, hymns, and spiritual songs, as you praise the Lord with all your heart. Always use the name of our Lord Jesus Christ to thank God the Father for everything.

Honour Christ and put others first. A wife should put her husband first, as she does the Lord. A husband is the head of his wife, as Christ is the head and the Saviour of the church, which is his own body. Wives should always put their husbands first, as the church puts Christ first.

A husband should love his wife as much as Christ loved the church and gave his life for it. He made the church holy by the power of his word, and he made it pure by washing it with water. Christ did this, so that he would have a glorious and holy church, without faults or spots or wrinkles or any other flaws.

In the same way, a husband should love his wife as much as he loves himself. A husband who loves his wife shows that he loves himself. None of us hate our own bodies. We provide for them and take good care of them, just as Christ does for the church, because we are each part of his body. As the Scriptures say, 'A man leaves his father and mother to get married, and he becomes like one person with his wife.' This is a great mystery, but I understand it to mean Christ and his church. So each husband should love his wife as much as he loves himself, and each wife should respect her husband.

EPHESIANS
6.10–18

Put on all the armour that God gives, so you can defend yourself against the devil's tricks.

VIOLENCE AND
WARFARE

GOD'S ARMOUR

Finally, let the mighty strength of the Lord make you strong. Put on all the armour that God gives, so you can defend yourself against the devil's tricks. We are not fighting against humans. We are fighting against forces and authorities and against rulers of darkness and powers in the spiritual world. So put on all the armour that God gives. Then when that evil day comes, you will be able to defend yourself. And when the battle is over, you will still be standing firm.

Be ready! Let the truth be like a belt around your waist, and let God's justice protect you like armour. Your desire to tell the good news about peace should be like shoes on your feet. Let your faith be like a shield, and you will be able to stop all the flaming arrows of the evil one. Let God's saving power be like a helmet, and for a sword use God's message that comes from the Spirit.

Never stop praying, especially for others. Always pray by the power of the Spirit. Stay alert and keep praying for God's people.

GOD'S HUMILITY

PHILIPPIANS
2.1–11

Paul had an eventful time when he was at Philippi and the church was clearly very dear to him. As he wrote to thank them for a gift they had sent, he urged them to keep going in their new faith.

Don't be jealous or proud, but be humble and consider others more important than yourselves.

W. BLAKE
CHRIST OFFERS TO
REDEEM MAN
MUSEUM OF FINE
ARTS
BOSTON
1808

Christ encourages you, and his love comforts you. God's Spirit unites you, and you are concerned for others. Now make me completely happy! Live in harmony by showing love for each other. Be united in what you think, as if you were only one person. Don't be jealous or proud, but be humble and consider others more important than yourselves. Care about them as much as you care about yourselves and think the same way that Christ Jesus thought:

Christ was truly God.
But he did not try to remain equal with God.
Instead he gave up everything and became a slave, when
 he became like one of us.
Christ was humble.
He obeyed God and even died on a cross.
Then God gave Christ the highest place and honoured his
 name above all others.
So at the name of Jesus everyone will bow down, those in
 heaven, on earth, and under the earth.
And to the glory of God the Father everyone will openly
 agree, 'Jesus Christ is Lord!'

CHRIST IS ABOVE EVERYTHING

COLOSSIANS
1.15–20

Although Paul never visited the church at Colossae, he wrote this letter because he was concerned that the Christians there were incorporating strange ideas into their faith.

All things were created by God's Son, and everything was made for him.

Christ is exactly like God, who cannot be seen.
 He is the firstborn Son, superior to all creation.
Everything was created by him, everything in heaven and
 on earth, everything seen and unseen, including all

See also
GENESIS 1.1–2.4,
JOB 38,
JOHN 1.1–5

forces and powers, and all rulers and authorities.

All things were created by God's Son, and everything was made for him.

God's Son was before all else, and by him everything is held together.

He is the head of his body, which is the church. He is the very beginning, the first to be raised from death, so that he would be above all others.

God himself was pleased to live fully in his Son.

And God was pleased for him to make peace by sacrificing his blood on the cross, so that all beings in heaven and on earth would be brought back to God.

1 TIMOTHY
3.1–13

ADVICE FOR CHURCH LEADERS

Timothy was a young man and valued assistant to Paul in his ministry. Paul wrote this letter to give him practical advice about running a church.

And they must have a clear conscience and hold firmly to what God has shown us about our faith.

It is true that anyone who desires to be a church official wants to be something worthwhile. That's why officials must have a good reputation and be faithful in marriage. They must be self-controlled, sensible, well-behaved, friendly to strangers, and able to teach. They must not be heavy drinkers or troublemakers. Instead, they must be kind and gentle and not love money.

Church officials must be in control of their own families, and they must see that their children are obedient and always respectful. If they don't know how to control their own families, how can they look after God's people?

They must not be new followers of the Lord. If they are, they might become proud and be doomed along with the devil. Finally, they must be well respected by people who are not followers. Then they won't be trapped and disgraced by the devil.

Church officers should be serious. They must not be liars, heavy drinkers, or greedy for money. And they must have a clear conscience and hold firmly to what God has shown us about our faith. They must first prove themselves. Then if no one has anything against them, they can serve as officers.

Women must also be serious. They must not gossip or be heavy drinkers, and they must be faithful in everything they do.

Church officers must be faithful in marriage. They must be in full control of their children and everyone else in their home. Those who serve well as officers will earn a good reputation and will be highly respected for their faith in Christ Jesus.

HEBREWS
1.1–14

JESUS – GOD'S LAST WORD

This letter was written to Jewish Christians. Its aim was to show how Jesus was the fulfilment of all prophecy in the Old Testament. All that had happened in the past was a shadow of what was now taking place.

But now at last, God sent his Son to bring his message to us. God created the universe by his Son, and everything will some day belong to the Son.

Long ago in many ways and at many times God's prophets spoke his message to our ancestors. But now at last, God sent his Son to bring his message to us. God created the universe by his Son, and everything will some day belong to the Son. God's Son has all the brightness of God's own glory and is like him in every way. By his own mighty word, he holds the universe together.

After the Son had washed away our sins, he sat down at the right side of the glorious God in heaven. He had become much greater than the angels, and the name he was given is far greater than any of theirs.

God has never said to any of the angels, 'You are my Son, because today I have become your Father!'

Neither has God said to any of them, 'I will be his Father, and he will be my Son!'

When God brings his firstborn Son into the world, he commands all his angels to worship him.

And when God speaks about the angels, he says,

'I change my angels into wind and my servants into flaming fire.'

But God says about his Son,

'You are God, and you will rule as King for ever!

Your royal power brings about justice.

You loved justice and hated evil, and so I, your God, have chosen you.

I appointed you and made you happier than any of your friends.'

The Scriptures also say,

'In the beginning, Lord, you were the one who laid the foundation of the earth and created the heavens.

They will all disappear and wear out like clothes, but you will last for ever.

You will roll them up like a robe and change them like a garment.

But you are always the same, and you will live for ever.' God never said to any of the angels, 'Sit at my right side until I make your enemies into a footstool for you!'

Angels are merely spirits sent to serve people who are going to be saved.

HEBREWS
10.1–18

But Christ offered himself as a sacrifice that is good for ever.

JESUS' UNIQUE DEATH

The Law of Moses is like a shadow of the good things to come. This shadow isn't the good things themselves, because it cannot free people from sin by the sacrifices that are offered year after year. If there were worshippers who already have their sins washed away and their consciences made clear, there would not be any need to go on offering sacrifices. But the blood of bulls and goats cannot take away sins. It only reminds people of their sins from one year to the next.

When Christ came into the world, he said to God,

'Sacrifices and offerings are not what you want, but you have given me my body.

No, you are not pleased with animal sacrifices and offerings for sin.'

Then Christ said,

'And so, my God, I have come to do what you want, as the Scriptures say.'

The Law teaches that offerings and sacrifices must be made because of sin. But why did Christ mention these things and say that God did not want them? Well, it was to do away with offerings and sacrifices and to replace them. That is what he meant by saying to God, 'I have come to do what you want.' So we are made holy because Christ obeyed God and offered himself once for all.

The priests do their work each day, and they keep on offering sacrifices that can never take away sins. But Christ offered himself as a sacrifice that is good for ever. Now he is sitting at God's right side, and he will stay there until his enemies are put under his power. By his one sacrifice he has for ever set free from sin the people he brings to God.

The Holy Spirit also speaks of this by telling us that the Lord said,

'When the time comes, I will make an agreement with them. I will write my laws on their minds and hearts.

Then I will forget about their sins and no longer remember their evil deeds.'

When sins are forgiven, there is no more need to offer sacrifices.

FAITH

FROM
HEBREWS
11.1–40

*Faith makes us sure
of what we hope for
and gives us proof
of what we cannot
see.*

Faith makes us sure of what we hope for and gives us proof of what we cannot see. It was their faith that made our ancestors pleasing to God.

Because of our faith, we know that the world was made at God's command. We also know that what can be seen was made out of what cannot be seen.

Because Abel had faith, he offered God a better sacrifice than Cain did. God was pleased with him and his gift, and even though Abel is now dead, his faith still speaks for him.

Enoch had faith and did not die. He pleased God, and God took him up to heaven. That's why his body was never found. But without faith no one can please God. We must believe that God is real and that he rewards everyone who searches for him.

Because Noah had faith, he was warned about something that had not yet happened. He obeyed and built a boat that saved him and his family. In this way the people of the world were judged, and Noah was given the blessings that come to everyone who pleases God.

Abraham had faith and obeyed God. He was told to go to the land that God had said would be his, and he left for a country he had never seen. Because Abraham had faith, he lived as a stranger in the promised land. He lived there in a tent, and so did Isaac and Jacob, who were later given the same promise. Abraham did this, because he was waiting for the eternal city that God had planned and built.

Even when Sarah was too old to have children, she had faith that God would do what he had promised, and she had a son. Her husband Abraham was almost dead, but he became the ancestor of many people. In fact, there are as many of them as there are stars in the sky or grains of sand along the beach.

Every one of those people died. But they still had faith, even though they had not received what they had been promised. They were glad just to see these things from far away, and they agreed that they were only strangers and foreigners on this earth. When people talk this way, it is clear that they are looking for a place to call their own. If they had been talking about the land where they had once lived, they could have gone back at any time. But they were looking forward to a better home in heaven. That's why God wasn't ashamed for them to call him their God. He even built a city for them.

What else can I say? There isn't enough time to tell about Gideon, Barak, Samson, Jephthah, David, Samuel, and the prophets. Their faith helped them conquer kingdoms, and because they did right, God made promises to them. They closed the jaws of lions and put out raging fires and escaped from the swords of their enemies. Although they were weak, they were given the strength and power to chase foreign armies away.

Some women received their loved ones back from death. Many of these people were tortured, but they refused to be released. They were sure that they would get a better reward when the dead are raised to life. Others were made fun of and beaten with whips, and some were chained in jail. Still others were stoned to death or sawn in two or killed with swords. Some had nothing but sheep skins or goat skins to wear. They were poor, ill-treated, and tortured. The world did not deserve these good people, who had to wander in deserts and on mountains and had to live in caves and holes in the ground.

All of them pleased God because of their faith! But still they died without being given what had been promised. This was because God had something better in store for us. And he did not want them to reach the goal of their faith without us.

JAMES 2.14–26 ## FAITH AND ACTIONS

James wrote this letter to explain that good behaviour should always be a consequence of true Christian faith. Where there was no evidence of a changed lifestyle, James questioned whether there really was true faith in Jesus.

Faith that doesn't lead us to do good deeds is all alone and dead!

See also JOSHUA 2.1–24, 6.22–25, MATTHEW 1.5, HEBREWS 11.31

My friends, what good is it to say you have faith, when you don't do anything to show that you really do have faith? Can that kind of faith save you? If you know someone who doesn't have any clothes or food, you shouldn't just say, 'I hope all goes well for you. I hope you will be warm and have plenty to eat.' What good is it to say this, unless you do something to help? Faith that doesn't lead us to do good deeds is all alone and dead!

Suppose someone disagrees and says, 'It is possible to have faith without doing kind deeds.'

I would answer, 'Prove that you have faith without doing

kind deeds, and I will prove that I have faith by doing them.' You believe there is only one God. That's fine. Even demons believe this, and it makes them shake with fear.

Does some stupid person want proof that faith without deeds is useless? Well, our ancestor Abraham pleased God by putting his son Isaac on the altar to sacrifice him. Now you see how Abraham's faith and deeds worked together. He proved that his faith was real by what he did. This is what the Scriptures mean by saying, 'Abraham had faith in God, and God was pleased with him.' That's how Abraham became God's friend.

You can now see that we please God by what we do and not only by what we believe. For example, Rahab had been a prostitute. But she pleased God when she welcomed the spies and sent them home by another way.

Anyone who doesn't breathe is dead, and faith that doesn't do anything is just as dead!

1 JOHN
1.5–2.2

HONESTY IS THE BEST POLICY

John wrote this letter at a time when some were questioning whether Jesus had truly been fully human. Speaking as a witness to all that Jesus did and said, John wanted to correct this way of thinking. He insisted that, just as Jesus lived and loved in tangible ways, his followers were to do the same.

But if we confess our sins to God, he can always be trusted to forgive us and take our sins away.

See also **Genesis 1.4, Isaiah 9.2, John 1.1–14, Ephesians 5.8**

Jesus told us that God is light and doesn't have any darkness in him. Now we are telling you.

If we say that we share in life with God and keep on living in the dark, we are lying and are not living by the truth. But if we live in the light, as God does, we share in life with each other. And the blood of his Son Jesus washes all our sins away. If we say that we have not sinned, we are fooling ourselves, and the truth isn't in our hearts. But if we confess our sins to God, he can always be trusted to forgive us and take our sins away.

If we say that we have not sinned, we make God a liar, and his message isn't in our hearts.

My children, I am writing this so that you won't sin. But if you do sin, Jesus Christ always does the right thing, and he will speak to the Father for us. Christ is the sacrifice that takes away our sins and the sins of all the world's people.

1 JOHN 4.7–21   GOD IS LOVE

The commandment that God has given us is: 'Love God and love each other!'

My dear friends, we must love each other. Love comes from God, and when we love each other, it shows that we have been given new life. We are now God's children, and we know him. God is love, and anyone who doesn't love others has never known him. God showed his love for us when he sent his only Son into the world to give us life. Real love isn't our love for God, but his love for us. God sent his Son to be the sacrifice by which our sins are forgiven. Dear friends, since God loved us this much, we must love each other.

No one has ever seen God. But if we love each other, God lives in us, and his love is truly in our hearts.

God has given us his Spirit. That is how we know that we are one with him, just as he is one with us. God sent his Son to be the Saviour of the world. We saw his Son and are now telling others about him. God stays united with everyone who openly says that Jesus is the Son of God. That's how we stay united with God and are sure that God loves us.

God is love. If we keep on loving others, we will stay united in our hearts with God, and he will stay united with us. If we truly love others and live as Christ did in this world, we won't be worried about the day of judgment. A real love for others will chase those worries away. The thought of being punished is what makes us afraid. It shows that we have not really learnt to love.

We love because God loved us first. But if we say we love God and don't love each other, we are liars. We cannot see God. So how can we love God, if we don't love the people we can see? The commandment that God has given us is: 'Love God and love each other!'

GREETINGS AND DECLARATION OF PRAISE

Written at a time when the church was established, Jude encouraged Christians to remain firm in their convictions despite an influx of teachings that contradicted what Jesus and the apostles had taught.

Offer praise to God our Saviour because of our Lord Jesus Christ! Only God can keep you from falling and make you pure and joyful in his glorious presence. Before time began and now and for evermore, God is worthy of glory, honour, power, and authority. Amen.

From Jude, a servant of Jesus Christ and the brother of James. To all who are chosen and loved by God the Father and are kept safe by Jesus Christ.

I pray that God will greatly bless you with kindness, peace, and love!

My dear friends, I really wanted to write to you about God's saving power at work in our lives. But instead, I must write and ask you to defend the faith that God has once for all given to his people. Some godless people have sneaked in among us and are saying, 'God treats us much better than we deserve, and so it is all right to be immoral.' They even deny that we must obey Jesus Christ as our only Master and Lord. But long ago the Scriptures warned that these godless people were doomed.

Don't forget what happened to those people that the Lord rescued from Egypt. Some of them did not have faith, and he later destroyed them. You also know about the angels who didn't do their work and left their proper places. God chained them with everlasting chains and is now keeping them in dark pits until the great day of judgment. We should also be warned by what happened to the cities of Sodom and Gomorrah and the nearby towns. Their people became immoral and did all sorts of sexual sins. Then God made an example of them and punished them with eternal fire.

The people I am talking about are behaving just like those dreamers who destroyed their own bodies. They reject all authority and insult angels. Even Michael, the chief angel, didn't dare to insult the devil, when the two of them were arguing about the body of Moses. All Michael said was, 'The Lord will punish you!'

But these people insult powers they don't know anything about. They are like senseless animals that end up getting destroyed, because they live only by their feelings. Now they are in for real trouble. They have followed Cain's example and have made the same mistake that Balaam did by caring only for money. They have also rebelled against God, just as Korah did. Because of all this, they will be destroyed.

These people are filthy minded, and by their shameful and selfish actions they spoil the meals you eat together. They are like clouds blown along by the wind, but never bringing any rain. They are like leafless trees, uprooted and dead, and unable to produce fruit. Their shameful deeds show up like foam on wild ocean waves. They are like wandering stars for ever doomed to the darkest pits of hell.

Enoch was the seventh person after Adam, and he was talking about these people when he said:

Look! The Lord is coming with thousands and thousands of holy angels to judge everyone. He will punish all those ungodly people for all the evil things they have done. The Lord will punish those ungodly sinners for every evil thing they have ever said about him.

These people grumble and complain and live by their own selfish desires. They boast about themselves and flatter others to get what they want.

My dear friends, remember the warning you were given by the apostles of our Lord Jesus Christ. They told you that near the end of time, selfish and godless people would start making fun of God. And now these people are already making you turn against each other. They think only about this life, and they don't have God's Spirit.

Dear friends, keep building on the foundation of your most holy faith, as the Holy Spirit helps you to pray. And keep in step with God's love, as you wait for our Lord Jesus Christ to show how kind he is by giving you eternal life. Be helpful to all who may have doubts. Rescue any who need to be saved, as you would rescue someone from a fire. Then with fear in your own hearts, have mercy on everyone who needs it. But hate even the clothes of those who have been made dirty by their filthy deeds.

Offer praise to God our Saviour because of our Lord Jesus Christ! Only God can keep you from falling and make you pure and joyful in his glorious presence. Before time began and now and for evermore, God is worthy of glory, honour, power, and authority. Amen.

REVELATION 5.1–14

HEAVEN'S WORSHIPPING COMMUNITY

Revelation contains glimpses of the world's end and the wonderful life in store for followers of Jesus. It was written at a time when the church was going through severe persecution, so the glorious vision it contained was aimed at inspiring and encouraging the Christians in their trials.

You are worthy to receive the scroll and open its seals, because you were killed. And with your own blood you bought for God people from every tribe, language, nation, and race.

DREAMS AND VISIONS

In the right hand of the one sitting on the throne I saw a scroll that had writing on the inside and on the outside. And it was sealed in seven places. I saw a mighty angel ask with a loud voice, 'Who is worthy to open the scroll and break its seals?' No one in heaven or on earth or under the earth was able to open the scroll or see inside it.

I cried hard because no one was found worthy to open the scroll or see inside it. Then one of the elders said to me, 'Stop crying and look! The one who is called both the "Lion from the Tribe of Judah" and "King David's Great Descendant" has won the victory. He will open the book and its seven seals.'

Then I looked and saw a Lamb standing in the centre of the throne that was surrounded by the four living creatures and the elders.

The Lamb looked as if it had once been killed. It had seven horns and seven eyes, which are the seven spirits of God, sent out to all the earth. The Lamb went over and took the scroll from the right hand of the one who sat on the throne. After he had taken it, the four living creatures and the twenty-four elders knelt down before him. Each of them had a harp and a gold bowl full of incense, which are the prayers of God's people. Then they sang a new song,

'You are worthy to receive the scroll
    and open its seals, because you were killed.
And with your own blood you bought for God people from
    every tribe, language, nation, and race.
You let them become kings and serve God as priests, and
    they will rule on earth.'

As I looked, I heard the voices of a lot of angels around the throne and the voices of the living creatures and of the elders. There were millions and millions of them, and they were saying in a loud voice,

'The Lamb who was killed
    is worthy to receive power, riches, wisdom,
strength, honour, glory, and praise.'

Then I heard all beings in heaven and on the earth and under the earth and in the sea offer praise. Together, all of them were saying,

'Praise, honour, glory, and strength
    for ever and ever to the one who sits on the throne
and to the Lamb!'

The four living creatures said 'Amen', while the elders knelt down and worshipped.

THE ENORMOUS CROWD

After this, I saw a large crowd with more people than could be counted. They were from every race, tribe, nation, and language, and they stood before the throne and before the Lamb. They wore white robes and held palm branches in their hands, as they shouted,

'Our God, who sits upon the throne,
    has the power to save
his people, and so does the Lamb.'

The angels who stood around the throne knelt in front of it with their faces to the ground. The elders and the four living creatures knelt there with them. Then they all worshipped God and said,

'Amen! Praise, glory, wisdom, thanks, honour, power, and strength belong to our God for ever and ever! Amen!'

One of the elders asked me, 'Do you know who these people are that are dressed in white robes? Do you know where they come from?'

'Sir,' I answered, 'you must know.' Then he told me:

'These are the ones who have gone through the great suffering.

They have washed their robes in the blood of the Lamb and have made them white.

And so they stand before the throne of God and worship him in his temple day and night. The one who sits on the throne will spread his tent over them.

They will never hunger or thirst again, and they won't be troubled by the sun or any scorching heat.

The Lamb in the centre of the throne will be their shepherd.

He will lead them to streams of life-giving water, and God will wipe all tears from their eyes.'

'The Lamb in the centre of the throne will be their shepherd. He will lead them to streams of life-giving water, and God will wipe all tears from their eyes.'

DREAMS AND VISIONS

THE END OF TIME

FROM REVELATION 21 AND 22

I saw a new heaven and a new earth. The first heaven and the first earth had disappeared, and so had the sea. Then I saw New Jerusalem, that holy city, coming down from God in heaven. It was like a bride dressed in her wedding gown and ready to meet her husband.

I heard a loud voice shout from the throne:

God's home is now with his people. He will live with them, and they will be his own. Yes, God will make his home among his people. He will wipe all tears from their eyes, and there will be no more death, suffering, crying, or pain. These things of the past are gone for ever.

Then the one sitting on the throne said:

I am making everything new. Write down what I have said. My words are true and can be trusted. Everything is finished! I am Alpha and Omega, the beginning and the end. I will freely give water from the life-giving fountain to everyone who is thirsty. All who win the victory will be given these blessings. I will be their God, and they will be my people.

But I will tell you what will happen to cowards and to everyone who is unfaithful or dirty-minded or who murders or is sexually immoral or uses witchcraft or worships idols or tells lies. They will be thrown into that lake of fire and burning sulphur. This is the second death.

I did not see a temple there. The Lord God All-Powerful and the Lamb were its temple. And the city did not need the sun or the moon. The glory of God was shining on it, and the Lamb was its light.

Nations will walk by the light of that city, and kings will bring their riches there. Its gates are always open during the day, and night never comes. The glorious treasures of nations will be brought into the city. But nothing unworthy will be allowed to enter. No one who is dirty-minded or who tells lies will be there. Only those whose names are written in the Lamb's book of life will be in the city.

I am Jesus! And I am the one who sent my angel to tell all of you these things for the churches. I am David's Great Descendant, and I am also the bright morning star.

The Spirit and the bride say, 'Come!' Everyone who hears this should say, 'Come!'

If you are thirsty, come! If you want life-giving water, come and take it. It's free!

INDEX OF THEMES

Genesis 40.1–23
Genesis 41.1–41
Judges 7.9–21
1 Kings 3.5–15
Isaiah 6.1–8
Jeremiah 33.14–22
Ezekiel 37.1–14
Ezekiel 43.1–9
Ezekiel 47.1–12
Daniel 2.1–13
Daniel 2.14–23
Daniel 2.24–49
Daniel 5.1–12
Luke 1.5–25
Luke 1.26–38
Matthew 1.18–25
Luke 2.8–14
Matthew 2.1–12
From Acts 6.8–8.1
Acts 9.1–9
From Acts 10.1–48
Acts 22.17–29
Revelation 5.1–14
Revelation 7.9–17
From Revelation 21 and 22

FARMING AND PRODUCE

Genesis 8.20–22, 9.8–17
Genesis 12.1–20
Genesis 37.1–11
Genesis 41.1–41
From Genesis 43.1–34
From Exodus 3.1–4.16
Exodus 9.13–10.29
From Judges 6.11–24
Ruth 2.1–13
2 Kings 4.8–37

Ezekiel 34.11–31
Luke 2.8–14
Mark 4.35–41
From Matthew 13.24–43
Matthew 21.33–46

FOOD AND DRINK

Genesis 2.4–25
Genesis 3.1–24
Genesis 24.1–27
Genesis 25.19–34
Genesis 27.1–41
Genesis 29.13–30
Genesis 40.1–23
Genesis 41.53–42.24
From Genesis 42.25–38
From Genesis 43.1–34
Exodus 12.21–34
From Numbers 13.1–33
Numbers 20.2–12
1 Samuel 1.1–20
1 Samuel 9.1–10.1
From 1 Samuel 17.4–39
1 Kings 17.1–7
1 Kings 17.8–16
1 Kings 19.1–16
Ezra 3.7–13
Nehemiah 2.1–8
Job 1.1–12
Job 1.13–22
Daniel 5.1–12
Matthew 3.13–17
Mark 2.23–3.6
John 6.1–15
From John 6.25–51
John 13.1–15
Matthew 26.26–29

Luke 24.13–35
John 21.1–14
John 21.15–22
Acts 2.36–47
From Acts 10.1–48
Acts 27.9–28.1
1 Corinthians 11.17–33

MARRIAGE AND FAMILY

Genesis 22.1–14
Genesis 24.1–27
Genesis 24.54–67
Genesis 25.19–34
Genesis 29.13–30
Genesis 37.1–11
Genesis 41.53–42.24
From Genesis 43.1–34
Exodus 1.1–22
Exodus 2.1–10
Exodus 12.21–34
Ruth 1.6–18
1 Samuel 1.1–20
From 2 Samuel 11.1–27
2 Samuel 12.1–14
Job 1.13–22
From Job 42.7–17
Jeremiah 33.14–22
Luke 1.5–25
Luke 1.39–56
Luke 1.57–80
Matthew 1.18–25
Luke 2.39–52
Luke 15.11–32
Matthew 21.28–32
Acts 5.12–26
Ephesians 5.1–33

INDEX

THE LAW

ELIJAH & ELISHA

EXILE AND RETURN

POETRY

THE SUFFERINGS OF JOB

DANIEL

OTHER PROPHETS

THE GOSPELS

JESUS' BIRTH

THE TEACHINGS AND MIRACLES OF JESUS

JESUS' LAST WEEK

JESUS' RESURRECTION

THE EARLY CHURCH

THE GOOD NEWS SPREADS

ADVICE TO THE FIRST CHURCHES